Praise for *Armies of Enablers*

"Amos Guiora's new book spotlights issues that are too rarely discussed. Frequently we think of the crime of sexual assault as involving only perpetrators and victims—ignoring how powerful institutions or individuals often enable those perpetrators to assault their victims. Springboarding from cases of sexual assault at Michigan State University, The Ohio State University, and Pennsylvania State University and in USA Gymnastics and the Catholic Church, Guiora illuminates how sexual assault survivors are harmed not only by the physical acts of those who violate them but also by those who empower sexual assault through silence and other failures to act. Using multiple and revealing interviews with survivors, Guiora asks them what they expected from the enabler—and the answers are new and surprising. Guiora's thoughtful exploration of these breaches of trust helps us understand these 'armies of enablers,' who too often make sexual assaults possible."

—Paul G. Cassell, Ronald N. Boyce Presidential
Professor of Criminal Law and University
Distinguished Professor of Law, S.J. Quinney
College of Law at the University of Utah

"Amos Guiora has captured in *Armies of Enablers* what happens when good people sit on the sidelines in the face of evil. His timing couldn't be better. As a critical hour has arrived in America, Professor Guiora presents to the nation and to the world too many examples where silence welds injustice because too few stood up. He answers the hard question of whether law and morality should compel action against the consequences of hatred and shows us why there can never be peace without justice."

—Avery Friedman, CNN Legal Analyst

"Guiora's book is a powerful, eye-opening condemnation of the role that educational and religious institutions, from staff to leadership, play in enabling and facilitating sexual predation. It is also a rallying cry for meaningful action, insisting that those in power do more to protect vulnerable members of their communities—and be held accountable when they don't. Guiora has done what university and faith leaders have so often failed to do: hear, believe, and stand with survivors in their quest to use their own experiences to help others. *Armies of Enablers* shines a vivid spotlight on the undeniable reality that, too often, those we entrust to protect our children and loved ones—educators, coaches, physicians, clergy, and university administrators—have not only betrayed that trust but are complicit enablers of sexual assault. Unlike so many books on sexual assault, *Armies of Enablers* does not focus on the harm done by the perpetrators. Instead, it explores the harm done by those who had power to stop the abuse but did nothing—or, even worse, discouraged, deceived, or punished those who reported the abuse. It is both a gut-wrenching account of survivors' stories and a roadmap for how we can, and must, do better. Everyone who works with, and cares for, young people should heed the lessons of the stories Guiora has collected, then work to ensure that the traumatic experiences recounted here never happen again."

—Adele Kimmel, Director, Public Justice
Students' Civil Rights Project

"We can't effectively address the damaging effects of complicity until we have a good understanding of the social and psychological dynamics of bystanders and enablers. Professor Guiora's timely work gets to the core of the relationship between liberty, social responsibility, and lawmaking. Heeding his call for greater proactive behavior from each of us will move our culture to higher levels of safety and productivity."

—Rep. Brian S. King, Utah State Legislature

"In *The Crime of Complicity*, Amos Guiora began a journey of self-discovery. Finding his voice, he challenged us all to find our own; silence is not an option. In *Armies of Enablers*, Guiora listens to and liberates the voices of others long silenced. We are challenged by his question that rings loud and clear: *Whose side are you on?*"

—Rev. Dr. John C. Lentz, Jr., Presbyterian
(USA) Pastor and Community Activist

"*Armies of Enablers* is essential reading for our times. A deeply moving book of testimonies from survivors of sexual assault and also a brilliant expose of how the predators can only perpetrate their crimes through their individual and institutional enablers, Guiora looks at the legal and moral issues of the enabler through the lens of the survivor. The book is a heart-rending and clear call to action, giving us a concrete legal plan to help achieve the goal: never again."

—Emily Mann, Director, Playwright, Screenwriter

"'It took a parish to molest me.' The voices of survivors and concrete blue-prints for change make Amos Guiora's searing book about sexual assault crucial reading for leaders and members of any institution. Exposing the necessary roles of bystanders and enablers in universities and churches, *Armies of Enablers* details proposals for legal change to end betrayals of trust and resulting trauma. The book draws upon Guiora's expertise on bystanders during the Holocaust and on extensive interviews with current survivors of sexual assault. Criminal liability for enablers and civil liability for failure to report abuse could crack deliberate silence and preference for 'brand protection' that make people complicit with violators."

—Martha Minow, 300th Anniversary University Professor, Harvard University and author of *Between Vengeance and Forgiveness: Facing History after Genocide and Mass Violence*

"At long last, an unflinching look at those who enable abusers, facilitate their access to children, overlook and hide their crimes, revictimize the abused and, all too often, evade scrutiny and accountability. One hopes this book shifts public attitudes, and that there can be criminal consequences for those who make this scourge possible."

—Walter V. Robinson, Editor at Large for *The Boston Globe* and editor of the Globe Spotlight Team that won the Pulitzer Prize for exposing the widespread cover-up of sexual abuse of children by the Catholic Church

"To see so many respected and responsible people in revered organizations with unfathomable blind eyes and deaf ears, failing so completely to protect vulnerable mostly child victims of the most heinous violations, is dumbfounding and infuriating. Something must be done, and Amos Guiora has a compelling recommendation. Reading this book has to instill in legislators, policymakers, and anyone who has a level of responsibility for the well-being of youth or other potential victims the courage to take action and try to put an end to these horrific nightmares."

—Daniel H. Sharphorn, University Attorney

AMOS N. GUIORA

Armies of
ENABLERS

Survivor Stories of Complicity
and Betrayal in Sexual Assaults

AMERICAN**BAR**ASSOCIATION
ABA Publishing

Cover design by Elmarie Jara/ABA Design

Printed in the United States of America.

24 23 22 21 20   5 4 3 2 1

A catalog record for this book is available from the Library of Congress.

Discounts are available for books ordered in bulk. Special consideration is given to state bars, CLE programs, and other bar-related organizations. Inquire at Book Publishing, ABA Publishing, American Bar Association, 321 N. Clark Street, Chicago, Illinois 60654-7598.

www.shopABA.org

To my late brother, Rami

Author's Note

The description of events discussed in this book was accurate at the time that the manuscript was submitted. It is inevitable that the issues examined within these pages will be subject to continued interpretation, due to subsequent judicial holdings, prosecutorial decisions, factual developments, government actions, civil lawsuits, and administrative rulings. The reader's recognition of the fluid nature of this complex topic is appreciated.

—Amos N. Guiora, April 2020

Contents

Preface

Working on this project has been eye opening on a personal level; there are endless emotions attendant to such an undertaking. Those emotions, part and parcel of any book project, were accompanied by significant life events that, no doubt, affected my approach to the issues at hand.

Sadly, one person who never had a chance to make the journey was my younger brother, Rami. I was three years old when he was born. We never met; I have never seen a picture of him. Rami died a few days after his birth in December 1960.

Because he was not circumcised, the Rabbinate in the city of our birth—Rehovot, Israel—refused to share with my grieving parents the location of Rami's grave. To this day, we do not know where Rami was buried. While I was writing this book, my mother mentioned this brutally painful fact to me for the first time. That discussion led me to do something I should have done long ago.

I dedicate this book to my late brother, Rami: although we never met, although we never exchanged a word with each other, as my brother, you too are a part of this journey.

Acknowledgments

The expression "it takes a village" is as true regarding this book as for its predecessor, *The Crime of Complicity: The Bystander in the Holocaust*. I am fortunate to be the beneficiary of a team that has made this project possible. This book truly could not have been completed without the wonderful collaborative spirit that very much defined the process.

The project required researching, organizing, and collating a significant amount of material, identifying the survivors we wanted to interview, working with their attorneys, preparing questions for the interviews, arranging interviews, and reading and re-reading drafts of the book in its various stages. This demanded sensitivity given the subject matter at hand. It goes without saying that an undertaking of this nature, in its complexity and its inherent sadness, has had its peaks and its valleys.

The list of those to whom I owe my deepest gratitude includes friends, colleagues, and former and current students. My heartfelt *thank you* goes to Scott Allen, Lauren Alllswede, Scott Balderson, Kate Charipar, Jessie Dyer, Madeline Harker, Christine Hashimoto, John Lentz, Brooks Lindberg, Noemi Mattis, Lynette Saccomanno, Dan Sharphorn, Dan Shoemaker, Maggi Spight, and Carrie Velez.

I am fortunate, also, that my editors, Bryan Kay and John Palmer, were fully engaged throughout the writing process. Their feedback was essential to the final product. Tanjam Jacobson's efforts in editing were also invaluable, and she has my utmost respect and gratitude.

For a book like this to happen, serendipity is important. Two small examples: While having coffee with my good friend Avery Friedman, he suggested I contact Tom Merriman regarding the survivors from The Ohio State University. I had not previously met Mr. Merriman, but during our call he recommended I call Adele Kimmel, who represents some of the Ohio State survivors. Ms. Kimmel, who has been beyond gracious and generous with her time and insight, also put me in touch with other attorneys who represent additional Ohio State survivors.

Similarly, after giving a talk (on the earlier book) at the Kansas University School of Law, my current dean, Elizabeth Kronk Warner (then an Associate Dean at University of Kansas School of Law) shared with me that my colleague and good friend Professor Paul Cassell was going to present at the School of Law at a conference hosted by the KU Journal on Law and Policy, and that one of the survivors from Michigan State University was scheduled to attend. Paul put us in touch, and in the course of our conversation, I learned that John Manley represented a number of Michigan State survivors. I contacted Mr. Manley, who, along with his colleague Alex Cunny, facilitated my meeting with their clients.

My work on *The Crime of Complicity*, while important personally, took on an added significance thanks to Utah State Representative Brian King, whom I met when working on a different legislative initiative. Rep. King began exploring the possibility of introducing legislation that would impose on the bystander a duty to act. I am deeply indebted to Rep. King for his decision to introduce House Bill 125, "The Duty to Assist in an Emergency," and subsequently to invite me to testify before the Utah House Judiciary Committee. Representative King did more than introduce the legislation; he truly became its champion.

Rep. King's bystander legislative effort serves as the natural segue for the proposal to criminalize the enabler. The two are directly related: criminalizing the enabler builds off criminalizing the bystander, and while there are differences between the two concepts, they are far outweighed by their similarities. The proposed legislation regarding the enabler that I discuss in the present book directly stems from Rep. King's bystander legislation.

In this way, Rep. King's efforts have helped give meaning to the suffering of my parents and other Holocaust survivors and serve as the basis for addressing the abuse caused to the survivors by their enablers. For that, I am most grateful to Representative King.

More than anything, however, this book owes its soul to the survivors who agreed to engage with me.

Introduction

Destruction of Trust

This book was not written out of the blue, quite the opposite. In 2017, my book *The Crime of Complicity: The Bystander in the Holocaust* was published. It explored whether the bystander, the individual who sees another in peril and chooses not to act on his or her behalf, is guilty of a crime. I argued in the affirmative and recommended that criminal codes incorporate a Duty to Act obligation.

In 2018, I was asked by Bryan Kay of the American Bar Association to consider a further writing project. We explored various themes; Bryan noted that as a sports junkie perhaps I might want to address the explosive situation of sexual abuse at Michigan State University (MSU). Like millions of others, I was vaguely familiar with the various news reports but did not have an in-depth understanding. I had indeed thought earlier of examining reported abuse in the Catholic Church, but had never fully engaged with that terrible issue.

But the more I thought about it, the clearer it became that exploring the sexual abuse cases at MSU and in the church was the natural next step after the first book. There is a link between the bystander and the enabler; while the former is present when another is in harm's way, the latter, as we shall come to see, creates the environment that facilitates that very harm. The enabler then is a natural extension of the bystander; recommending criminalizing the enabler is the logical progression after proposing the same regarding the bystander. There is a sequencing of the two—bystander and enabler—when examined through the lens of the person in peril. It is through that perspective that we shall engage in the Duty to Act question. That is why we will hear the survivors' voices throughout this book: the twin assaults—physical and emotional—they survived are the abuses that demand our attention.

The enabler and bystander have knowledge that another individual is at risk. We will discuss the different ways—whether directly or indirectly—in which they came to know of the peril. The critical fact is that they have knowledge. The question is, what did they do with that information? In deciding not to act on behalf of the person in peril, bystander and enabler alike facilitate the harm caused by the predator. It is my contention that both actors owe a duty to that person.

The failure to positively act—to provide assistance or prevent future harm—in accordance with that duty resulted in terrible consequences to an innocent person. Why? Because the enabler and bystander made the decision to walk away, literally and figuratively. That is the essence of *abandonment.* Both the bystander and the enabler are of paramount importance to the predator; that understanding directly contributed to my decision to pursue this project.

This book focuses on cases of sexual assault at Michigan State University (MSU), The Ohio State University (OSU), USA Gymnastics (USAG), the Catholic Church, and Pennsylvania State University (PSU).[1] In doing so, it in no way intends to ignore or exonerate the mind-numbing number of other sexual assault cases that occur every day, quite the opposite.[2] It is hoped that by shedding light on these institutions, greater attention will be paid to the vulnerability of survivors elsewhere and to the roles and responsibilities of those who could have acted to prevent the harm. These five institutions were chosen because of the sheer amount of available documentary material—special reports, grand jury reports, victim impact statements—that illuminates how enablers protect their institutions and the perpetrators at the expense of the survivors.

---

1. While I reference Penn State University in this book and cite material relevant to the crimes committed on its campus, I did not engage with any individual assaulted by Jerry Sandusky. I did, however, interact with journalists who have covered the story.

2. https://www.nsvrc.org/node/4737; https://www.huffpost.com/entry/sexual-assault-statistics_n_58e24c14e4b0c777f788d24f; http://worldpopulationreview.com/countries/rape-statistics-by-country/.

I stated in my acknowledgments that the survivors whom I interviewed are the "soul" of this book. I do not use that word lightly. It is intended to denote something significant, something powerful. For that is the reality of the subject matter at hand: the survivors with whom I spoke were sexually assaulted by people they trusted, in some cases, the people whom they trusted most. Were that not enough, the perpetrators were enabled by individuals whom the survivors similarly trusted. The theme of *trust*, then, is of paramount importance, for it is at the core of what was shattered by perpetrator and enabler alike. That is of great relevance in considering the consequences of the enabler's action: they violated trust no less than the perpetrator. Wherever a survivor turned, there was an enabler who made the conscious decision not to provide assistance, nor to prevent future attacks. The pattern repeated itself endlessly. Tragically, it will continue to repeat itself unless we, as a society, loudly and clearly say: *Enough.*

Just saying "enough" is insufficient, however; we need to take action. To understand why that is critical, one must hear the voices of the survivors; hear their pain; learn how they were abused; appreciate how deep that abuse cuts, physically and emotionally. In many cases, the emotional abuse presents a life-long struggle. The abuse is exacerbated because, as I came to learn, many survivors chose not to share their experiences with their families, or only did so many years—even decades—later.

The pain of carrying such a burden alone is something I cannot imagine. What added to the pain—what made the abuse much worse—was the fact the survivors were abandoned by those they most trusted. While the physical abuse was awful, the emotional abuse, it seems to me, was even more painful to bear. That is not intended to minimize the consequences of having doctors and priests assault their young bodies; rather, it is intended to emphasize the depth of the emotional abuse resulting from abandonment by the enabler. For the survivors, it was the utter violation of trust that cut so deeply into them. That is an abuse that, perhaps, has not been sufficiently understood regarding the enabler–survivor relationship. It is very much on the minds of the survivors.

But the question of trust went beyond that; the survivors were abandoned by the institutions they most loved. That, seemingly, made the insult deeper and more painful. They were harmed at the very places with which they so powerfully identified; the perpetrators and enablers were individuals who worked at these places.

The irony must not be lost: One day, these institutions held the survivors out as examples of "our" excellence; the next day, they shoved them out the door. The manner in which they did so only intensifies the abuse: with a couple of exceptions it was not a forceful kick in the ass, but rather, abuse in the form of abandonment. That is, those in positions of authority simply walked away from those in need. It was a figurative slap in the face. However, it may well have hurt more than a physical slap.

Broken trust demands *accountability*. The word "demand" is used deliberately; it was a theme survivors articulated loud and clear. Particularly painful is their recognition that the institutions to which they gave their hearts and souls have avoided accepting accountability for their suffering. That has only exacerbated their overwhelming sense of being abandoned.

The role of institutions is essential to our discussion; the survivors whose voices we shall hear are, for the most part, in great pain regarding the institutions they so dearly loved. Whether one was a Spartan, a Buckeye, an elite USAG athlete, or a deeply committed Catholic, it was understood that there was a clear relationship between the individual and their institution: a mutual relationship, reflecting two-way commitment and obligation. As an individual, one was all in; one thought they, the institution, was all in too. One committed to them, believed in them, was proud to wear their colors. There was a sense of pride, belonging, commitment, and loyalty. Coaches, priests, and senior officials created a team that one was a part of. Team and belonging were intrinsic to how these individuals understood the relationship and what their expectations were.

What they did not expect was that the institution to which they were committed and devoted, which they loved, would make the decision to enable a predator who was attacking them. They did not expect the institution, in the words of survivor Mattie Larson, to enable a predator to turn her body in his plaything.

Strong words. Awful words. But that is the consequence of the institutional enabling of predators. That is exactly how we must understand it. Otherwise, we will not fully appreciate or understand the degree of harm and abuse caused by perpetrator and enabler alike.

Tiffany Thomas-Lopez, another survivor, was blunt in describing the consequences of institutional enabling: "They super fucked me." Mattie and Tiffany's powerful words will serve as an important path when we consider enablers, individuals and institutions alike.

The list of enablers at the relevant institutions is extraordinarily long and far-reaching. This is one of the reasons survivors have such a tragically difficult time for many years: wherever they have turned, there has been another enabler. That abuse was in addition to the abuse suffered at the hands of the predator. That warrants criminalizing the enabler.

My decision to pursue this project was reinforced once I started watching victim impact statements of Larry Nassar's victims at Michigan State University; watching the women who appeared in front of Judge Rosemarie Aquilina in a Lansing, Michigan, courtroom compelled me to write this book. The themes of destruction of trust, lack of accountability, and abandonment were a constant refrain; they were expressed honestly, painfully, oftentimes with anger.

The statements were powerful. But, they were more than that: they were clear in pointing a finger at the enablers who facilitated Nassar's assaults on their young bodies. Their anger—Mattie Larson's words, "Do you know how much I fucking hate you?"—was obviously directed at Nassar. After all, he was the defendant and they were testifying as to his punishment. The victim impact statements were intended to convince Judge Aquilina to impose on Nassar the maximum punishment possible. However, they also left no doubt as to the anger directed towards Michigan State's coaches, trainers, and university officials, including President Lou Anna Simon. No enabler escaped unscathed. Names were named; people were called out.

While Nassar was the primary focus of the victim impact statements, no listener could fail to recognize the following: young boys and girls had been assaulted by unrelenting, adult male predators who had been enabled by adult males and females. Some of the survivors were assaulted hundreds of times over the course of a number of years. Others were assaulted "only" once.

Regardless of the number of assaults or the number of years, the people we will meet in this book are true survivors. Many of them have, literally, been to hell and back. Some, by their own testimony, are still working their way back to normal, healthy lives. The struggle reflects the consequences of the intersection of the themes outlined above. For some, the struggle has been just that, a terrible struggle. The pain and suffering many of the survivors have carried within them over the course of decades illuminates the cost of sexual assaults. That is something easily—perhaps—lost in an understandable focus on the attack. In reality, decades later, the pain and anger come through loud and clear.[3] It is unmistakable. It demands our attention.

We—society writ large—owe the survivors our fullest attention and willingness to roll up our sleeves and get to work on their behalf. Otherwise, not only will their pain remain unabated, but the pain of future survivors is completely foreseeable. One of the most powerful messages repeatedly expressed by survivors was a deep desire to be involved in efforts to address predators and enablers alike.

Sadly—that is, I think, the best word—some survivors hold themselves guilty for not having reported the crimes of the predator; from their perspective, had they done so, assaults that occurred years after they were attacked could have been prevented. The misplaced guilt survivors articulate is striking in comparison to the repeated denials uttered by the enablers, whether directly or through layers of lawyers, spin masters, and press statements. The candor with which the survivors describe their pain, and in certain cases, their guilt, is only "matched" by the pervasive, almost systemic, unctuousness of the enablers.

What stood out, perhaps more than anything else in my interactions with the survivors, is their clear recognition that two distinct actors caused them significant harm. The survivors confronted two distinct categories of evil: predator and enabler. While criminal law is fully equipped to prosecute predators, the gaps and loopholes available to the enabler must be addressed. Otherwise, not only will enablers continue with their lives while the survivors suffer, but future enablers will

---

3. For more on this, see research on Adverse Childhood Experience (ACE); I thank Rep. Brian King for drawing my attention to this.

follow in their footsteps. Decisions to prosecute MSU president Lou Anna Simon and MSU gymnastics coach Kathy Klages are obviously welcome; however, these two are but the tip of the iceberg. Underneath that tip is where we find the armies of enablers.

The word "armies" is intended to convey just that: an endless number of enablers, far more numerically significant and institutionally powerful than just one army. While one army is significant, several armies are, literally, insurmountable. They come at you from different directions, they use every strategic and tactical advantage possible, they have unlimited resources, they carry the "prestige" of seemingly reputable and esteemed institutions, they represent success and power. They are arrogant; they are dismissive; they are deceitful; they are punitive. They are adults in positions of authority.

And the survivor? The survivors we will meet were between seven and twenty years old when they were abused.

Who attacked the survivor? A predator known to the survivor and largely trusted by the survivor.

Who protected the predator? An enabler directly positioned to protect the survivor.

What did the enabler do? He or she protected their "hallowed" institution: protect the institution; enable the predator; abandon the survivor.

That needs to be framed as a crime. Not a moral or ethical crime, but a crime punishable to the fullest extent of the law. The more interviews I conducted with survivors, the greater my clarity regarding the need to create a framework facilitating criminalization of the enabler.

Without the enablers, the perpetrators would not have had the enormous confidence and impunity to act as they did. There is no question that the perpetrators we will encounter knew their actions would go unpunished. Their actions were akin to a running back with an open field ahead of him, unencumbered sprinting to the end zone with strong, powerful blockers clearing the path.

Because many of the survivors we will meet are athletes, the sports metaphor is applicable. The predators—Larry Nassar, Richard Strauss, Jerry Sandusky, and an endless array of priests—knew their path to the end zone was clear and uncluttered, as their "offensive line" had removed all possible obstacles. Waiting in the end zone were young bodies to which the predator would have full, unlimited, and endless access for purposes of satisfying their criminal perversions. That is the crux of the fate that awaited the survivors. It was enabled by those they trusted. That is why the theme of abandonment is so paramount.

Survivor Peter Pollard's phrase "destruction of trust" suggests that time and again the runner (perpetrator) and blocker (enabler) violated the trust they owed to the victim.[4] It is for that reason that the blocker must also be criminalized; without their blocking the path, the runner would not make it, untouched, to the end zone. This was a team effort. Sometimes enablers were coaches, sometimes trainers, sometimes priests, sometimes monsignors, sometimes bishops, sometimes cardinals, sometimes athletic directors, sometimes senior officials, even a university president. There was always a teammate the predator counted on to clear the path on the gallop to the end zone.

Peter and I agreed on one critical issue but disagreed on another. We agreed that the most important undertaking is to prevent such conduct in the future. We disagreed as to how to proceed. Perhaps that is a reflection of our different disciplines and professions, since Peter is a social worker and I am an attorney. I believe in criminal codes as a deterrent; Peter is committed to principles of restorative justice and efforts to change human behavior. Perhaps the two means are not mutually exclusive, as our common focus is to ensure that what happened to these survivors will not happen to others.

I approached the interviews with a fair amount of trepidation, clearly compounded by the fact those who agreed to be interviewed had suffered terribly. While my previous books involved interviewing a wide range of people, including Holocaust survivors, meeting with sexual assault survivors was a new experience for me. That is not to compare one group of survivors with another or to suggest the pain of one survivor is more acute than that of another. I had previously addressed questions of bystander complicity, but the role of the enabler in sexual assaults was a new undertaking.

---

4. This phrase was used by Peter Pollard in describing the enabler. Skype conversation, October 18, 2019.

To say that I am humbled by the survivors agreeing to speak with me is an understatement. I have tried to do justice to their voices, which must be heard. Their voices are essential in an effort to examine three distinct issues: criminalizing bystander and enabler complicity; extending the Statue of Limitations; and clarifying the Title IX obligations of American universities.

To truly understand the importance of these issues, particularly their urgency, we must listen to and learn from the survivors. Otherwise, the discussion is abstract, theoretical, and devoid of context. It is not my intention to use the survivors' voices in making the legal argument; it is absolutely my intention to ensure their voices are heard when the public debates these issues. This is a fine line: to incorporate survivor voices is not to make this a book about survivors.

My intention is to press upon the reader, through the survivors' voices, the obligation to ensure enablers be penalized in the future, and institutions be held accountable when they choose to protect themselves rather than vulnerable members of their communities. For those two reasons we must listen to the survivors. Otherwise, we cannot truly understand the consequences of tolerating enabler conduct and failing to impose accountability requirements on institutions.

We must not allow ourselves to casually shrug our shoulders, as if to say, "Yes, this is terrible, but these are all special circumstances that do not represent mainstream society." That specious argument fails to understand a tragic reality: the combustible combination—from the survivor's perspective—of perpetrator and enabler is not limited to "special" circumstances. It can happen here, there, anywhere. *That is the point.* That is what demands our attention. We can no longer allow ourselves the comfort—perhaps "arrogance" is a better word—of the bland statement offered to me on more than one occasion, "This couldn't happen at my institution."

Such an argument reflects denial, whether deliberate or not is irrelevant, of a reality that is staring us in the face. A casual glance at any news source should make this self-evident. Time after time we are confronted with accounts of how sexual assaults were enabled by those who were in a position to act on behalf of the survivor. However, what stands out more than anything else is the fact that we are not really surprised.

It is a source of deep concern that people in positions of power hold on to a myth that their institution has enough protocols, safety measures, and other means to ensure sufficient protection to those for whom they are responsible. Listening to the survivors makes clear how empty many of the oft-repeated assurances are.

As difficult as the conversations were for me, I can only imagine how painful they were for the survivors. Actually, I cannot imagine; it would be presumptuous. That was made repeatedly clear to me in my interactions with the survivors. These were women and men who had been violated by people they trusted, or at least had every reason to trust. The perpetrators were their physicians or religious leaders.

Moreover, the people we will meet in this book were young, sometimes very young, when they were abused. The youngest survivor was seven when her priest started abusing her, and that abuse lasted for seven years.[5] To understand the severity of the injury, to truly appreciate the depth of the physical and emotional hurt, requires focusing on the enabler.

That is why the question I posed to the survivors was, "What did you expect from the enabler?" In other words, what did you expect from the person who enabled the perpetrator who assaulted you? The term "enabler" perhaps sounds somewhat passive, as if that person were not fully engaged and not directly responsible for the harm caused. Something akin to, "Oh yes, that is really terrible. . . . What's for dinner?"[6]

Nothing could be further from the truth; nothing could be more incorrect from the survivor's perspective. To be clear: for the survivor, the enabler was critical to the assault. Theirs was not a passive role; it was an active role: Person A tolerated or facilitated the assault of person B by person C. That is not some casual spectator at a sporting event, disinterested in the final score. On the contrary, to understand the enabler we must recognize that they could have acted to prevent a terrible act but made the decision not to do so. In making that fateful decision, they enabled a crime.

In my conversations with the survivors, the role of the enabler was front and center. As awful as the assaults were, the survivors pointed an

---

5. That is not to suggest that children under the age of seven were not attacked; but I did not interview any survivor who was younger than seven when attacked.
6. When I shared excerpts of the manuscript with some of the survivors, a number of them noted how much this sentence resonated.

accusatory finger at their enablers. The phrase "*their* enabler" is perhaps jarring, because the enabler might be considered more accurately aligned with the perpetrator. However, I deliberately use "their enabler" when referring to the survivor, because that individual enabled the assault that occurred to them. The pronoun "their" is important for it suggests the enabler had a duty to the survivor but chose not to honor that obligation; in that context, the enabler became "their" enabler. This was the person the survivor thought would protect them; the person they assumed owed them—and not the perpetrator—a duty.

The word "their" is powerful, because it means there is a direct relationship between two individuals, devoid of an intermediary. It is a possessive, akin to "mine" or "my." That is what makes the enablers conduct so devastating to the survivors. The enabler is not some remote figure, residing on a different planet, speaking an incomprehensible language, practically or intellectually. Not in the least. The enabler was within arm's reach. There was a relationship even though the enabler, in contrast to a bystander, did not see the crime committed. None of these enablers was present when young bodies were assaulted. But they were told directly by those who they knew (the survivors), for whom they had a responsibility, to whom they owed accountability.

The survivors with whom I spoke did not walk up to random strangers in the street and say, "You won't believe what just happened to me!" Nor did they stand on the rooftops and yell to the broader public. Not at all. They did exactly what any young victim should do: go to an individual in a position of authority whom they trusted to act in their best interests and put an end to predators assaulting their bodies. They reported to the person they believed was best positioned to protect them.

In the case of survivors who did not complain, who did not understand they were being assaulted, under no condition are "their" enablers to be understood as innocent. As we shall come to see, coaches, trainers, and senior officials who were not told still established the toxic and dangerous environment that enabled the predator. Of that, there must be no doubt.

To ignore this is, from the survivor's perspective, to miss a critical component of the assault. As I came to learn from the survivors themselves, the enabler's decision not to protect is no less painful and traumatic than the actual physical attack. It is perhaps the most heart-breaking, if not devastating, aspect. For the survivor, the two are intertwined and must be so viewed: Without the enabler, there is no perpetrator.

In focusing our conversation on "What were your expectations of the enabler?" I did not intend to minimize the consequences of the harm caused by the perpetrator. I wished to focus on the enabler and the harm that individual or institution caused the survivor. In some cases, survivors shared with me the actions and harms of the perpetrators; others chose not to share these details. That was not, however, the primary issue at hand. After all, the perpetrators have been identified, prosecuted, convicted, and incarcerated.[7] The decision to address the enabler reflected my commitment to the survivors to bring the harm done to them by their enablers to the public's attention. That is the reason the reader will hear—in the survivors' unfiltered language—and learn about enablers, rather than perpetrators.

Some of the survivors allowed me to use their names; others requested anonymity. The decision was theirs. Where the survivor is referenced anonymously, I have noted that in the text. Our communications included in-person meetings, Skype calls, and cell phone calls. With the survivors' permission, I took notes during our conversations.

Some of the survivors made clear our communication would be limited to one interaction; with others, there were follow-up communications, by Skype or email. With those who agreed, I shared drafts of the book, requesting their comments and feedback. While I am sure reading this material was difficult for them, their comments were of the utmost importance, as they brought my attention to important matters that otherwise were incorrect or reflected my failure to understand particular points they had previously expressed. On matters of interpretation, disagreement is always possible.

The structure of the book is as follows. Chapter 1, "Holocaust Bystander to Contemporary Enabler," traces the development of the idea of complicity from the survivor's perspective from my earlier work on complicit bystanders in the historical context of the Holocaust to

---

7. The obvious exceptions are Dr. Richard Strauss, who committed suicide, but not before assaulting Ohio State University students; and the Catholic priests who have escaped justice.

complicit enablers in contemporary society. The enabler may be identified both as an individual and as an institution. Chapter 2, "From Impunity to Accountability," examines the consequences to the survivor of the perceived impunity of the enabler, and argues for the need to hold the enabler accountable. Chapter 3, "Enough," discusses the anger rightly voiced by the survivors toward their enablers and the need to make their voices heard. In Chapter 4, "Survivor Expectation," we hear in survivors' own words and from their stories about the athlete–coach relationship and the culture of enabling that is hidden behind a veil of institutional secrecy. Chapter 5, "Where the Hell Are the Adults?" focuses on USA Gymnastics' dereliction of duty in giving Larry Nassar total and unsupervised access to the young women gymnasts training under their care. Chapter 6, "Complicity," documents the pervasiveness of complicity in enabling sexual assault. It examines its nature, and how it is experienced by the survivor.

Chapter 7, "The Bystander Duty to Act," takes a close and practical look at the complexity of criminalizing bystanders, based on my active engagement with Representative Brian King of the Utah State Legislature to enact bystander legislation; research conducted over the years; and a law review article co-authored with my research assistant, Jessie Dyer. It argues that bystander Duty to Act legislation is a logical precursor to enabler Duty to Act legislation. Chapter 8, "Criminalize the Enabler," discusses legislative proposals with respect to protecting the vulnerable, while Chapter 9, "Sexual Assault and Enabling at Universities: Title IX," discusses existing Title IX legislation and suggests measures that could heighten universities' obligations of protection to their students. Chapter 10, "The Challenges Ahead," recaps the main points of enabler complicity from the survivor's perspective and looks to the future.

In the epilogue I discuss a specific meeting with a survivor that shows the courage and strength of all the survivors discussed in this book. The book ends with a piece titled "Violated by Water" meant to showcase the emotions portrayed throughout this book.

Such is the nature of this undertaking, which builds off my previous book, *The Crime of Complicity*. It is in some ways a sequel. The first book was more personal in nature, as I explored in great detail my parents' travails and experiences during the Holocaust. The oft-used term, which in reality says very little, to capture the horror of the Holocaust is "unimaginable." Frankly, the phrase "unimaginable suffering," however well intentioned, has become, for me, meaningless. Terminology matters. Words have meaning.

This is particularly the case when bringing to the fore the suffering of another human being. To understate their plight, however unintentionally, results in minimizing their suffering. It is for that reason that I recoil when people—innocently, no doubt—refer to Holocaust "victims" who "died." No, they did not die: THEY WERE MURDERED. To phrase it in any other manner is historically incorrect. It also fails to capture the essence of the Holocaust.

In the same vein, there is significance in the use of the terms "victor," "survivor," and "victim." While the common expression is "Holocaust survivor," my 87-year-old mother is adamant in referring to herself as a "Holocaust victor." Similarly, the women attacked by Nassar refer to themselves as an "army of survivors." They eschew the word "victim." On more than one occasion, I was reminded of this important terminological distinction. In using the term "survivors" in this book, I honor their request. More than that: while not in any way minimizing the harm done to them, there was never a sense of "woe is me." In that sense, those with whom I spoke are truly survivors, badly injured by two different actors: one in physical terms, both in emotional terms.

Perhaps that was a result of our deliberate focus on the survivors' expectation of the enabler. Posing the "expectation" question inevitably leads to examining what duty was owed to the survivors. That is particularly relevant when considering the consequences of the decision to not provide assistance. The question of imposing a duty to act on the enabler is a theme we will explore throughout this book. It builds off the duty question developed in *The Crime of Complicity* regarding bystander obligation. In that sense, imposing Duty to Act requirements on the enabler can be understood to be the logical step after imposing Duty to Act requirements on the bystander.

There is a direct relationship between the two, despite the differences in how the two actors came to learn of the peril of another human being. In addition to the question of knowledge, there is another important difference between bystander and enabler: the former was "by chance" at the scene when a person was in need of assistance, the latter was in a position of authority and facilitated the attack by refusing to act when informed of the harm, or deliberately ignored a known danger.

Duty to act is even more pronounced when the person in peril is a child and the enabler is an adult in a position of authority tasked with responsibility for that child's health and welfare. Individually and collectively, these individuals must affix to their clothing the scarlet *A* that Hester Prynne was forced to wear in Nathaniel Hawthorne's classic.[8] More important, enablers and bystanders must also be brought to justice.

Otherwise we shall do nothing more than perpetuate the complicity of enablers and bystanders. The duty to act owed to the injured, regardless of age, gender, status, sexual orientation, and/or race must outweigh any other consideration—with the caveat that there is no requirement that the enabler or bystander put themselves in harm's way. That is the only circumstance that would justify their not acting.

To create additional exceptions is to enhance and to tolerate the peril of the vulnerable.

---

8. Nathaniel Hawthorne, *The Scarlet Letter* (1850).

"We stood in line awaiting our slaughter."
—*Tiffany Thomas-Lopez*

"I have never been more disgusted or angry towards the people that let this go on. Larry Nassar was first accused in 1994, and by 1997, was working for MSU. One accusation went by and nothing was done but neglected and pushed aside. By 1998 there were even more, and one was even a six-year-old. Yet, once again, nothing was done. I hope you know what you have done by not investigating this man so much earlier. If you had, there would have been so many girls safe from the pain."
—*Erin Blayer, victim impact statement*

— 1 —

Holocaust Bystander to Contemporary Enabler

My interest in the concept of complicity and its status as a crime under law was born while training for the Salt Lake City Marathon. To pass the time on one of our long runs, my running partner asked me conversationally about the Holocaust, "How did this happen?" I floundered as I realized that, even as the child of Holocaust survivors, I could not answer her question.

From this seed planted in my mind, the question slowly morphed into a slightly different one: "How did they let this happen?" I was not sure who "they" were; I also had little awareness of what "they" could, or could not, have done. Nevertheless, the question increasingly became a focus of what I chose to read. And the more I read, the more I started thinking about the bystander and his or her complicity.

While reading about the Holocaust with an eye toward the bystander, I started thinking about the bystander in contemporary society. As an educator, I was well aware of sexual assaults on college campuses. They are, literally, a matter of daily coverage in the media and very much on the minds of students and parents. Innumerable widely publicized attacks; public focus, if not criticism; and judicial proceedings have brought into sharp light a critical issue that demands the time of college officials. This requires implementing concrete measures significantly extending beyond mantras and slogans. As we shall come to see, public imaging serves as a lightning rod for survivors, who angrily dismiss what they perceive to be mere posturing.

As I was researching this book, University of Utah student Lauren McCluskey was murdered on campus by a former non-student boyfriend.[1] The murder galvanized students, who were concerned that fears expressed by McCluskey and her friends regarding threats directed at her were not fully and satisfactorily addressed by relevant university officials.[2] The following semester, I taught a course at the university's Honors College on "The Bystander" (based on my earlier book, *The Crime of Complicity*). McCluskey's murder was a prime source of class discussion addressing a number of issues relevant to sexual assaults and campus safety. For students enrolled in the course, this was a topic of utmost importance.

The connection building in my mind between the bystander in the Holocaust and the bystander in contemporary society, however, was as yet insufficient. Over time, I came to realize that the missing piece of my puzzle was the survivor: the person whom the bystander chose deliberately to avoid; the person in whose pain and suffering the bystander is complicit by failing to intervene on their behalf.

Critical to me, in examining bystander complicity, is the question of consequences. This, more than anything else, became the focus of my inquiry. That is, I came to understand that bystander complicity was not without cost—it was not an abstract concept, but rather a topic that warranted examination under bright lights, if not harsh glare. While there was no doubt regarding the direct responsibility of the perpetrator, there was an additional actor without whom the perpetrator would have been hard pressed to act.

The more I read about the bystander, the more obvious became the centrality of the role. It was not important to me whether the perpetrator

---

1. https://www.cnn.com/2018/10/24/us/lauren-mccluskey-university-of-utah-fatal-shooting /index.html; https://www.news965.com/news/national/report-campus-cop-shared-explicit-photos -utah-student-lauren-mccluskey-days-before-her-murder/VZ4wHqRp9EBuYv4seShC2N/; https://www.deseret.com/2019/5/31/20675000/what-really-happened-to-lauren-mccluskey-the -inside-story-of-her-tragic-death.
2. A lawsuit filed by Ms. McClusky's parents is pending before the courts.

and bystander had a relationship, for that is not a significant factor from the perspective of the person in peril. Whether or not the perpetrator and the bystander knew each other, that person was endangered both by the attacks by the former and the complicity of the latter.

After I decided to explore sexual assaults on college campuses—in particular, Vanderbilt[3] and Stanford[4]—I expanded my scope to include the rape and murder of seven-year-old Sherrice Iverson by Jeremy Strohmeyer in Nevada. Although deplorable, Strohmeyer was not of interest to me; it was his friend David Cash who attracted my attention. David Cash, perhaps more than any other bystander I examined, came to embody the absolute requirement to punish the complicit bystander.

Cash had followed Strohmeyer into the bathroom after the latter had grabbed Sherrice and stood on a toilet seat in the adjacent stall while Strohmeyer sexually assaulted the young child, at which point Cash left the bathroom. Shortly thereafter, Strohmeyer rejoined him. Cash inquired as to her fate, and Strohmeyer straightforwardly informed Cash that he had raped, strangled, and murdered the child. Cash and Strohmeyer's actions are best described as callously indifferent. It is a theme that dominates Cash's retelling of the events in an interview with Ed Bradley on *60 Minutes*.[5]

While Strohmeyer was convicted of first-degree murder, Cash was not prosecuted, for there is no bystander obligation law in Nevada. In the interview with Bradley, Cash dismissed any duty he may have had, casually stating he did not know the child, and therefore his only loyalty was to his friend.

The Bystander

For any child of Holocaust survivors, the expression "we live in the shadow of the Holocaust" is particularly apt, even seven decades later. In pursuing the research that would lead to my book *The Crime of*

---

3. https://www.tennessean.com/story/news/2015/01/25/bro-code-inaction-vandy-rape-case
-sparks-anger/22318275/.
4. https://www.theguardian.com/society/2016/aug/26/brock-turner-stanford-sexual-assault
-victim-testimony-laugh.
5. https://www.youtube.com/watch?v=KqTdXOQmXrc.

Complicity, the more I read about the Holocaust, the more I realized the events of 1933–1945 could not be fully understood without examining the issue of bystander complicity. I found that I was not interested in the perpetrators—Hitler, Himmler, Auschwitz accountants—who had in any case been covered in voluminous literature. It was the bystander who most grabbed my attention.

As I came to learn, the book would be the first to explore the legal aspect of the bystander in the Holocaust. Of course, others had already written on the topic, notably Dr. Victoria Barnett and Professor Raul Hilberg. Their path-breaking books, *Bystanders: Conscience and Complicity during the Holocaust*, and *Perpetrators Victims Bystanders: The Jewish Catastrophe 1933–1945*, provided me with a wealth of material, insights, and perspectives.[6] Meeting with Dr. Barnett at the U.S. Holocaust Museum significantly enhanced my understanding of the bystander in the Holocaust and was crucial to the decision to undertake the project.

A central focus of my research was the effort to understand the decision of an individual to act when another human being, in immediate proximity, is in distress. I approached the question from the perspective of those who saw my parent's travails but chose not to act. While I understood all the reasons "why not" to intervene—fear, incapability, identification with the perpetrator—I was nevertheless fascinated by the individual who sees another in harm's way and yet chooses not to act. The decision to do nothing is as much an act as the decision to do something. If we do not acknowledge this, we let the person who chose not to act off the hook in excusing their behavior.

In the earlier book, I was particularly focused on the situation where the bystander was physically present and therefore had firsthand knowledge of the peril and was in a position to act. The concept of physicality was of particular importance and relevance to my assessment of bystander complicity. Without doubt, that was a direct result of my efforts to understand what happened to my parents. Consequently, I did not inquire into the roles and actions of the International Red Cross, the Hungarian or U.S. governments, the Catholic Church. I was not

---

6. Victoria Barnett, *Bystander: Conscience and Complicity during the Holocaust* (Greenwood Press, 1999); Raul Hilberg, *Perpetrators Victims Bystanders: The Jewish Catastrophe 1933–1945* (Harper Collins, 1992).

interested in the complicity of institutions, nation states, or large organizations because the distance between an institution and the person in immediate peril struck me as too remote.

Whether to define the bystander by his or her physical presence at another person's peril, or to extend the definition beyond geographical immediacy, is a thorny question. It is, obviously, of far more relevance today than it was seventy-five years ago, in large part because we live in an age of social media. While the role of the bystander was as relevant historically as today, the advent of modern means of communication raises an additional point of inquiry. It is tempting to argue that a duty to act should be imposed regardless of location, particularly when imagining a person in extreme peril. But given the practical uncertainties in extending the duty beyond a "physically present" test, it is highly unlikely that legislators would look favorably on such a proposal.

For that reason, I rejected the notion that an individual sitting at home and watching scenes of barbarism in Syria on CNN is a complicit bystander. It is all too easy to say that person should have "done something." But what burden of obligation could we reasonably impose: Call President Assad? The UN Secretary-General? The president of the United States? However terrible the acts portrayed, there is nothing the individual could immediately do to alleviate the harm of the moment. The same holds true for the so-called Facebook bystander, in large part because of legitimate concerns regarding the veracity of what appears to be shown. The premise that observing a purported scene on social media qualifies one as a bystander—underlying criminalization of a "911 obligation"—is an unjustified and unenforceable proposition. The essence of the bystander is being physically present, with knowledge of the peril and the capability to act.

The intimacy of the physical space shared by victim and bystander increasingly drew my attention. Even though they may not have had a prior relationship, circumstances somehow brought them together. I was particularly struck by the immediacy and randomness of their "interaction," though there was no real, substantive engagement between them. The bystander is there and in a position to act even if the two individuals did not exchange a word, much less a glance. The duty to act is the consequence of a fleeting moment.

That is not the case with the enabler. The complicity of the enabler is of a quite different nature.

The Enabler

In contrast to the randomness of the bystander narrative, the enabler narrative is predicated on crimes that occur between two individuals who knew one another. We must also recognize the symbiotic relationship between predator and enabler; without the latter, the former is unable to commit brazen crimes over so many years on a, literally, endless—actually, unfathomable—number of victims.

Examination of the harms done at Michigan State University, The Ohio State University, and Pennsylvania State University, in USA Gymnastics, and in the Catholic Church reveals the power of institutions and how individuals working within these institutions interpret the question of to whom they owe a duty. In case after case, the answer was clear: "I owe my duty to the institution." In case after case, that decision had devastating consequences for the individual in peril. Exalting the institution over the individual is the essence of the institutional enabler.

That is not to suggest that there was no one in a position of authority who sought to do the "right thing." But they were clearly in the minority. The sheer number of individuals harmed speaks loudly to that fact.

As we shall come to see, there was nothing heroic demanded of the enabler. The enabler was merely required to recognize to whom he or she owed a primary duty. There really should not have been anything complicated in this. After all, in many instances perpetrator and survivor were brought together under everyday circumstances. The students, student athletes, and elite gymnasts at Michigan State, Ohio State, and USA Gymnastics whom we will encounter in the coming pages met with a physician whom they knew for what should have been a routine physical examination. But that is not what occurred. As we have come to learn, these interactions were nothing but pretexts for sexual assault. And what did the enablers do? Protect the institution.

The same pattern applies to the situations in the Catholic Church and Penn State. In the context of seemingly everyday interactions—physical examination, medical treatment, pastoral care—innocent children were sexually assaulted by adults enabled by individuals who were in a position to prevent the assaults but who made the deliberate decision not to do so.

Superficially, Penn State aside, none of these interactions should have been anything but routine. Moreover, the survivors' own understanding of the nature of these interactions was clear: doctor and pastor were respected members of the community, entrusted with addressing particular issues. Larry Nassar was viewed as "iconic"; athletes were considered fortunate to be treated by him. Parents drove their children hundreds of miles to have him "fix" their daughter's gymnastics-related injuries.

There was no obvious cause for concern or mistrust: an athlete is treated by the team doctor; a young Catholic meets with the priest, pastor, or bishop. Physicians are expected to treat; church leaders are expected to provide religious and spiritual guidance. There was no one more "safe," no one more "trustworthy," no one whom parents could be more "pleased," if not "honored," that their child was spending time with.

That was particularly true of single-parent families, especially mothers raising their children alone. In these cases, a priest could provide a much-needed adult male role model in place of the missing father. The abusive priests knew their audience all too well. They knew whom to target and how to play on their vulnerabilities and weaknesses. Richard Strauss and Nassar, in the world of athletics, were no different.

However, for such relentless criminal activity to proceed unabated for so long a time, there was need of an additional actor. In addition to the survivors, who were groomed, manipulated, and attacked, the predators needed an additional audience: the enabler.

The word "audience" is used deliberately, if with caution. Clearly, neither survivors nor enablers were sitting passively in a theater, programs in hand. Quite the opposite: the survivors were deliberately targeted; the enablers, actively enabled. Therefore, the word is used to reference two groups that the predators had to play to in order to commit their crimes. To ensure success, they needed both groups and had to be confident of how the enablers would react.

The reported number of victims at Ohio State, Michigan State, USA Gymnastics, and the Catholic Church does not reflect the actual number of individuals who have suffered so terribly. Their suffering is twofold: at the physical hands of the perpetrator and at the intangible hands of the enabler. Dual abuse was a theme survivors consistently emphasized, describing both their immediate pain at the hands of the predator and their long-term suffering at the "hands" of the enabler.

Willie Jones[7] was a swimmer at The Ohio State University when Coach Dick Sloan said, "Captains lead the team to the physical." In return, one of the captains said to Jones, "Stay away from Strauss, because he'll play with you." Jones noticed there was a "race" amongst the older team members to avoid being treated by Strauss, who was referred to as "Grabby Hands." According to Jones, during the 10-12 minutes he was in Strauss's examination room, he could clearly hear his teammates laughing, as if he was undergoing a "rite of passage." He fully expected that someone would say something; that a member of the coaching staff—who had to have known—would do something. While Willie Jones was unable, either at the time or today, to define what that "something" was, his clearly articulated expectation was that a person in a position of authority would act on his behalf.

In response to my question "Who are the enablers?" Jones suggests the following: the OSU officials who employed and/or worked with Strauss, but did not say a word. "How do you justify yourself?" Jones asks plaintively. While Jones does not have "hard-core" proof that the athletic director and other officials knew—a recurring theme that we will address—he is correct in asserting that "others had to know," given how openly Strauss's conduct was discussed.

Painfully, for there is no better word, Jones describes the enabler both as an individual and as a system that allowed him to be "ambushed." The word "ambush" is important, for it indicates that the enabler knew of the predator's actions and chose to abandon the survivor. "How do you, the enabler, not do something?" Jones is left to wonder. From his—the survivor's—perspective, those in a position of authority, tasked with protecting him, made the decision to protect the predator and their institution instead.

---

7. This is a mutually agreed upon pseudonym; the individual's true identity is known to me. Jones and I Skyped on August 23, 2019.

When asked, "What should the enabler do?" Jones is clear: Never send a swimmer to Strauss. After all, the primary obligation of a coach is to protect the athlete for whom he or she has assumed responsibility. As he noted, parents send their children to an institution such as OSU, with a coach such as Dick Sloan, with the expectation and understanding that the coach will protect their children.

Jones trusted the coach who sent him to the team doctor. From there, his life spiraled out of control: Jones quit the swim team and then dropped out of OSU. Notably, none of his coaches called him after he suddenly left the team. Jones went from respecting authority to becoming skeptical; today he sees his primary duty as protecting children.[8]

The disconnect that Jones was forced to face between his legitimate expectations and his experience was profound and life changing: not only was he assaulted, but he was failed by those who he believed were obligated to protect him. Time after time, survivors expressed this same belief that those in a position to provide assistance—trainers, coaches, bishops, senior administrators—would do so, and then the same realization that this was not to be the case. "Like lambs to the slaughter" was a familiar refrain.

In their book *Soldiers: German POWs on Fighting, Killing and Dying*, Professors Sönke Neitzel and Harald Welzer stress the importance of "reference" when examining individual actions.[9] They propose four frames of reference:

1. The broad sociohistorical backdrop against which people of a given time operate;
2. Frames that are more concrete in a historical, cultural, and often geographical sense;
3. Concrete constellation of sociohistorical events within which people act;
4. Special characteristics, modes of perceptions, interpretative paradigms, and perceived responsibilities that an individual brings to a specific situation.[10]

8. Jones, by his own account, came from a "Yes, Sir; No, Sir" culture.
9. Sönke Neitzel and Harald Welzer, *Soldiers: German POWs on Fighting, Killing, and Dying* (Signal, 2012).
10. Neitzel and Welzer, *Soldiers*, 10.

By shedding light on the relevance of context, circumstances, and conditions in assessing motivation, this schema is helpful in assessing the actions of the perpetrator, and by extension, those of the enabler. To the extent that one's focus is on what caused the bystander or enabler to ignore the cries of the survivor, in whatever manner they were articulated, this is of great importance. However, from the survivor's perspective, there must be no understanding of why the bystander or enabler chose not to act. For the survivor, the only issue of relevance is whether the person who could have provided assistance did so.

The Survivor's Perspective

While the title of this book, *Armies of Enablers*, highlights the enabler, it is crucial to understand that we are examining the enabler *from the perspective of the survivor*. This necessarily shapes the approach of the book. This insight was provided by Adele Kimmel, a senior attorney with the nonprofit legal advocacy organization Public Justice, who represents two of the survivors portrayed in this book. She made the compelling argument that, as the focus of this book is on the survivor, to interact with enablers would deflect from the primary intent: to illustrate the consequences of bystander and enabler complicity through the survivors' voices. It is for that reason that I have not reached out to enablers or perpetrators. Although the bystander and enabler are clearly essential to the inquiry, the centerpiece is the survivor; it is his or her pain that we must understand.

This pain was made graphically clear to me by Tiffany Thomas-Lopez. In one of our many Skype conversations during the summer of 2019 we were discussing "enabler impact," when Tiffany literally grabbed her throat. The point was driven home when she explained that *twenty years later* her enablers—the Michigan State University athletic trainers to whom she had confided what Larry Nassar was doing to her—were "still grabbing me by the fucking throat." This was not an intangible; this was visceral and graphic demonstration of the ongoing impact that the enabler has on the survivor.

A consistent theme brought up by survivors in discussions about their enablers is their sense of abandonment. This is brilliantly captured in the following passage from *Betrayal: The Crisis in the Catholic Church,* which exposed the sexual assaults committed by Catholic priests in Massachusetts, and was the basis for the award-winning movie *Spotlight*.[11]

> For Peter Pollard, that moment from 1967 is indelibly imprinted in his memory. The sixteen-year-old altar boy and Rev. George Rosenkranz were alone in the church basement just after midnight on Easter Sunday morning, in the obvious early stages of a sexual encounter, when the pastor of the parish walked in on them.
>
> Much like his peers were accustomed to doing, Monsignor William McCarthy pretended not to notice Pollard and Rosenkranz. And very much like the bishops and cardinals who have long known about the unchecked sexual yearnings of some of their priests, McCarthy side-stepped the opportunity to put a stop to it. As the Catholic Church has done for so long, McCarthy turned his back on the victim. "Could you put out the light when you are finished?" Monsignor McCarthy asked nonchalantly as he turned and walked away from Rosenkranz and his quarry.
>
> Not long after the light was extinguished, Pollard descended into darkness. He had been an honor student at his high school in Marblehead, north of Boston, before Rosenkranz coaxed him into his first sexual experiences. But after that betrayal, his grades plummeted and his ambitions evaporated.
>
> "I kissed a girl for the first time in the winter of 1967. I got my first kiss from Rosenkranz a few months earlier," Pollard recalled.
>
> Pollard started college but stayed less than two months. He moved around the country, by his own description an itinerant hippie who took odd jobs so he could feed himself. After the sexual abuse by a priest he had trusted, he chose to live a celibate, ascetic life for several years. His withdrawal from the world around him was so complete that even when he encountered strangers at a bus stop, he opted to stand well behind them. It was nearly two decades before Pollard reclaimed his life, secured the education he had long

---

11. The Investigative Staff of the Boston Globe, *Betrayal: The Crisis in the Catholic Church* (Little, Brown and Company, 2002). For *Spotlight,* see https://www.imdb.com/title/tt1895587/plotsummary.

postponed, started a family, and threw himself into a life's vocation—working with abused children.

By the time Pollard went to the Boston archdiocese in 1988 to complain about Rosenkranz, Monsignor McCarthy was long dead. But sitting in for McCarthy, with much of the same indifference, was [Cardinal] Law's, deputy Rev. John B. McCormack.

Pollard remembered McCormack saying that Rosenkranz had some "sexual issues," but they were not cause to remove him from parish work.

Although Pollard informed McCormack that Rosenkranz, after the kissing and fondling, had asked him to masturbate for him, McCormack had a ready defense for his fellow priest. "He said some individuals growing up formed relationships with George Rosenkranz in which [Rosenkranz] might have expressed affection, and they might have interpreted these acts as sexual involvement," Pollard recalled. Besides, McCormack informed Pollard, Rosenkranz had denied the charges. "My experience is that if they are guilty, they admit it," the future bishop told the stunned Pollard. McCormack, he said, added that even if Pollard was telling the truth, the sexual activity was, in McCormack's view, consensual.

Only after other complaints against Rosenkranz surfaced three years later did the archdiocese quietly remove the priest from his parish and commission a nun to let Pollard know that his initial complaint had been handled "inappropriately." "From my perspective," said Pollard, "McCormack basically abused me again. For me, the emotional and spiritual scarring came from the betrayal, and my betrayal by [Cardinal] Law and McCormack was as damaging as what Rosenkranz did."[12]

In assessing the relationship between bystander or enabler and survivor, my only consideration in the present inquiry is that the bystander is an individual who knows the victim is in distress and, in the overwhelming majority of cases in contemporary society, has the capability to provide assistance. It is of no relevance whether the parties had ever interacted or were even aware of each other before the incident.

---

12. Boston Globe, *Betrayal*.

It is unimportant what circumstances caused the victim's need for assistance: a crime, an unfortunate fall, a sudden medical condition, or anything else. That is what drives the legal proposition to impose an obligation to act on the bystander. Bystander Duty to Act legislation mitigates punishment if an actor responsible—directly or indirectly—for the peril alerts law enforcement regarding the victim's need for assistance.

Nevertheless, it is important to remember that the number of reported assaults, daunting as it is, does not represent the full picture at any of these institutions discussed in this book. A recurrent theme in the interviews I conducted for this book and its predecessor was that many survivors either never shared their experiences, even with their families, or only did so decades later.

For a variety of reasons, the "cost" of sharing was too great. In some cases, survivors did not think anyone would believe them; in other cases, family members or other authority figures directly told the survivors they did not believe them;[13] some survivors felt terrible shame;[14] some wished to put their past behind them in an effort to "move forward."[15]

It is to be hoped that over the coming years, with increasing publicity and greater public awareness and understanding, others will come forward. Any undertaking that facilitates survivors' willingness to come forward is of great importance; not only can it serve an important therapeutic purpose for the survivor, but it can also lead to identification of perpetrators and enablers who would otherwise continue to harm the vulnerable.

Confronting the Issue

In researching and writing my earlier book, *The Crime of Complicity*, I learned a great deal about the Holocaust in general, and my family in particular. In that sense, the first book was a "journey." And the journey continued after the book was published. Indeed, for me, the most powerful

---

13. Tragically, this is true of at least one Nassar survivor: https://www.youtube.com/watch?v=Q0_qzIsQtkI.
14. This was a theme expressed primarily, but not exclusively, by male athletes.
15. My parents fall into this category.

moments were the book talks: sometimes overwhelming, often poignant. I was caught off guard. Holocaust survivors, rape survivors, children and friends of survivors reached out to me in person or in writing, sharing their stories and family pictures, and occasionally asking assistance in tracking down long-lost families. I found this beyond humbling. My primary motivation in writing the book was to honor my dying father. I had never expected these kinds of personal connections with strangers.

The book and my talks also led to ugly death threats. Again, I was caught off guard, surprised that an academic book would elicit such reactions. An anonymous letter sent from Cleveland, Ohio, assured me that the next Holocaust was only a matter of time, and I would be one of its victims. Another letter guaranteed my public hanging.

I am grateful to the concern expressed by law enforcement officials to whom I reported such communications. But if the intention was to shut me down, these threats decisively failed. I decided that if sharing my parents' Holocaust experiences and urging criminalization of bystander complicity resulted in such hate, then the only thing to do was to plow ahead. Following my own logic, allowing myself to be silenced would make me complicit.

The question was how best to respond? My answer was to keep writing and keep talking. I accepted interviews in local, national, and international media on the question of bystander complicity. Whether my arguments were convincing was not foremost in my mind; for me, the most important point was to have the discussion. I am forever grateful to the people who made these occasions possible. In intimate conversations in living rooms and talks before audiences of hundreds, I was able to present and develop my argument.

Of course, I encountered skeptics and critics. They primarily focused on the complexity and danger of legislating bystander obligation to act. One commentator suggested I was proposing the creation of a "reporting (nanny) state"; others argued that such a duty to act is exclusively a *moral* obligation. In other words, for many of the critics, imposing a legal obligation, subject to criminal penalty, on the bystander for failing to provide assistance to a victim was a step too far.

Several people accused me of cheapening my parents' misfortune, of "using" their Holocaust experiences to make a "point" about contemporary society. They contended that I was basing a legal argument on human emotions. This was a criticism I was not prepared for. Although the book examined the bystander in a historical context—through the lens of the death march my father survived and two attempts to kill my mother—the ultimate focus was a legal question regarding bystander complicity. If my parents' experiences explain my perspective in approaching the bystander question and serve as an impetus for my working with legislators to criminalize complicity, then that is the best way for me to honor those experiences.

When I was researching *The Crime of Complicity*, I visited my father's hometown in eastern Hungary. I wanted to find my father's childhood home; to retrace my grandparents' walk on May 26, 1944, from their home to the train station from which they were deported to Auschwitz; to stand on the platform and visualize the Hungarian gentile bystander watching them being forcefully pushed onto the train; and in the Jewish cemetery, to find my grandparents' names on the memorial commemorating all the towns' Jewish residents who were murdered in Auschwitz.

When I finally found their names, I recited the mourner's *Kaddish*:

> *Glorified and sanctified be God's great name throughout the world*
> *which He has created according to His will.*
> *May He establish His kingdom in your lifetime and during your days,*
> *and within the life of the entire House of Israel, speedily and soon;*
> *and say, Amen.*
> *May His great name be blessed forever and to all eternity.*
> *Blessed and praised, glorified and exalted, extolled and honored,*
> *adored and lauded be the name of the Holy One, blessed be He,*
> *beyond all the blessings and hymns, praises and consolations that*
> *are ever spoken in the world; and say, Amen.*
> *May there be abundant peace from heaven, and life, for us*
> *and for all Israel; and say, Amen.*
> *He who creates peace in His celestial heights,*
> *may He create peace for us and for all Israel;*
> *and say, Amen*[16]

---

16. https://www.myjewishlearning.com/article/text-of-the-mourners-kaddish/

It was important for me to do so, for it enabled me to directly confront their fates. Although I know that both my grandparents were murdered on the day they arrived at Auschwitz, the details of my grandfather's final moments are lost to history. One fact that remains present today, however, is that a bystander facilitated my grandparents' murder. The bystander saw them walking to the train station and chose not to offer solace or assistance; the bystander stood on the station platform and watched them be pushed onto the train taking them to their deaths. That was the bystander of May 1944.

As we turn our attention in the present book to addressing the crime of complicity in contemporary society, we are once again confronted with the reality of the bystander. We must acknowledge that bystander and enabler complicity enhances the peril of the vulnerable individual in need of assistance. This is a *legal*, not just a moral, crime. In examining complicity, we must recall the consequences of inaction from the perspective of the individual in peril.

Today, as we examine our society and the world we live in, examples of complicity are plentiful. It is not by chance that "complicity" was chosen as the "word of the year" in 2017.

On August 16, 2018, the *Washington Post* published an op-ed by retired U.S. Navy admiral William H. McRaven, the commander of U.S. Joint Special Forces Command from 2011 to 2014. In that capacity, he oversaw the operation to kill Osama bin Laden. McRaven was writing in the aftermath of President Trump's decision to revoke the security clearance of former CIA director John Brennan. Because of the relevance of his words to the themes discussed in this book, I include it in its entirety:

Dear Mr. President:

Former CIA director John Brennan, whose security clearance you revoked on Wednesday, is one of the finest public servants I have ever known. Few Americans have done more to protect this country than John. He is a man of unparalleled integrity, whose honesty and character have never been in question, except by those who don't know him.

Therefore, I would consider it an honor if you would revoke my security clearance as well, so I can add my name to the list of men and women who have spoken up against your presidency.

Like most Americans, I had hoped that when you became president, you would rise to the occasion and become the leader this great nation needs.

A good leader tries to embody the best qualities of his or her organization. A good leader sets the example for others to follow. A good leader always puts the welfare of others before himself or herself.

Your leadership, however, has shown little of these qualities. Through your actions, you have embarrassed us in the eyes of our children, humiliated us on the world stage and, worst of all, divided us as a nation.

If you think for a moment that your McCarthy-era tactics will suppress the voices of criticism, you are sadly mistaken. The criticism will continue until you become the leader we prayed you would be.[17]

McRaven's letter reflects the tension confronted by bystanders: Do I act or do I not?

---

17. https://www.washingtonpost.com/opinions/revoke-my-security-clearance-too-mr-president/2018/08/16/8b149b02-a178-11e8-93e3-24d1703d2a7a_story.html.

"You don't know this about me, but I was raped. The devastation is incalculable. DECADES later—well, a life-time later, I am still surprised by all of the ways this still impacts my life. My story does not involve enablers, but I can only imagine what it would feel like if it did—the betrayal would be soul crushing, nowhere to turn. I think many (most?) people do not know how devastating sexual assault can be on a person's psyche. I am so fortunate that I found wonderful men in my life and I could go on. I told NO ONE for decades. If I hear one more joke about 'Oh, come on, she enjoyed it!'; or 'What's the big deal?'; or 'Get over it!' I might become homicidal."

—*Anonymous; identity is known to me*

"Nobody did anything, no. The coaches, I think, that was— I know they're probably listening and watching—the people I was the most disappointed in because they were supposed to protect us, and they just decided that it was more important to have functioning athletes, and their reputation was more important than our well-being, and how we felt. Really, that was the thing that broke my heart I think was that they let me down, and I want to say this because I think in all sports now, especially with this happening, I think it's important that the coaches really try to be there for the athletes, and not think about the sport and the competition and the notoriety of how great they are over the fact that they are working with children. They are coaching children, they are leaving their children in care of somebody like Larry, and they're just brushing it all aside, and I don't want that to ever happen to anybody else."

—*Melissa Imrie, victim impact statement*

— 2 —

From Impunity to Accountability

The freedom to act with utter impunity is a disturbing and tragic reality of the role of the enabler. Enablers knew, or easily could have discerned, who was at risk, who was responsible, what harm was inflicted, and how to aggressively bring the crime to a screeching halt. Enablers chose not to act to mitigate the ongoing harm. This choice had profound consequences, and accordingly enablers must be held accountable.

The title of this book is a reference to Tiffany Thomas-Lopez's powerful victim impact statement (VIS), in which she referred to the "army" that Nassar created when he abused hundreds of victims: the army of enablers. The army of enablers includes trainers, coaches, senior university officials, bishops, and others who turned their back on those in peril.

Their actions reflected both personal and institutional failures. On the basis of survivors' testimonies, court records, and media coverage, it is possible to identify four main categories of enabler: *dismissive, discouraging, punitive,* and *deceitful.* Enablers were dismissive when survivors shared with them what had been done to them. Enablers actively discouraged survivors from reporting the crimes visited upon them; they were punitive when they suggested there would be negative consequences to the survivor should they pursue recourse. Enablers deceitfully claimed not to believe what they heard. Enablers "addressed" the harm by moving the assailant to another location, where additional crimes could be committed. Enablers placed protecting an institution above protecting a survivor. More than anything, the pain—physical and emotional—inflicted on the survivors was facilitated by the army of enablers that surrounded, embraced, protected, covered for, and "understood" the perpetrators. These enablers bear significant responsibility for the evils perpetrated on the innocent.

The extent of this pain became dramatically clear in a Lansing, Michigan, courtroom when woman after woman stood in front of her abuser, Larry Nassar, and detailed the horrors she had endured. Some had been assaulted hundreds of times. It is hard to listen to the victim impact statements; the women are direct, honest, unsparing, and above all brave. Their bravery puts them in direct contrast to the enablers; Lindsey Lemke, captain of Michigan State University's women's gymnastics team, made powerfully clear in her VIS that the litany of enablers who ignored her and her sister survivors were cowards.[1] Despite the power conferred by their positions of authority, they stood as cowards behind the protective wall provided by the institution, rather than protect those to whom a duty was owed. In Lemke's words:

> You [Lou Anna Simon, former president of MSU] say you aren't responsible for this. I wish you would come up to this podium and be half as brave as all of us have had to be the past year-and-a-half. . . . To be brave enough to come up here and confidently tell us the reasons why you don't think that you are responsible.[2]

Perhaps it is convenient to hide behind the façade of an institution? Certainly it is a pattern that repeats itself over and again, even though it casts the enablers in highly negative light. It is indicative of a failure to recognize who is in the wrong and who was harmed and is at risk. It reflects a stunning inability to understand the consequences of failing to protect present and future targets, and as such, it merits punishment.

---

1. https://www.youtube.com/watch?v=c6yFL18aSJE.
2. https://www.thecut.com/2018/01/usa-gymnastics-larry-nassar-trial-aly-raisman-mckayla-ma roney.html.

Lindsey's description regarding enablers at Michigan State holds equally true for Penn State. The following account adapted from a news story at the time could be applied to any of the institutions examined in this book:

Penn State's former president and two other ex-administrators were sentenced Friday to at least two months in jail for failing to report a child sexual abuse allegation against Jerry Sandusky a decade before his arrest engulfed the university in scandal and brought down football coach Joe Paterno.

"They ignored the opportunity to put an end to his crimes when they had a chance to do so," Judge John Boccabella said as he lambasted the three defendants and the Hall of Fame coach over a delay that prosecutors say enabled Sandusky to molest four more boys.

Boccabella said he was "appalled that the common sense to make a phone call did not occur," a transgression that "sort of robs my faith in who we are as adults and where we are going."

The case hinged on coaching assistant Mike McQueary's claim that he witnessed Sandusky—a retired member of the coaching staff who ran a charity for youngsters—molesting a boy in the team showers in 2001. Prosecutors said that after McQueary recounted what he saw, the three administrators decided not to report it to authorities to protect the university's reputation.

Sandusky was not arrested until 2011, after a prosecutor got an anonymous email tip. Sandusky was found guilty the next year of sexually abusing 10 boys and is serving 30 to 60 years in prison.

Both the judge and prosecutors Friday thrust blame onto Paterno himself. Paterno was fired but never charged with a crime; he died of lung cancer at age 85 two months after Sandusky's arrest.

Paterno "could have made that phone call without so much as getting his hands dirty," Boccabella said. "Why he didn't is beyond me."

Prosecutor Patrick Schulte said Curley at one point had drawn up a plan to report Sandusky to state authorities, but "something changed after talking to coach Paterno."

"What was it about that conversation that made you change your mind?" Schulte said, referring to the ex-athletic director.

Prosecutors reserved some of their harshest words for Spanier (PSU President—ANG), with Chief Deputy Attorney General Laura Ditka saying he was "a complete and utter failure as a leader when it mattered most." She said his inaction "allowed children to be harmed."[3]

The Freeh Report, which addressed the culpability of Penn State officials in the Sandusky scandal is quite clear: "The most saddening finding by the Special Investigative Counsel is the total and consistent disregard by the most senior leaders at Penn State for the safety and welfare of Sandusky's child victims."[4] That is the most succinct description of the enabler: an individual who makes an unconscionable and willful decision to protect the perpetrator, thereby exacerbating the harm caused by the predator.

It is astonishing to imagine how, time after time after time, the enabler cast asunder cries for help. Looking Nassar in the eye, Mattie Larson slowly, emphatically, and deliberately told him, "You have no idea how much I fucking hate you."[5] She left no doubt as to the overwhelming pain he had caused her and the depth of her anger. However, it is crucial to recognize that without enablers, Larry Nassar could not sexually assault hundreds of girls, some of them hundreds of times; Jerry Sandusky could not rape boys in the shower at Penn State and in his basement; Richard Strauss could not assault hundreds of athletes at Ohio State; and Catholic priests could not rape thousands upon thousands of boys, girls, and nuns worldwide.

Only by hearing the survivors and seeing the pain deeply etched into their faces can one begin to grasp the enormity of the crime. What stands out when listening to the VISs and reading the grand jury reports is the ease with which the enablers ignored the pain of other human beings. In contrast to bystanders who, under certain circumstances, can argue their failure to act is justified because of potential harm to themselves

---

3. https://www.nbcsports.com/philadelphia/penn-state-nittany-lions/3-ex-penn-state-officials-sent-jail-jerry-sandusky-scandal.

4. Freeh Report. See https://www.washingtonpost.com/blogs/on-parenting/post/penn-state-report-are-they-glad-they-tried-to-protect-their-reputations-now/2012/07/12/gJQAnV9sfW_blog.html.

5. https://www.youtube.com/watch?v=gsEVmL02AZg&t=50s.

or their families, these enablers were protected by the fact that they held positions of authority in their respective institutions. The caveat in the bystander obligation—that one should not endanger oneself—does not apply to the enabler obligation. Perhaps, referencing Lindsey Lemke, this is the essence of the enabler as coward: knowing someone is in harm's way and yet making the decision to ignore their peril, thereby both protecting the institution and facilitating additional harm.

On May 9, 2019, Pope Francis made it mandatory for Roman Catholic clergy to report clerical sexual abuse and cover-ups of such abuse. Though undoubtedly important, this action was a day late and a dollar short. Actually, it is hundreds of years late and, from the perspective of an unfathomable number of survivors, tragically short. Boys and girls alike were allowed to fall prey to tens of thousands of priests, enabled by an overwhelming number of bishops, cardinals, and other high-ranking church officials.[6] A clerical leader is a person of enormous importance among the faithful; for some, the divine's representative on Earth. It is thus all the more reprehensible that the hierarchical structure of the Catholic Church made possible the institutionalization of sexual assault.

Ignoring the pain and distress of another is a puzzling human characteristic; ignoring a child in distress is incomprehensible. Nevertheless, that is precisely what the enablers of Nassar, Sandusky, Strauss, and the priests did. Though they may have had different reasons for their actions, it appears that the principle motivations were instinctively either to protect the institution or to protect the perpetrator.

Their failure to act was a deliberate and calculated choice. In some cases, the enablers held lengthy meetings to determine their course of action; in others, emails were sent exploring how to protect the perpetrator and the institution; in yet others, the victim was waved off with a flick of the hand. It is hard to determine which is more reprehensible: the calculating enabler or the nonchalant enabler. Perhaps there is no need to

---

6. https://www.nbcnews.com/news/religion/nearly-1-700-priests-clergy-accused-sex-abuse-are -unsupervised-n1062396, https://www.usatoday.com/in-depth/news/nation/2019/11/11/catholic -sexual-abuse-accused-priests-arent-sex-offender-registry/4012206002/. https://www.usatoday.com /story/news/nation/2019/11/11/catholic-sex-abuse-why-dont-accused-priests-go-jail /3997022002/.

categorize enablers; maybe it is sufficient to point a finger at the enabler and say, "J'accuse."

Regardless of why the enabler chose not to act, the consequences of their inaction are consistent and predictable: by escaping punishment, the perpetrator is free to assault the next innocent victim. In *The Crime of Complicity* I recommended adoption of Duty to Act legislation that would impose on the bystander the obligation to dial 911 when he or she sees another person in peril. The proposed bar is very low: make a phone call. In the pages ahead, we shall introduce proposed legislation criminalizing the enabler who failed to act.

In both cases—bystander and enabler—the duty to act imposes minimal obligation and would significantly mitigate the peril facing the survivor. Some have suggested, evidence notwithstanding, that we can rely on people to know to do the right thing. They argue that individuals are sufficiently moral that it is unwarranted to impose a legal duty to act. If only this were true. Ask any gymnast assaulted by Nassar, any boy raped by Sandusky, any child violated by priests, any student assaulted by Strauss, and he or she will tell you that the "right thing to do" is a myth—a "feel good" myth.

Of course, some people will step up and do the right thing and will be praised for doing so. No doubt there are heroes who are not afraid to endanger themselves on behalf of others. Truly those people are to be lauded.

However, while we note those who do take action, history reveals, time and time again, that they are alarmingly outweighed by the majority who stand by. I have been one among them. Many are good people who see themselves as bound by a strong moral compass and able to distinguish between right and wrong. Much consideration has been given to why, in the bystander's mind, the potential for personal harm far outweighs the possible benefit to the survivor. This is a balancing argument that cannot be discounted out of hand. However, the Talmud (the body of Jewish civil law) offers guidance in resolving this tension: "Whoever destroys a soul, it is considered as if he destroyed an entire world. And whoever saves a life, it is considered as if he saved an entire world."[7]

---

7. https://judaism.stackexchange.com/questions/74049/anyone-who-saves-a-life-is-as-if-he -saved-an-entire-world-jewish-life-or-any.

This book builds the case against such individuals who turn their heads or walk away. The charge is distinct from participating in a conspiracy, or aiding and abetting, or other crimes reflecting actions of two or more individuals with a common purpose to commit a wrong. Rather the crime of enabling is more in line with the crime of the bystander, for both are predicated on a duty to act, reflective of an obligation to protect the person in peril. The proposal is best understood as extending the scope of who and what harmed the survivor beyond the perpetrator. Far from diminishing or minimizing the attacker's criminal conduct, it acts in parallel to point a guilty finger at the enabler.

Until enabling is recognized as a criminal act, we—intentionally or otherwise—enable the enabler to continue enabling. As a result of our continued unwillingness to demand enablers be penalized for their actions, we fail the survivors. That is something that must no longer be tolerated. Speaking to survivors, one hears the voices of stolen childhoods, damaged dreams, and memories of unspeakable perversions that will forever remain with them. These are the voices of the vulnerable who were ignored when they cried out for help.

We cannot undo the damage they suffered, but by truly listening to them we can prevent future offenses. The enabler did not commit sexual assault, but when the survivor turned to the enabler with the legitimate expectation that he or she would mitigate the harm, the enabler did not do so. Such failure must be punished. In recommending imposition of punishment, the intent is unequivocal: You failed the survivor, you chose to protect the institution, you pay the price.

This is the key to understanding the enabler from the perspective of the survivor. Punishing the predator is essential, but insufficient. Punishing the enabler is equally important, for predator and enabler *together* are responsible for the assault. Hearing these survivors' stories in their own words graphically illustrates why society has an obligation to punish the enabler.

"The day I finally told someone (my stepdad) and was told to keep it to myself because it will only upset my mom (it was her father who abused me) is forever etched in my mind. Later, when she found out, she was angry at me for ruining her vision of her father and for interrupting her idea of her happy little family. Nowhere did anyone consider the consequences it had on me or how their further relationship with him would almost destroy me. Living with the anger at that inner circle is truly as abusive as the acts themselves!!! I still live with that pain."

—*Anonymous; identity is known to me*

"The investigation done by MSU was brief and sloppy, and it left me feeling disposable and worthless. After asking a few of his friends if what he did was inappropriate and getting a collective answer of, 'Well, I would've done it differently, but I guess what he did was okay,' Larry Nassar was cleared to practice again under new guidelines that were never actually enforced. . . . When Larry Nassar sexually assaulted me and MSU covered for him, they altered the entire course of my life."

—*Amanda Thomashow, victim impact statement*

— 3 —

Enough

The main point of my undertaking in this book is to show that enough is enough. The survivors I have met with are articulate, intelligent, thoughtful, and insightful. I promised that their words would be shared with the reader in as unfiltered a manner as they spoke with me.[1] Jamie Dantzscher asked Larry Nassar, "How fucking dare you say you are sorry?"[2] I see no reason to filter the language, to tone down the anger, to "clean up" the vocabulary. It would be disrespectful to do so and would deny the reader the opportunity to appreciate just how deeply the survivors have been hurt and how truly angry they are.

These emotions are directed at both enabler and predator, sometimes with greater intensity at the former. I had not expected that. It was only while watching the victim impact statements that I began to understand the extent to which the survivors blamed the enablers for their plight. As I interacted with them, that anger was repeatedly reinforced, expressed directly, and often mixed with sadness. In one of the most painful interactions, one of the survivors came to the realization that a revered and much-loved coach was nothing more than an enabler. For her, it was excruciating. And it impressed upon me the power of the enabler.

---

1. While writing the book, I met with a psychologist whose practice focuses on survivors of sexual assault. He was not surprised to learn of the direct language in which my interviewees expressed their emotions. Indeed, he encouraged me to understand that it can be therapeutic, for it enables survivors to "release" their anger.
2. https://www.youtube.com/watch?v=pUWuN371hio&t=129s.

I was fortunate in being able to spend considerable time with these badly injured survivors, and thus to begin to truly understand the costs they had incurred as a consequence of their enablers' decisions. The emotions they expressed cover the gamut. In many cases, the painful road to recovery will last a lifetime; some survivors doubt whether they will ever lead normal, healthy lives. Some survivors are currently in an abusive personal relationship, sometimes one in a series of abusive relationships, unable to break the cycle. Some survivors have strained relations with their parents; whether because the parents feel they did not sufficiently protect their children is an open question. For some, going public with their stories has strained their marriages, and their experiences have affected their relationships with their own children. Survivors of abuse by priests have, in some cases, developed great anger against the church.

I am not the emissary for the survivors; for that, they do not need me. I have no interest in recounting what sexual predators did to them. Indeed, I believe they were relieved when they learned that was not my focus. In approaching the survivors whom I interviewed for this book, I made it clear that while I am deeply sympathetic to the terrible pain caused by their perpetrator, my primary interest was the person who enabled the perpetrator. There is no doubt regarding the depravity of a sexual predator, but the enabler is only half a step behind.

Although the enablers hid behind various cloaks, many of their survivors today call them out by name. This book joins in that effort. In making the decision to name names, my intention is clear: to ensure that the reader understands how institutionalized the culture of assault was and how deeply invested enablers were with their institutions. Their allegiance was clear; their identification was absolute.

Court documents filed on behalf of survivors make clear the overwhelming odds they faced. The enablers literally overwhelmed them. Not only were there a seemingly endless number of enablers, but their status at the relevant institutions enabled them to clear the path for the predator and give the survivor not a chance. Until now.

Whether the enablers feel shame and embarrassment is unclear, safe to assume they have convinced themselves they either did not know or were not in a position to do anything. In listening to and reading their comments, there were times I wanted to shout, "Stop, just stop!" for no statements, however artfully drafted by lawyers or crisis management experts, can explain or excuse their actions. They are nothing more than empty words intended to sway the court of public opinion. I would be remiss were I not to single out USA Gymnastics as the absolute "master" of empty ad hominems,[3] but the other institutions discussed here follow close behind.

In spite of persistent best efforts to dodge, bob, and weave, none of the enablers has Muhammed Ali's ability to forever "float like a butterfly," though some have clearly stung the survivors "like a bee." Larry Nassar's former dean, Dr. William Strampel, was convicted in a court of law for "misconduct in office and willful neglect of duty."[4] Former Michigan State University president Lou Anna Simon is on trial, as is former MSU gymnastics coach Kathy Klages. Others must join them as defendants, not only individuals but also the institutions behind them. Their actions clearly warrant prosecution. It is my hope this book will facilitate the bringing of these enablers to justice.

The report of the Independent Investigation, "The Constellation of Factors Underlying Larry Nassar's Abuse of Athletes," was submitted on December 10, 2018, by the law firm Ropes and Gray. Written by Joan McPhee and James P. Dowden, it addresses both USA Gymnastics and Michigan State University. Of USAG, the report stated:

> The institutional failures, however, extended beyond weak structural elements, governance deficiencies and failures of oversight. In the summer of 2015, when the National Team member allegations of sexual assault were squarely presented to USAG and the USOC [United States Olympic Committee], the two organizations, at the direction of their respective CEO's, engaged in affirmative efforts to protect and preserve their institutional interests—even as Nassar retired from the sport with his reputation intact and continued to have access to girls and young women at the college, club and high school levels. The actions of these organizations, their CEO's and other senior personnel reveal that, apart from USAG's referral

3. https://www.dailymail.co.uk/news/article-6292789/USA-Gymnastics-head-hid-remote-cabin-indicted-larry-nassar-cover-up.html.
4. https://edition.cnn.com/2019/06/12/us/msu-strampel-conviction-nassar/index.html.

to law enforcement in the summer of 2015 and again in the spring of 2016, USAG and the USOC took no meaningful steps to protect athletes from the danger presented by Nassar. Rather, these organizations, each in their own way, maintained secrecy regarding the Nassar allegations and focused on controlling the flow of information about his alleged misconduct.[5]

I Skyped with a Michigan State survivor, JD1,[6] on March 20, 2019. In the course of our conversation, she pinpointed the distinction between the bystander and the enabler from the survivor's perspective: the bystander *saw* and chose not to mitigate immediate or present harm, the enabler *was told* and chose not to do so. An enabler is not a bystander, but a bystander who chooses not to act becomes an enabler. JD1 knew who Nassar's enablers were, but no bystander directly witnessed Nassar abusing JD1.

Like many other survivors, JD1's anger is directed primarily at the enablers who protected the institution, rather than at the perpetrator. As survivors consistently emphasized, enablers were adults in positions of authority. Unlike the bystander, who in the overwhelming majority of cases is randomly at the scene, the enabler, although not present, has the ability to make important decisions regarding the perpetrator based on information received, directly or indirectly. The enablers at whom JD1 pointed an accusatory finger were Michigan State University officials—trainers, coaches, senior administrators, including former president Lou Anna Simon—who made the deliberate decision to protect the "brand" rather than protect the victim. In the eyes of JD1 and the other survivors, the enabler repeatedly had the opportunity to act but chose not to do so.

JD1 was raised a Spartan and loved Michigan State University. Nevertheless, when asked how she currently felt about the university, her response was direct: "Burn the fucking place down." This blunt expression of the sense of betrayal was reiterated by other survivors in relation to individual enablers and institutions alike.

---

5. Independent Investigation, "The Constellation of Factors Underlying Larry Nassar's Abuse of Athletes," submitted on December 10, 2018.
6. Survivor's identity known to the author.

The "Status of the Independent Special Counsel's Investigation into Michigan State University's Handling of the Larry Nassar Matter" was submitted on December 21, 2018, by William Forsyth, independent special counsel. Of MSU, Forsyth wrote:

> Amid the multitude of stirring accounts of how MSU's premier sports medicine doctor sexually abused scores of young women, the MSU Board of Trustees sent a written request to the Attorney General [of the State of Michigan], asking him to investigate "MSU's handling of the Nassar situation." The Board pledged that it "stood ready to fully cooperate with (the Attorney General Office's) review"
>
> Unfortunately, the University failed to live up to this pledge by: (1) issuing misleading public statements, (2) drowning investigators in irrelevant documents, (3) waging needless battles over pertinent documents, and (4) asserting attorney-client privilege even when it did not apply. These actions warrant extended discussion because they highlight a common thread we encountered throughout the investigation into how the University handled allegations against Nassar. Both then and now, MSU has fostered a culture of indifference toward sexual assault, motivated by its desire to protect its reputation.[7]

Forsyth's assessment is echoed by the survivors. In her victim impact statement, Olivia Cowan, a former gymnast, was forceful in addressing USA Gymnastics and Michigan State University. "I now view green and white in the same way I view Larry Nassar," she said. Acknowledging that MSU had apologized for Nassar's action, she noted that MSU officials needed to "look in the mirror and take ownership."

"Where were you when we needed you?" Cowan asked. "If you had only believed the women who brought complaints forward."[8]

---

7. Forsyth, p. 2.
8. https://www.mlive.com/news/2018/01/nassar_sentencing_victims.html.

> "I wanted someone to do something; to
> shut Larry the fuck down."
> —*Conversation with Tiffany Thomas-Lopez, June 4, 2019*

"Why has the US Olympic Committee been silent? Why isn't the USOC here right now? Larry was the Olympic doctor and he molested me at the 2012 London Olympic Games. They say now they applaud those who have spoken out, but it's easy to say that now. When the brave women started speaking out back then, more than a year after the USOC knew about Nassar, they were dismissed. At the 2016 Olympic Games, the president of the USOC said that the USOC would not conduct an investigation. It even defended USA Gymnastics as one of the leaders in developing policies to protect athletes. That's the response a courageous woman gets when she speaks out? And when others joined those athletes and began speaking out with more stories of abuse, were they acknowledged? No. It is like being abused all over again. I have represented the United States of America in two Olympics and have done so successfully. And both USA Gymnastics and the United States Olympic Committee have been very quick to capitalize on and celebrate my success. But did they reach out when I came forward? No."

> —*Aly Raisman, victim impact statement*

— 4 —

Survivor Expectation

Based on thousands of pages of grand jury indictments, civil lawsuits, criminal prosecutions, special reports, media accounts, and personal interaction with sexual assault survivors and their attorneys, I formulated one critical question: What are the survivor's expectations of the enabler or bystander?

In response, interview after interview shed compelling light on two fundamental points: First, this question had not been previously posed. Second, survivors were desperate for protection and support that never materialized. In Tiffany Thomas Lopez's words, "I wanted the enabler to fucking do something." Because that almost never happened, the perpetrator benefited from the complicit cowardice of enablers, both individual and institutional. From the survivors' perspective, both perpetrator and enabler bear responsibility for their plight and must be held accountable.

Anger at a perpetrator is understandable. Emotions regarding the enabler range from deep disappointment to seething anger to profound frustration. All reflect a sense of abandonment by someone who was in a position to alleviate pain and suffering. Most of the athlete survivors with whom I engaged reported the abuse they suffered to their coaches and trainers, because they trusted them. They expected them to act on their behalf. They certainly did not expect them to turn away and side with the perpetrators.

Coaches and trainers play a crucial role for athletes. The same is true of the relationship between priests and their parishioners. These are relationships of trust and respect. For many, the dependence extends well beyond the playing field or matters of faith. In addition to being mentors, coaches can be both significant gatekeepers—protecting their athletes from outsiders—and door-openers—making opportunities available to them. By best positioning young athletes, coaches can be conduits to athletic scholarships or bring them to the attention of higher-level coaches and trainers. Such successes reflect well on coach and athlete alike, creating a symbiotic relationship. However, as we have come to learn, coaches—like others in positions of authority, including in the Catholic Church—can fail their athletes, violate their trust, and become enablers.

Context is important in discussing the issue of sexual abuse in the athletic world. Young athletes are in their physical prime; their bodies are at their peak and are a source of personal and family pride. For many, their body is their identity. And in a sports loving (if not crazed) culture such as the United States, athletes are critical to fans' identity with their team. Because of the overwhelming importance athletes place on their bodies, they are naturally hesitant to report injury or weakness; that is, to admit they might be damaged goods. Most of the survivors I talked with did not initially share their experiences with their families or their teammates.

On the one hand, the survivors I interviewed included America's most renowned athletes, who enjoyed success and fame on a level most of us will never attain, much less truly understand. On the other hand, though, these were young people, vulnerable on two distinct but inter-twined levels: to sexual predation and to abandonment by the people they trusted most. Their devastation was overwhelming. Many have lost their ability to trust anyone, even after decades have passed.

In the following extracts, four former athletes express their thoughts on the athlete-coach relationship:

> I think that the initial trust and relationship between coach/trainer and athlete prior to the sexual assault is what enables the coach/trainer to get away with it. These coaches/trainers are predatory

and carefully plan and build up to the attacks. They have the time to do so because sports consume so much time, and I think sports make athletes more vulnerable and open to forming close bonds/relationships to those that share in the experience. They form these relationships with coaches/trainers over time, and after this relationship has developed, the athlete is probably less likely to report sexual assault because of the relationship. It may seem more justifiable and less like an attack. So in a way sports is a perfect medium for sexual predators.

. . . Sports being so physical, there are more opportunities to gradually cross lines or provide rationale for doing so, so logistically sexual assault seems easier in a sports context also.

I would love to learn more about why players don't tell teammates about sexual assault. Does it vary in individual vs. team sports? Maybe players in individual sports are less likely to confide in teammates because there is more competition and less camaraderie? I would like to think I would tell a teammate if I was sexually assaulted by a coach, but maybe I wouldn't.[1] (Division One women's soccer player)

I had only female coaches (and trainers) in college and never came close to anything like this. So I don't want to comment on the aspects of the sexual abuse. *But* I can relate to the trusting/mentor relationship with coaches, wanting to do anything to please them, hesitation in reporting injury, identity as an athlete, etc. Those were all *very* real to me and I think the way you describe them is right. One aspect that I'm not sure I agree with at least personally, is in the last paragraph that the trainer/team doctor was expected to be emotionally available and would understand your fears and anxieties. . . . Maybe it's because I was never really injured and wasn't generally around trainers on a regular basis, but I don't think I ever relied on them to understand everything going on with me beyond my physical health. This goes back to your

---

1. Email forwarded to me by teammate of the writer. All such extracts have been lightly, but not substantively, edited.

earlier point that athletes don't want to report injuries or weakness, including anxiety, self doubt, other emotional things.

Additionally, I'm not sure this really needs to be included in this part/your book in general, but I would say that I felt more empowered being on a team with 30 other women compared to individual sports like gymnastics where they are all constantly competing against each other. I wonder if instances of sexual assault happen as much on team sports?[2] (Division One women's lacrosse player)

I hesitate in casting a wide net over coaches who prey upon the athletes. The relationship between coach and athlete is built by both parties and the foundation is added to by both parties. The number of victims is not proportionate to the number of perpetrators. I think the more valuable point is that a few individuals can get away with ruining so many victims' hopes and dreams and prior realities and that those individuals need to be stopped because they are bad (for lack of a better word) individuals, not because they are coaches or trainers. They use the position that they are in to take advantage of the athletes.[3] (Female college swimmer)

I believe that when questioning how a coach/trainer can get away with such unfathomable acts, one must acknowledge that numerous elements are routinely at play. In most cases, the appeal of the coach/trainer to the public, the role of the coach/trainer, and whether the athlete plays an individual or team sport lend to the enabling of a predator coach/trainer. . . .

Certain aspects of the general role of the coach/trainer can also enable sexual attacks. Both the coach and the trainer have impactful roles in regards to the athlete, but they manifest in different ways. Metaphorically speaking, if the coach is the bad cop, then the trainer is the good cop. Perpetrators can benefit from either role. The coach tends to play a parental role for the athlete. With this comes authority and the desire of the athlete to please coach which can quickly escalate to emotional manipulation and abuse. A coach also has control over the athlete's playing time, scholar-

---

2. The identity of the writer is known to me.
3. The identity of the writer is known to me.

ship amount, spot on the roster. On the other hand, the essence of the trainer's job is to make the athlete feel good. Not only does the trainer perform physical adjustments and treatments on the athlete's body to provide relief, but the trainer often can be an emotional outlet for the athlete. This is a formidable combination when abused and the unique relationship between trainer and athlete can make for a slippery slope. . . .

Regarding the emotional impact, I personally struggle more with my feeling towards the enabler than the abuser. The abuser became the bad guy the second he acted. The enabler, when faced with the choice between right and wrong, chose wrong. To me, that is arguably more betraying than the act itself. (Division One, female, track and field athlete)[4]

Throughout the interview process, coaches were frequently described as "father figures." The desire to please the coach, the ultimate determinant of playing time, was paramount; conversely, angering the coach was to be avoided at all costs. In some cases, the coach took on mythic status. To be on a Division One team was a source of enormous pride to the athlete and his or her family and friends. For non-scholarship athletes, to be a "walk-on" on a Division One team was to have, at best, a tenuous hold on one's standing.

In this context, trainers were also of great importance: they provided an "ear" for an athlete's fears, anxieties, and pain. Similarly, Larry Nassar gained the trust of the gymnasts he was "treating." After all, he was a good guy, always ready with an encouraging word, happy to sneak some food to the girls, whose food intake was closely monitored and an endless source of anxiety. Given the very competitive nature of Division One sports and elite gymnastics, the belief that a trainer or team doctor was emotionally available to an athlete was crucial. The idea that they were on the athlete's side and would "understand" their fears and anxieties was a critical component of the athlete's assumed support system.

It is therefore understandable that when Ron McDaniel, then a member of The Ohio State University's tennis team, was abused by Richard Strauss during a medical exam, he went directly to head tennis coach

---

4. The identity of the writer is known to me.

John Daly.[5] McDaniel reports that standing with Daly were OSU's athletic director, Hugh Hindman, and sports information director, Steve Snap. Their response? Some combination of ignoring, dismissing, and walking away. None saw fit to directly address McDaniel's serious complaint.

From McDaniel's perspective this is what happened: Strauss sexually assaulted him, he immediately reported the assault to his head coach, the university's sports information director, and, perhaps most important in the enabler context, the athletic director. The athletic director, particularly at an institution that places extraordinary emphasis on athletics, such as Ohio State, wields significant institutional power. Beyond the considerable resources for which they are responsible and the absolute control they have over the hiring and firing of coaches, the athletic director is one of the most publicly recognized individuals—and often the target of an irate and noisy fan base—at a Division One school, second only to the head coach of the dominant sport. While John Daly was McDaniel's head coach, and therefore the person most directly responsible for his own college athletic career, development, and well-being, there is no comparison between Hindman's institutional power and prestige and that of Daly.

Remarkably, both men chose to ignore McDaniel's report and his statement that he would never again allow himself to be examined by Ohio State's sports medicine doctor, an associate professor of medicine at the university, because of Strauss's inappropriate conduct. Rather than taking any steps to protect either McDaniel or other students including athletes, for whom they were responsible in the future, Hindman, Daly, and Snap walked away.

From the survivor's perspective, "walking away" has both physical and psychological meaning. Both McDaniel's coach and the most senior official in the university's athletic department turned their backs on him. That survivors who "dared" to complain were ignored, marginalized, minimized, denigrated, humiliated, or banished by their enablers is a recurring theme. Underlying this theme is the devastating reality that these people should have had the survivors' best interests at heart. The

5. Skype conversation with Ron McDaniel, June 12, 2019.

enablers were not random individuals whom the survivors bumped into on the way to the grocery store after an assault.

On November 13, 2018, a First Amended Complaint was filed in the U.S. District Court for the Southern District of Ohio against The Ohio State University on behalf of a number of plaintiffs, including Ronald McDaniel and Steve Snyder-Hill.[6] Snyder-Hill had reported his abuse by Strauss to the director of the university's Student Health Services. The complaint speaks volumes regarding the relationship between the perpetrator and enabler, and the extent to which the survivor is violated both physically and emotionally.

Coach John Daly knew of the abuse to which a player on his team was subjected, yet failed to take any action on McDaniel's behalf. In terms of the paradigm of "dismissive" and "discouraging" enablers, Daly would be categorized as dismissive. He did not actively discourage McDaniel from filing a complaint against Strauss, but tacitly suggested that there was no need, because what happened to McDaniel was not a big deal. From McDaniel's perspective, this was abandonment by a person positioned to protect him from harm, who instead chose to be complicit in his abuse.

That same "indictment" applies to Hugh Hindman and Ohio State athletic director Andy Geiger, who were both informed by student athletes of Strauss's conduct:

> Student-athletes informed OSU athletic administrators and staff, including, but not limited to, Athletic Director Andy Geiger, Assistant Athletic Director Archie Griffin, Track and Field Coach Frank Zubovich, Tennis Coach John Daly, Swimming Coach Dick Sloan, and Fencing Coach Charlotte Remenyik, that Dr. Strauss's conduct seemed inappropriate and made them uncomfortable.[7]

The word "indictment" is used deliberately. The list above reflects what survivor JD1[8] articulated in distinguishing between bystanders and enablers: these coaches and senior administrators were not casual bystanders; they were classic, complicit enablers. Each one held a position

---

6. Case: 2:18-cv-00736-MHW-EPD Doc # 27. Filed: 11/13/18.
7. Case: 2:18-cv-00736-MHW-EPD Doc #: 27. Filed: 11/13/18, p. 17.
8. Survivor's identity known to the author.

of status and responsibility from which they were well placed, and could have been expected, to act on behalf of Strauss's victims.

It is interesting to give pause and ponder whether Daly would have acted differently were he a bystander who chanced upon a person in peril, rather than an institutional enabler familiar with the parties involved. Ironically, he might have found it more instinctual to provide assistance to a random individual who was being sexually assaulted.

In fact, Daly failed his own athlete. Moreover, he used Strauss's known malfeasance as a punishment. According to McDaniel, "if you did something wrong, 'You need to see Strauss'" was a common refrain. Track and field athletes who also were required to be examined by Strauss were warned, "Drop the baton, get your nuts checked." Joking is an inherent part of athletic culture, but this is not good humor. These coaches were clearly articulating two things: they knew what Strauss was doing, and they recognized that the athlete understood the consequences of being examined by Strauss. However the coaches perceived such an examination, McDaniel leaves little doubt that he and other athletes perceived it as abuse.

McDaniel suggests an atmosphere where Strauss's actions were a standard operating procedure facilitated by an uncomfortable reality: seeing Strauss was required of athletes in particular sports and training in specific locations on the Ohio State campus. Tellingly, when I asked what he would like to see result from the court case, McDaniel answered, "To clean house." This response is based on his conviction that "lots of shit is hidden," and that "OSU knew."

Likewise, in regard to sexual abuse in the Catholic Church, the Pennsylvania grand jury stated:

> We saw from diocesan records that church officials, going back decades, were insisting that they had no duty to report to the government when they learned of child abuse in their parishes. New laws make it harder to take that position; but we want them tighter. . . . Make it clear that the duty to report a child abuser continues as long as there's reason to believe he will do it again—whether or not he's "active" on any particular day, and whether or not he may pick a different kid next time.[9]

---

9. PA GJ, p. 8.

The issue of "duty" is of prime importance. Duty to whom? In reality, there should be no need to ask this question. As a survivor, Tiffany Thomas-Lopez cut to the heart of the matter: "I wanted someone to do something; to shut Larry the fuck down."[10] From the survivors' perspective, there is no dilemma regarding what duty was owed and to whom: enablers were obligated to protect the vulnerable, not the predators or institutions that employed the enablers.

The report of the Independent Investigation examining the sexual abuses committed at The Ohio State University by Richard Strauss was written by the law firm of Perkins Coie, LLP. Submitted by its principal authors, Caryn Trombino and Markus Funk, on May 15, 2019, it noted:

> We find that [Ohio State] University personnel had knowledge of Strauss' sexually abusive treatment of male student-patients as early as 1979 but that complaints and reports about Strauss' conduct were not elevated beyond the Athletics Department or Student Health until 1996. Specifically, in January 1996, the University suspended Strauss from his activities as a treating physician at OSU after a Student Health patient accused Strauss of fondling him during a genital examination. At that time, the University undertook a very limited investigation of Strauss' complaint history. Although the University's 1996 disciplinary action resulted in Strauss' permanent removal from Athletics and Student Health, his status as a tenured faculty member remained unaffected.[11]

Similarly, the law firm of Freeh Sporkin & Sullivan, LLP, on July 12, 2012, submitted its "Report of the Special Investigative Counsel Regarding the Actions of The Pennsylvania State University Related to the Child Sexual Abuse Committed by Gerald A. Sandusky." The executive summary reports what has now become a familiar tale:

> On November 4, 2011 the Attorney General of the Commonwealth of Pennsylvania ("Attorney General") filed criminal charges against Gerald A. Sandusky ("Sandusky") that included multiple counts of involuntary deviate sexual intercourse, aggravated indecent

---

10. Conversation with Tiffany Thomas-Lopez, June 4, 2019.
11. OSU PC report, Executive Summary, p. 1.

assault, corruption of minors, unlawful contact with minors and endangering the welfare of minors. Several of the offenses occurred between 1998 and 2002, during which time Sandusky was either the Defensive Coordinator for The Pennsylvania State University ("Penn State" or "University") football team or a Penn State professor Emeritus with unrestricted access to the University's football facilities. On November 4, 2011 the Attorney General filed criminal charges against the University's Athletic Director ("AD") Timothy M. Curley ("Curley") and Senior Vice-President Finance and Business ("SVP-FB"), Gary C. Schultz ("Schultz") for failing to report allegations of child abuse against Sandusky to law enforcement or child protection authorities in 2002 and for committing perjury during their testimony about the allegations to the Grand Jury in Dauphin County, Pennsylvania, in January 2011.[12]

While many of us sit in our living rooms and cheer on elite athletes, we rarely ask ourselves, "What did it take to get there?" For an outsider, it is almost impossible to truly understand the discipline, focus, tolerance of pain, mental toughness, and determination required to succeed in the world of elite gymnastics. All of this is compounded by the fact that elite gymnasts are identified very young and henceforth largely separated from their peer group, except fellow gymnasts. Their entire day revolves around practice, and their families' lives revolve around them.

The all-out commitment required to succeed comes at significant cost: financial sacrifices by parents, burdens on families, strains on marriages, and long-term physical and emotional tolls on the athletes themselves. These sacrifices are justified by the winning shot, the fourth down pass, the seamless dismount from balance beam, the perfect dive, the putt on the eighteenth hole. The notion of sacrifice is central to understanding elite athletes. But however commendable their willingness to push their bodies, this must never be used to justify mental, physical, or emotional abuse.

Behind the public face of the athletic events watched by millions lurks another, underreported aspect of the undertaking that is deeply problematic and carries terrible consequences. This "veil of secrecy" enables the

---

12. Freeh Report, Executive Summary, p. 13.

perpetrator to commit terrible crimes with the twin confidence that the majority of survivors will not report them, and that if and when a report is made, the enabler will make the wrong decision. In the cases before us, most of the victims were children or young adults. They were vulnerable, carefully groomed by their attackers, chosen with an expert's eye, and manipulated, initially by the perpetrator and subsequently by the enabler. The attacks occurred in athletic training rooms, in showers, in physician offices, in back rooms, in basements, in hotel rooms—places where adults never should have been allowed to be alone with children.

Tragically, such activity behind closed doors reaches well beyond the athletic arena. Thousands of pages of documents graphically detailing abuses in the Catholic Church are irrefutable proof that the pattern of perpetrator's crime and enabler's complicity is repeated time and after time. The Pennsylvania grand jury was adamant:

> We, the members of this grand jury, need you to hear this. We know some of you have heard some of it before. There have been other reports about child sex abuse within the Catholic Church. But never on this scale. For many of us, those earlier stories happened someplace else, someplace away. Now we know the truth: it happened everywhere.[13]

The ugly and painful truth that emerges from the voluminous court record and media reports on all the institutions discussed in this book is that in this sad pattern, one can merely substitute name *A* with name *B*.[14]

Was it a matter of convenience for those in positions of authority to enable the perpetrator? Did the adults in some way benefit from the harm caused? I have found no suggestion in discussion with the survivors or elsewhere that the enablers had a prurient interest in the acts of the perpetrators. And although there is little doubt regarding the sexual

---

13. Pennsylvania GJ, p. 1. https://www.attorneygeneral.gov/report/.
14. One can also throw into the mix the University of Southern California (https://www.npr .org/2018/06/11/618950892/we-are-at-a-breaking-point-pressure-builds-at-usc-over-gynecolo gist-scandal); and the University of California, Los Angeles (https://www.insidehighered.com /news/2019/06/12/ucla-doctor-accused-sexual-violence-only-latest-series-incidents-college -campuses).

gratification of the predators, there is no indication the survivors knew intimate details of the predators' actions with others.[15]

That was left to the survivors who chose to speak with their coaches, trainers, and clerical leadership. But, as repeatedly documented, such reporting did not have the desired effect. After Willie Jones shared with Coach Richard Sloan the abuse he had just suffered at the hands of Strauss, Sloan told Willie Jones to "get in the fucking pool." We must never forget it was Sloan who sent Jones to see Strauss. And yet, his message to Jones, in front of his teammates, was clear: there was no room for complaining. There was no thought given to the young person's needs, fears, and best interests.

Truth be told, from the survivors' perspective, protecting the institution was the only thing that matters to the enablers. The institutional enablers chose either to dismiss their complaints or to discourage them from coming forward. There was a determined effort to undermine the survivor, reflecting a commitment to protect the institution.

Thus, in searching for the primary motivation of these enablers, the notion of "brand protection" must not be dismissed. It is the one factor that applies in all the cases under consideration and explains why the reaction is disturbingly similar in each. Major institutions—in higher education, in religious communities, in elite athletics—go into "protect" mode by hunkering down in a determined and unsparing effort to save the brand.

Think, for example, of Tiffany Thomas-Lopez in a Florida hotel room, physically demonstrating to Lianna Hadden, a Michigan State University trainer, what Nassar was doing to her. According to Thomas-Lopez, Hadden "turned bright red—blushed, started crying, said, 'That's not supposed to happen. You need to talk to Destiny' [Teachnor-Hauk, another MSU trainer]." But when Thomas-Lopez shared her experience with Destiny Teachnor-Hauk, her response was that of the

---

15. I did not engage with a survivor (unless he or she chose to do so) in discussion of predator sexual gratification, as that was not the focus of our conversation. Some survivors suggest the phrase "sexual assault" misrepresents the predator's actions, for there was nothing sexual in what the predator did. From their perspective, the encounter was an assault and must be understood as such.

classic discouraging enabler: "Tiffany, why are you confused? Why do you think you are not getting relief [for your injury]?" She added threateningly: "If you file a report [against Nassar], it will be bad for your family, the Doctor. Are you sure?"

Hadden and Teachnor-Hauk abandoned Thomas-Lopez in her greatest hour of need. In suggesting that Tiffany share the details with Teachnor-Hauk, Hadden chose the easy way out; that she appeared sympathetic is irrelevant. There are no "merit" points for being horrified and upset. Both women ultimately followed the classic path of the institutional enabler: protect the institution and its reputation. And indeed, Michigan State University failed to punish either trainer when informed of their actions.[16]

From Tiffany's perspective, she experienced two levels of harm, one more egregious than the other: her body was violated 150 times by Larry Nassar, and she was abandoned by Lianna Hadden and Destiny Teachnor-Hauk. In spite of the full and graphic knowledge they had, these women made the decision not to protect her. In doing so, both of them made very clear their priorities: MSU and Nassar over Tiffany. This was not an impulsive, one-off reaction, but was reflective of a determined effort with a clear goal. Otherwise, it is likely that either Hadden or Teachnor-Hauk would have mitigated their responses.

Teachnor-Hauk is a metonym for the armies of enablers that the survivors encountered. She knew, she belittled, she discouraged, she dissed, she sided with the predator and the institution. As inexcusable and damaging as her actions were, they are instructive in shedding light on how enablers respond when survivors confront them with the intimate details of the crimes committed against their bodies. Their instinctive response is the dual protection model: protect predator and institution alike.

---

16. In February 2019, "Michigan's Licensing and Regulatory Affairs and the Michigan Attorney General are serving administrative complaints to Michigan State University athletic trainers Destiny Teachnor-Hauk and Lianna Hadden, alleging they lied to investigators about what they knew about the sexual abuse of students by Nassar. The complaints, announced Wednesday, are being forwarded to the disciplinary subcommittee of the Michigan Board of Athletic Trainers for determination of whether to impose a sanction that could include a fine, license suspension or revocation, or probation with terms or a limitation on the licensee"; https://www.detroitnews.com/story/news/local/michigan/2019/02/20/state-accuses-2-msu-trainers-lying-nassar/2929458002/.

There is a clear sequential process resulting in the abandonment of the survivor. It is in that context that we must consider Tiffany's words: "I wanted someone to do something; to shut Larry the fuck down." She and the thousands of other survivors confronted armies of enablers who followed through on a game plan that was as well executed as it was prepared. This is beyond outrageous. It is criminal activity.

In their zeal to protect Michigan State University rather than the athlete entrusted to their care, Hadden and Teachnor-Hauk created an environment in which Nassar had unfettered access to Tiffany's body. Hadden was not Tiffany's peer; she was a professional trainer, employed by Michigan State University. Her failure to act directly on Tiffany's behalf, despite her evident shock and dismay, is a form of enabling. Hadden handed Tiffany off to Teachnor-Hauk, whose dismissiveness and discouragement proved devastating. There is no evidence that Teachnor-Hauk feared personal repercussions for her conduct. She appears to have been fully confident that her employer was in agreement with her response.

Technically, the two trainers engaged in different forms of enabling. However, from Tiffany's perspective their roles were the same. Neither provided assistance, neither rectified the situation, neither took measures to ensure Nassar would not assault student athletes in the future. Individually and collectively, the trainers dramatically worsened Tiffany's situation. They acted with impunity. This is, without doubt, a form of complicity.

In case after case examined for this book, the brazenness with which the enabler disregarded, dismissed, and discouraged the survivor is a powerful motif. The modus operandi is to ignore the plight of the survivor and implement systematic protections that will save and shield the institution and the perpetrator. Among the many constants are the empty words, public relations platitudes, and posturing of institutions, reflecting their unabashed and self-serving damage control.

Lindsey Lemke, in her victim impact statement, addressed USA Gymnastics:

To USAG:
I'm just going to be blunt and start by calling you out for paying athletes millions of dollars to stay quiet about Larry Nassar.

Thank you for proving to us why you are indeed responsible and need to be held accountable.

Steve Penny, you are a coward. Resigning from your position to give responsibility to someone else for creating the environment to let this monster thrive.

You, as in USAG, came to court this week, I'm assuming because you felt like you had to, not because you wanted to.

You hid in that back corner, hoping no one would see you or recognize you.

Well I hope the way you feel right now, the way you are hiding, being evasive, being cowards, sits with you heavy because that's how we women feel and some have felt for the past 20+ years.

Scared of the public and scared to speak up, just like you are right now.

Well you better learn to step it up and stop feeling sorry for yourselves.

Because for all of the women who have been able to speak and share their story, we are the survivors and I'm here to tell you we don't feel sorry for ourselves anymore because, we are working on healing.

So no, you don't deserve to feel sorry for yourselves.

I see USAG being praised on social media for their new focus to "better secure their athletes." You're already being praised when all you've done is talk? That's disgusting. And what a slap in the face to us.

When you personally reach out to each and every survivor and make it up to every girl and their families, which will never be able to happen, that's maybe when the 100+ women and I will be able to forgive you.

But I don't see that as a possibility.

We went through this for years, so I hope that you are ready to spend decades trying to make up for what you have done.[17]

---

17. Lemke, Victim Impact Statement. https://www.youtube.com/watch?v=c6yFL18aSJE.

Lemke's words could describe any of the institutions addressed in this book. Earnest officials make promises, utter words, draft statements, and gravely pronounce that lessons have been learned, mistakes internalized, protocols drafted, meetings convened, victims listened to. It is an empty ritual that offers zero respite to the survivor and does nothing to protect the next survivor. Rather than bringing the culprit to legal justice, the first impulse is for institutions to engage in self-congratulatory behavior predicated on avoiding direct engagement with the wrongdoer and dismissing the cries of the survivor.

Much later, if the institutions find themselves confronted either in a court of law or in the court of public opinion, they begin to back down and seek to buy their way out. Michigan State settled for $500 million; Penn State fired Joe Paterno; USA Gymnastics accepted the resignation of Steve Penny. But in laying all the blame on the predator, the institutions protect themselves more broadly. The enablers hide behind the depravity of the perpetrator. This is truly heinous: when the survivors came forth to report crimes, the enablers dismissed, discouraged, or were deceitful or punitive.

Lindsey Lemke was identified at an early age as an elite gymnast, training for years at the Twistars USA Gymnastics Club located near Lansing, Michigan. She received her first college scholarship when she was 14 years old, and committed to the University of North Carolina at the age of 15, enrolling as a freshman at 18. After three semesters, she transferred to Michigan State University, where, after an initial period as a walk-on, she was awarded a full ride scholarship and was ultimately named captain of the Michigan State women's gymnastics team. Lemke shared with the MSU gymnastics coach, Kathy Klages, the sexual abuse that Nassar subjected her to over a number of years. When I asked Lemke what she expected from Klages at this meeting, her answer was twofold: support and protection. Klages offered neither.[18]

---

18. In addition to specifically calling out USGA president Steven Penny and Coach Klages (https://www.oxygen.com/martinis-murder/who-is-coach-kathie-klages-and-did-she-know -about-larry-nassar-abusing-gymnasts), Linday Lemke directed comments at former Michigan State University president Lou Anna Simon (https://www.lansingstatejournal.com/story /news/local/2019/04/08/msu-michigan-state-lou-anna-simon-larry-nassar-lying-to-police-presi dent/3244729002/), and Bob Geddert, owner of Twistars Gym.

Lindsey estimates that Nassar sexually assaulted her over 100 times, from when she was ten years old through her time as team captain. The coach's response? To cast doubt in Lindsey's mind as to the veracity of her report and to suggest she had not done the required research to understand the validity and viability of Nassar's method of "treatment." According to Coach Klages, Lindsey was not in a position to pass judgment on the nature of the medical examination.

Klages was not a bystander. She had never been in the examination room when Nassar attacked Lemke. However, as gymnastics coach, she was employed by Michigan State not only to develop the physical abilities of student athletes but also to ensure their physical, mental, and emotional well-being. In responding to Lindsey as she did, Klages deliberately chose the enabler's path of protecting Nassar and the institution.

Indeed, Klages made two additional comments indicative of the dismissive enabler. She intimated that she would need to talk with Lindsey's parents, and she asked Lindsey to consider how a complaint might impact Nassar's family. Her priorities were clear: Nassar's reputation, and by extension that of the university, were paramount. Klages's sole intention was to dissuade Lindsey from taking any action, even though she had no reason *not* to believe Lindsey. Clearly, she did not feel she owed Lindsey a duty of protection in the face of the larger interests at stake.

In our conversation, I suggested to Lindsey there are two types of enablers: those who are dismissive of the survivor's complaints and those who discourage the victim from complaining, sometimes in a manner suggesting consequences to the survivor and their family. Lindsey gave me an example of the second option. After Lindsey went public with her complaint against Nassar, Klages hinted that she might lose her athletic scholarship: "You need to fight to continue earning this scholarship."

Perhaps if Klages were not so dedicated to her employer (Michigan State) or her colleague (Nassar), she might have had the humanity to see that there was a student athlete—*her* student athlete—who deserved her full and undivided attention. Lindsey needed her in a way that Nassar and MSU did not.

In the case of abuse in the Catholic Church, the Pennsylvania grand jury noted:

> We came across a file in which the diocese candidly conceded that "this is one of our worst ones"—but of course told no one about him. Actually we came across the same statement in the files of other priests. Then there was the file with the simple celebratory notation: "bad abuse case. (Victim) sued us . . . we won." And this happy note, in a case in which a seven-year-old girl was molested by a priest from outside the diocese.[19]

What were they thinking? The following account may provide some clues:

> Former USA Gymnastics chief executive Steve Penny consulted with W. "Jay" Abbott, the special agent in charge of the FBI's Indianapolis office as early as July 2015, a month after Penny was first informed of allegations that Nassar had sexually assaulted gymnast Maggie Nichols at a U.S. national team training camp at the Karolyi Ranch.
>
> In a July 29, 2015 email to Abbott, Penny wrote, "Below are two pieces of our communication strategy moving forward. We wanted to share them with you for your quick review to be sure they are consistent with FBI preferences. Please let us know if you concur with our messaging."
>
> Then USA Gymnastics board chairman Paul Parilla, an Orange County attorney, and Scott Himsel, an attorney representing USA Gymnastics, were copied on the email.
>
> Abbott replied to Penny later that day "certainly respond as you deem appropriate."
>
> A day later Penny emailed Abbott again.
>
> "I am so sorry to continue bothering you with this issue. . . . As you can see below, we have a very squirmy Dr. Nassar. Our biggest concern is how we contain him from sending shockwaves through

---

19. PA GJ, pp. 10–11.

the community. In our conversations with Scott, we are trying to make sure any correspondence with him is consistent with FBI protocol. Right now we are looking for a graceful way to end his service in such a manner that he does not 'chase the story.'"[20]

20. https://www.ocregister.com/2018/11/06/all-olympia-agrees-to-pay-nassar-survivor-mattie-larson-1-million/.

"They forgot we were young kids away from home."
—*Mattie Larson, Skype conversation, July 17, 2019*

"Lastly, shame on MSU, USAG, and the United States Olympic
Committee for this gross, inexcusable negligence, for allowing this pedophile to flourish for this long, and for all of these
poor victims to be abused. They, and every one of the people
who enabled this, are responsible for this. It wasn't just Larry,
it was all the people, including USA Gymnastics, and I see that
you're representing them there? They are accountable. They
are accountable, and I don't want to hear any more statements
from everybody else. 'We're doing this,' and 'We're doing that.
We have a safer place now.' It's too late now. That's fine, we
need to make a safer place, but all the people at USAG and
MSU and United States Olympic Committee who covered it
up and allowed this negligence and abuse to happen to children
are responsible, and they have to take responsibility for it."
—*Gina Nichols, victim impact statement*

"USA Gymnastics and the United States Olympic Committee did not provide a safe environment
for me and my teammates and friends to train."
—*Maggie Nichols, victim impact statement given on
her behalf by her mother, Gina Nichols*

— 5 —

Where the Hell Are the Adults?

I met Jamie Dantzscher on June 3, 2019. She won a bronze medal in the 2000 Sydney Olympic Games. She is also one of the survivors of Larry Nassar's assaults. Our conversation focused on the culture at the Karolyi Ranch, located in unincorporated Walker County, Texas. The sole purpose of the ranch was the training of elite female gymnasts, under the guidance of Bela and Marta Karolyi, with the goal of making the U.S. Olympic Team.[1] It was deliberately in the middle of nowhere, removed from civilization, let alone comfort and care.[2] Parents were not allowed to be there, food was heavily regulated, punishment was routine. In retrospect, abuse was inevitable.

The Karolyis, world famous gymnastic coaches credited with developing iconic Olympians such as Nadia Comaneci and Mary Lou Retton, were given free rein by USA Gymnastics, which operates under the auspices of the U.S. Olympic Committee (USOC). USA Gymnastics functionaries were focused on one thing: medals. Whatever facilitated winning medals was acceptable; failure was not tolerated. Indeed, these

---

1. For further reading, see https://edition.cnn.com/2018/02/02/us/karolyi-ranch-gymnastics
-abuse-allegations/index.html; https://www.houstonchronicle.com/sports/article/Law-firm-s-report
-on-Larry-Nassar-case-critical-13455692.php; https://people.com/sports/aly-raisman-karolyi-ranch
-larry-nassar/.
2. https://www.youtube.com/watch?v=Vd70wzP4Asg.

functionaries, some of whom drew very handsome salaries, had much at stake. Their financial well being, sense of self, and presumed prestige was dependent on the girls' success.

USAG officials visited the ranch, but they did not interfere with the Karolyis' practice. Nor did USOC officials exercise either control or supervision. The Karolyis, in particular Marta, had total control over the U.S. elite gymnastics program. As long as the U.S. team succeeded, all was well.

As discussed in the previous chapter, elite athletes have a rare combination of talent and dedication that separates them from the good, even great, athlete. Their training regimen is different. Their willingness to commit themselves to an unparalleled degree is understood as necessary to achieve their goals. All that is widely recognized as the price to be paid for an Olympic gold. However, there are limits.

Training is an all-encompassing term, extending beyond the endless hours of actual practice to the physical and emotional welfare of the whole person. Standing firm with respect to what can and cannot be done is no less important than standing on the podium to receive a medal. Setting boundaries and enforcing them is the responsibility of mature adults charged with the care and training of young people. In an all-encompassing competitive environment where maximum effort is the minimum expectation, it is an absolute requirement.

The reality of the ranch was that USA Gymnastics, under the banner of the U.S. Olympic Committee, failed to protect the children in their care and allowed them to fall prey to those seeking to benefit from their successes. No one gave a damn what it took to achieve those successes.

The young girls were expected to perform at an elite level, regardless of injury or pain. And if there was need for medical treatment, Larry Nassar was always there. He was revered as the best gymnastics doctor in the United States. The fact he had total access to the girls never seems to have struck any of the adults as problematic. There is no evidence that a single official over the years stopped for a second to ask the question posed by survivor Mattie Larson: "How the fuck did they let a minor be alone in a hotel room with an adult?"

Such a colossal failure can only occur if enabling is deeply ingrained in an institution's culture. The actions (or inactions) of USA Gymnastics reflect, in Mattie's words, "an unwillingness to take responsibility." The costs are terrible, as pointed out by Olympic gold medalist Simone Biles:

> We've done everything they asked us for even when we didn't want to. And they couldn't do one damn job. . . . You had one job. You literally had one job and you couldn't protect us. . . . You feel everything at once. It hits you like a train wreck and it was really hard for me to train.[3]

The ranch was focused on training champions. Jamie Dantzscher paints a difficult picture: screaming coaches, humiliating training sessions, with the girls expected to be "robotic." All methods of training were on the table, no matter the physical and emotional consequences. Jamie described the culture at the ranch as a "mind fuck." Compounding the stress, anxiety, pain, and humiliation were the "treatments" Nassar performed on the young girls in their cabins and treatment rooms.[4] According to Jamie, the nature of Nassar's treatments were known to the Karolyis and to Nassar's assistant, Debbi Van Horn. Of Van Horn, Jamie is succinct: "She kept her mouth shut and had no personality." Mattie Larson described Van Horn in similar terms.[5]

On March 28, 2017, Dantzscher testified before the United States Senate Judiciary Committee:

> I made the USA Junior National Team for the first time when I was just 12 years old. It was in Palm Springs, California. . . .
>
> I made the USA National Team every year after that, all the way up to the Olympics. It was then that I was introduced to the U.S. National Team Physician, Dr. Larry Nassar.
>
> What I have only recently come to understand is that the medical treatment he performed for my back pain and other injuries was sexual assault. Dr. Nassar abused me at the USA National Center in Texas, he abused me in California and at meets all over the world. Worst, he abused me in my hotel room in Sydney at the Olympic Games. . . .

---

3. https://nypost.com/2019/08/08/simone-biles-slams-usa-gymnastics-over-larry-nassar-scandal/.

4. Mattie Larson discussed and described an "end room"; see graphic p. 57.

5. Mattie Larson and I met June 3, 2019.

Children often don't speak up when they are abused. They suffer in silence. They are taught to honor the authority of adults. This is especially true in the hyper-competitive world of elite gymnastics. Women do speak up and that is why I am here today. USA Gymnastics failed its most basic responsibility to protect the athletes under its care. They failed to take action against coaches, trainers, and other adults who abused children. And they allowed Dr. Nassar to abuse young women and girls for more than 20 years.[6]

Dantzscher compellingly articulates her pain. What should have been a crowning achievement—winning an Olympic medal—was forever overshadowed by the repeated violations to her body. But the crux of the matter is that not only did Nassar sexually assault her for so many years, those who could have prevented him failed to do so. Those who were in a position to protect the vulnerable failed in this primary obligation. The individuals whom Jamie calls out facilitated Nassar in the same manner as Kathy Klages, Lianna Hadden, and Destiny Teachnor-Hauk enabled Nassar at Michigan State University.

The complicated and controversial issues surrounding the criminalization of bystander and enabler complicity require resolving many dilemmas regarding the degree of responsibility that members of society owe to one another. Undertaking this analysis demands stating without hesitation that both harms caused by the perpetrator and those caused by the enabler demand response. To impose punishment only on the attacker, thereby excusing the enabler, facilitates further attacks by the protected and emboldened predator. It is through this prism that the concept of duty is best understood.

Someone knew, someone heard, someone saw. By choosing to ignore this knowledge, the bystander or enabler exacerbated the harm. This fact was clearly expressed by Mattie Larson, a former U.S. National Champion gymnast, who won a silver medal at the World Championships in 2010. Like the other survivors with whom I met, Mattie was identified at an early age as an elite gymnast and undertook the same rigorous training regimen required to become an Olympic athlete. Because of

---

6. Jamie Dantzscher, Congressional testimony. https://www.judiciary.senate.gov/imo/media/doc/03-28-17%20Dantzscher%20Testimony.pdf.

her demonstrated excellence, Mattie was invited to train at the Karolyi Ranch four to five days a month; the rest of her training took place at a local gym. Our discussion focused on the ranch, where Larry Nassar repeatedly assaulted her. She stated that activities at the ranch were observed by USA Gymnastics officials, but they did not intervene in the Karolyis' training methods. This mirrors Jamie Dantzscher's description.

Mattie suggested that the unhealthy environment at the ranch—"perfectly insane," were her words—was based on a conspiracy of silence that enabled abusive behavior and, ultimately, sexual abuse. She specifically named Marta Karolyi, Kathy Kelley, Debbi Van Horn, Gary Warren, and Steve Penny as enablers of Nassar's assaults. Of these officials, Penny was the most senior USAG official, and Marta Karolyi was the coach.

Mattie described Nassar's treatments as "weird, but not 'Oh, shit!'"[7] She noted that since some of the exams were conducted in full view of others (see layout), in these cases USA Gymnastics officials should have stepped in to protect the girls. [8]

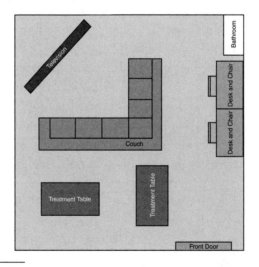

7. In my July 17, 2019, Skype conversation with Mattie Larson, we made air quotes when using the word "treatment," but Larson expressed discomfort with both the word and the air quotes. Her discomfort is understandable and well expressed. While from the perspective of Nassar and USAG the meetings with the gymnasts were for purposes of medical treatment, in reality the sessions were sexual assaults, and that is how the survivors understand them today. Accordingly, there is uncertainty as how best to refer to these interactions, whether as understood at the time or in light of what is known now.
8. With thanks to Noah Herron for developing the computer graphic illustrating Mattie Larson's drawing.

However, she emphasized that many of Nassar's assaults occurred when he was alone in a hotel room with a gymnast, that is, *a child*, ostensibly conducting treatments. In reality, Nassar was digitally penetrating these young girls with his bare hands.

The image of Mattie alone with Nassar in a hotel room is not merely disturbing and sobering, it is painful and outrageous. There is no evidence, direct or indirect, to suggest that any USAG official, any coach, or trainer asked the girls about Nassar's treatments, whether they were comfortable with them, or whether they wanted another adult in the room with them. Nor do they appear to have discussed these issues among themselves. If they did, they did not act on their concerns.

Once practice sessions ended, Mattie explained, the coaches and USA Gymnastics officials would leave the ranch. The only adult who remained with the girls was Larry Nassar. Even if Nassar was not assaulting the girls, it defies logic that no thought was given to the inherent impropriety of leaving a group of young girls in the sole care of an adult male. This was total abandonment of any duty of care. It represents a colossal failure on both personal and institutional levels.

The only plausible explanation for this failure is that Steve Penny and his colleagues saw the girls as a commodity from which they would benefit. They did not see them as vulnerable human beings, young girls, who happened to be extraordinary athletes. I have no evidence, direct or indirect, that USA Gymnastics officials had a prurient interest in Nassar's criminal behavior, nor that there was any physical interaction between USAG officials and the girls. The only individuals, other than Nassar, who engaged with the girls were their trainers and coaches.

When I asked Mattie what she expected from USAG officials, she was clear: "[To] keep me safe and protected, especially when children travel with adults." The fact that she felt she had to ask for such a basic right highlights the extent to which Nassar's behavior was enabled. It is therefore no surprise that Mattie said she felt "abandoned" by USA Gymnastics, and thought of as "disposable." They let a predator have unrestricted access to her body, no questions asked, and allowed the predator to prey on his victims at the training center, the Karolyi Ranch.

This raises the question, to whom did Nassar's enablers owe a duty? From Mattie Larson's perspective, the obvious answer is "to me." As a child, notwithstanding her status as an elite gymnast, she deserved the full protection of each and every adult affiliated with USA Gymnastics. In fact, the duty owed is not just "deserved," but rather should be understood as a demand. That is, it is something that the law must guarantee, with clear consequences for failing to fulfill the demand.

From Mattie's perspective, no one wanted to assume responsibility for the girls: neither the USA Gymnastics coaches nor the gymnasts' personal coaches, from their home gyms, who attended training sessions at the ranch. Moreover, neither set of coaches expressed any concern or interest in them outside the actual training sessions. In other words, they were on their own.

The callousness with which the coaches treated their gymnasts is illustrated by Mattie's experience with her personal coaches, Galina Marinova and Artur Akopya. Although they freely used her name to advertise their California-based gym, when she performed poorly at the World Championships held in The Netherlands, Marinova "turned" on her and Akopya shunned her:

> All Olympia Gymnastics Center, the world renown Hawthorne academy, recently finalized a $1 million settlement with World Championships silver medalist Mattie Larson, her attorney confirmed to the Southern California News Group
>
> The settlement stems from Larson's lawsuit in Los Angeles Superior Court against AOGC and its directors Artur Akopya and Galina Marinova that alleged their treatment of Larson led to her being sexually abused by former U.S. Olympic and USA Gymnastics national team physician Larry Nassar. While Akopya and Marinova agreed to pay Larson $1 million in June the deal was only recently completed.
>
> The suit alleged All Olympia and Akopya and Marinova "fueled an abusive, harassing and degrading environment." That environment "allowed, concealed and promoted abusive behavior" by Nassar, former U.S. national team directors Bela and Martha Karolyi and USA Gymnastics. Specifically, the suit alleged Akopya and Marinova "directed degrading, abusive, and harassing comments and actions towards" Larson.
>
> . . .

"It is a sad day when Southern California looses (sic) a gym that has been so instrumental for the development of gymnastics," Carol McIntyre, president of the So Cal Women's Gymnastics Coaches Association, wrote in an email Monday to the Southern California gymnastics community. "I can't imagine how devastating this is to Galina.

". . . With USA Gymnastics being in the hot seat once again, Let's work together and show the pride and Class Southern California is famous for. We have always been the leaders of the country. Let's rise above the negative perception that has been bestowed on our beautiful sport by no fault of our own. Let's all remember we are competitive, but we are colleagues first. Athletes will come and go but we will all remain.

"Let's band together and show the country we will not buckle under the pressure. We will hold our heads high and continue to show this country and community true leadership."

McIntyre said Tuesday night that the letter "was supposed to be so positive and supportive and (encouraging) coaches (from other gyms) not to vulture children (from AOGC). It had nothing to do with abusing children."

But John Manly, an attorney for Larson and dozens of other survivors, said McIntyre's comments were "emblematic of the culture of USA Gymnastics where athletes come and go sort of like cattle and that's how they look at them. It's an abusive culture."

"People," Manly added, "don't pay a million dollars if they didn't do anything wrong."[9]

Mattie and her fellow gymnasts were vulnerable, away from their families, and without recourse while on the ranch. They felt they were on their own, but crucially, that should not have been the case. Ostensibly, they were under the care and supervision of trainers and coaches who were responsible for their welfare. There must be no doubt as to whom these adults owed their primary obligation. That duty went

9. https://www.ocregister.com/2018/11/06/all-olympia-agrees-to-pay-nassar-survivor-mattie-larson-1-million/.

beyond improving gymnasts' skills, positioning them to qualify for the Olympics; it was fundamentally a duty to protect the girls.

The duty requirement is relevant to bystander and enabler alike. While there are distinctions between the two, the duty principle must be applied to both, otherwise there are no consequences to what happened to Mattie Larson. Larson was just a child training under the auspices of USA Gymnastics. She was not at the ranch as a free agent, but had been specifically selected by USAG on the basis of her demonstrated abilities to represent the United States in the Olympics. And she ended up as a vulnerable child left to a predator surrounded by enablers. Though the USA Gymnastics officials, the coaches, and the trainers were not bystanders to Nassar's assaults on the vulnerable young gymnasts, they enabled those assaults by not protecting the girls.

It is important to realize that if the duty to act to protect an individual in distress is not rigorously enforced, the vulnerability of the survivor is heightened by the perpetrator being enabled. For this reason, the duty to act must go beyond a moral obligation, predicated on ethical considerations and principles of compassion. Although these are admirable and compelling concepts, reflecting well on aspirations of an enlightened society, they are not sufficiently pinned down to ensure accountability when the enabler or bystander ignores the survivor's peril. The duty to end abuse must not be framed in purely moral terms, for these are, ultimately, devoid of practical substance.

Mattie needed someone to put an immediate stop to Nassar's unsupervised access to her body in a hotel room. The failure to do so cannot be vaguely dismissed as a moral failure; it must be reframed as a legal obligation with clear consequences under the criminal code for failure to act. Otherwise, we will have learned nothing.

The differences between a moral and a legal duty are significant. They must not be smoothed over or minimized; doing so would blur their distinctions and obscure the thrust of the proposal: the bystander or enabler who fails to intervene must face criminal sanctions. Framing the obligation in legal, in addition to moral, terms would be a major step in protecting the vulnerable. The most effective means of doing so is by legislating consequences for failure to act, including incarceration.

One person is in a direct position to mitigate the harm of another. The decision to not intervene, assist, and protect must be met with severity. The enabler or bystander would face a criminal penalty, a significant consequence in itself, but arguably less significant than the twofold consequences to the survivor of the bystander's or enabler's actions plus the perpetrator's crime. The survivor pays the price when the bystander walks away or the enabler makes the decision to facilitate the crime. The survivor's voice guides us in advocating criminal penalties against those who fail in their duty to act.

In this context, "walking away" is not just a turn of phrase, but a practical, oftentimes painful reality for the victim. Surprisingly, while there have been many studies of the plight of survivors, very little attention has been paid to the expectations that survivors have of the bystander or enabler. In my many interactions with survivors in the course of my research, it has been made clear that, from their perspective, their hopes and expectations have been dashed. Across the board, this has been devastating, in some cases, life-altering—perhaps more so than the assaults themselves. While criminal codes address the perpetrator's actions, the fact the bystander-enabler is not punished for their failure is, from the survivor's perspective, a wrong that must be addressed.

It is in that spirit that the recommendation for the imposition of criminal sanctions must be understood. The motivation is the survivor who has been abandoned by those in a position and with a duty to protect. The failure to act in accordance with this duty must be recognized in the law. The most suitable mechanism is a codification of criminal law that has two clear purposes: to punish the negligent bystander or enabler and to deter future wrongdoers. Deterrence, after all, is one of the intended goals of legislation that criminalizes conduct. We punish the offender, and thereby deter other members of society from committing the same offense.

This chapter has focused on enabler complicity and survivor expectation in the context of the particularly egregious conduct of USA Gymnastics and other participants at the Karolyi Ranch. But it must never be forgotten that these issues are raised every day, everywhere. While writing this book, I requested feedback from someone I had met at an event for my previous book and had kept in touch with regarding issues related to complicity.[10] In response, this individual shared with me the

---

10. Name and email exchanges in author records.

consequences of sexual abuse suffered as a child. I share the following account with permission:

> I was sexually abused by my grandfather beginning at age five. I kept the abuse a secret and hoped/waited for someone to step in. That did not happen and finally as a teenager I wrote a letter to my stepdad whom I trusted. I do not remember the details of the letter but I do clearly remember how he called me out to the barn and threw my letter into the fire. He simply stated that my mother could never handle this truth about her father. He said it was best to keep quiet and move on. His response was a shock to me and nearly crushed me. I spent the next few years lost in the pain of both the abuse and the realization that my parents would not choose to protect me.
>
> Looking back I now know I suffered from depression and PTSD. Later on my mother did learn of the abuse and was quick to show her anger, shame and resentment. It seemed as though I ruined the image of her father and that she was ashamed of me. In the days after, she announced that I should get counseling but that I'll need to pay for it myself. Again, the realization and heartache of knowing I was still alone in picking up the broken pieces was incredibly overwhelming! My parents continued their relationship with my grandparents and they were often invited to vacation at our home.
>
> Over and over again my parents had a chance to do the right thing and they did not. This reality is just as damaging as the sexual abuse. I continue to struggle to fully trust those closest to me. Depression and complex PTSD are my reality; however, I will always wonder if some of this pain could have been lessened by my parents.
>
> The day I finally told [of the sexual assault] someone (my step dad) and was told to keep it to myself because it will only upset my mom (it was her father who abused me) is forever etched in my mind. Later when she found out, she was angry at me for ruining her vision of her father and for interrupting her idea of her happily little family.
>
> Nowhere did anyone consider the consequences it had on me or how their further relationship with him would almost destroy me. Living with the anger at that inner circle is truly as abusive as the acts themselves!!!
>
> I still live with that pain.

"It took a parish to molest me."

—PV1, Skype conversation; individual is known to me

"You could've been stopped back in 1997. You know that a teammate and I brought concerns about what you were doing to Kathy Klages on the same night. She was a person I looked up to. She was a person I thought had my back. But instead of notifying authorities or even my parents, we were interrogated. Imagine that. . . . We were led to believe that we were misunderstanding a medical technique. Do you know how she came to that conclusion? Was it when she called you and talked to you about it? She conducted her own unqualified investigation. She humiliated and silenced me as she began to call in all of my Spartan Youth teammates into her office. While I sat there in humiliation, she asked them in small groups if they ever felt uncomfortable with the treatments from you. All but the one other girl said no. . . .

Kathy continued her interrogation of us by pulling the MSU college-level gymnasts into the office. She left the room, we sat on the green carpet in her office, talking to these girls that we looked up to. Can you even for one second begin to imagine the humiliation I felt when the college gymnasts came into Kathy's office to explain their treatments with you?"

—Larissa Boyce, victim impact statement

"As if what Larry Nassar did isn't bad enough, it is horrifying that MSU and USAG isn't stepping up to the plate to admit their wrongdoing."

—Lindsey Cowan, victim impact statement

"This was a priest, a holy man who not only was a breath away from God himself, but also someone who was powerful, chaste and to be revered. Saying you were hurt by someone wearing the collar was almost sacrilegious."

—Sarah Shiley, email, December 7, 2019

— 6 —

Complicity

Writing my previous book, *The Crime of Complicity*, made me all too aware of the prevalence of complicity. My interactions with survivors in researching the present book drove the point home.

It was a dominant theme in our conversations; a common refrain when survivors described the assaults committed on their bodies, whether in East Lansing, Michigan; the Karolyi Ranch; hotel rooms at gymnastic competitions; Columbus, Ohio; State College, Pennsylvania; or a church rectory. Lindsey Cowan's victim impact statement, which reads like an indictment, could well carry the title, "Complicity."[1] Without complicity, Lindsey would not have been subject to hundreds of assaults on her young body. Those who are complicit—trainers, coaches, USA Gymnastics officials, priests, bishops, university presidents, athletic directors, senior university officials—bear a significant burden in the harm caused by the perpetrators.

The epigraphs to this chapter capture that reality. In the case of PV1, those who knew about his ongoing abuse, lasting for over three years, included priests, bishops, and members of the parish. From his perspective, it took an entire parish to molest him. While the actual molestation was committed by a single priest, those criminal acts were enabled by an entire community.

The same theme defines the abuse committed by Larry Nassar. He alone committed the crime of sexual assault, but entire communities

---

1. https://www.youtube.com/watch?v=c6yFL18aSJE; https://www.youtube.com/watch?v=g08X RqEX9yo; https://www.youtube.com/watch?v=THaacQ0R15E.

enabled his criminal actions at Michigan State University and USA Gymnastics. In Mattie Larson's words, "it took an entire USAG infrastructure" to enable Nassar's assaults. According to Tiffany Thomas-Lopez, "it took MSU trainers" to enable his actions.

All these accounts reflect a line of connection: survivor–enabler–complicity–perpetrator. And this relationship has important and painful consequences: it empowers the perpetrator and heightens the vulnerability of the survivor.

As we have come to learn, a seemingly endless parade of bystanders and enablers made the decision not to act. It would be patently incorrect to suggest that a perpetrator was emboldened by the action of a single person. Rather, armies of complicit individuals failed to protect the survivor. It is critical to note the similarity of patterns among the institutions, the perpetrators, and the enablers. Ron McDaniel was a tennis player for The Ohio State University; Lindsey Lemke, Jamie Dantzscher, and Jeanette Antolin were USAG gymnasts; Tiffany Thomas-Lopez was a softball player for Michigan State; but the manner in which their abuse occurred and was facilitated at all three institutions literally follows the same script.

In all these situations there was a clear power imbalance between survivor and perpetrator. At Michigan State University, Pennsylvania State University, The Ohio State University, in USA Gymnastics and the Catholic Church, all the abusers were in positions of authority over the survivors. They were fully capable of preventing the harm, and indeed, as personnel empowered to act on behalf of a child or young adult at their institutions, they were mandated to do so. The duty to act could not be more obvious.

This power imbalance is the crucial difference between the cases discussed in this book and the "classic" peer-to-peer campus sexual assault, where alcohol, drugs, and hormones are the well-documented catalysts.[2] In the peer-to-peer narrative, all three parties—victim, perpetrator,

---

2. https://www.theatlantic.com/education/archive/2017/09/the-uncomfortable-truth-about-campus-rape-policy/538974/; https://www.theatlantic.com/education/archive/2017/09/the-bad-science-behind-campus-response-to-sexual-assault/539211/. The prevalence of sexual assault on campuses is staggering: https://www.rainn.org/statistics/campus-sexual-violence; https://www.alcohol.org/effects/sexual-assault-college-campus/. Unfortunately, the same holds true for society at large: https://www.nsvrc.org/node/4737; https://www.msn.com/en-us/health/medical/17-staggering-sexual-assault-statistics-everyone-should-read/ar-BBVK6WB.

complicit enabler or bystander—are college students or college-age individuals. The innumerable instances in which survivors report losing consciousness, being in a haze, waking up not remembering events from the previous evening, speaks loudly to the tragic impact of date rape drugs.[3] In that context, the predator is enabled by the complicity of peers who saw a "roofie" slipped, unbeknownst to the drinker, into the victim's drink; by those who saw the potential victim sufficiently inebriated not to be in full control of their faculties; by those who knew the behavior of the predator and yet chose not to intervene.[4] Such examples have prompted much discussion and attention, including the development of bystander programs intended to heighten awareness and teach methods of intervention.[5] These efforts are of great importance.

In the majority of peer-to-peer assaults, however, there are no "adults" involved.[6] Moreover, the notion of an enabler, as distinct from a bystander, is largely irrelevant. By contrast, our present focus is on situations in which adult enablers facilitate adult perpetrators. Many of the survivors we are examining were children assaulted by adult authority figures, enabled by other adult authority figures (Penn State, USA Gymnastics, the Catholic Church). The survivors at Michigan State and Ohio State were largely (though not exclusively) athletes assaulted by a university faculty member to whom they were sent, who was enabled by adults in positions of authority. In the preponderance of cases, the survivors had no choice: coaches directed their athletes to Dr. Nassar and Dr. Strauss. Ohio State students who were not athletes were also referred to Dr. Strauss by the university's Student Health Services. The abuse of athletes in the closed world that defines elite level performances,

---

3. https://www.drugfreeworld.org/drugfacts/prescription/rohypnol.html; https://www.thecut.com /2014/10/what-you-might-not-know-about-getting-roofied.html.

4. https://www.youtube.com/watch?v=LskOE9xDuzQ; https://www.youtube.com/watch?v=Lq0 9VT3zaww.

5. https://www.jsonline.com/story/news/solutions/2019/09/03/campus-violence-bystander -intervention-programs-not-enough-their-own/2029094001/; http://www.ncaa.org/sport-science -institute/topics/bystander-intervention.

6. The word "adult" is intended to reference a person in a supervisory position as compared to an individual's age. The age of majority (21) is not relevant to the supervisory position discussion.

and similarly the abuse of children by priests in the Catholic Church, is distinct from the classic college interaction gone awry.[7]

Larry Nassar was a revered doctor; it was considered a privilege to be treated by him. A student athlete or elite gymnast would not question his credentials or his methods. Yet those who were directly informed— Kathy Klages, Lianna Hadden, Destiny Teachnor-Hauk, John Daly, Hugh Hindman, Andy Geiger, Dick Sloan, amongst others—made the conscious decision not to believe what they were hearing from those for whom they were responsible. The enablers refused to believe the vulnerable.[8] This institutionalized belittling is a recurring theme voiced by survivors, enhancing their sense of abandonment.

In truth, the "I don't believe you" of these adults should be understood as dismissing a legitimate complaint. It is the epitome of enabling. Survivors were made to feel that complaining was a risky proposition. To be perceived as a "whiner" could have negative consequences to playing time, visibility, peer respect, recognition, and self-worth. To be sidelined on account of a perceived bad attitude was something to be avoided at all costs. As we have come to learn, most of the USA Gymnastics and Michigan State athletes whom Nassar treated never shared their concerns. Those who did were swiftly shut down. The message is clear and devastating: You don't know what you are talking about. Sarah Shiley, a survivor of clerical abuse, puts the matter succinctly:

> As any adult survivor would tell you. . . . We don't always come forward until we are at a time in our lives where we feel mentally safe, emotionally supported to do so. There are still some who question me about why they never saw, why I still smiled as a child, how I hid the pain. That's when I point to basic trauma survival statistics.[9]

---

7. PV1 attested that the closed world setting applies to the relationship between priests and their victims.

8. https://medium.com/@sheriheller/hard-to-believe-conditions-that-discredit-victims-of-sexual-harassment-assault-c8d7b076aad; https://spec.hamilton.edu/not-being-believed-a-survivors-account-of-injustice-8110e59064cb; https://edition.cnn.com/interactive/2019/12/us/salesians-of-don-bosco-intl/.

9. Email received Dec 7, 2019.

For Tiffany Thomas-Lopez, standing with other female Michigan State athletes outside Nassar's office felt like "awaiting our slaughter."[10] Knowing what would happen once she was on the examination table, she felt the walls closing in. The "closing in" was the realization that there was no one to talk to. According to Tiffany, the girls standing in line never discussed the nature of the physical examination that awaited them. Other survivors concurred. Some were of the belief that they alone were subject to such examinations.

In some cases, this closing off from others has resulted in "survivor's guilt." These survivors are convinced that had they acted sooner, had they raised their voices, had they spoken out regarding the examinations, then other individuals would not have been harmed in the future. Survivor's guilt is yet another layer of harm caused by enablers, as well as predators. The survivors bear no responsibility for what was done to them and should never be allowed to think themselves responsible for future harms to others.

Indeed, the notion of survivor's guilt highlights the insidiousness of the situation. After all, it was the *enablers* who made the deliberate decision to fail the survivor and protect the institution. In Tiffany's case, Teachnor-Hauk's decision to protect Nassar and Michigan State took on an added twist. After Teachnor-Hauk dismissed the complaint, Tiffany believed Nassar physically punished her in subsequent examinations. Her sense of vulnerability was compounded by her feeling that, "Nassar had a fucking army and I had nothing but my talent." Furthermore, she noted that, "the army shifted from protecting Nassar to protecting MSU." As a result, Nassar assaulted Tiffany Thomas-Lopez approximately 150 times over the course of two years.

---

10. The other female athletes with whom Thomas-Lopez stood in line were members of Michigan State University's soccer, crew, track and field, and softball teams. She did not see male athletes. With respect to the crew team, in July 2019 MSU fired its long-time and highly successful coach Matt Weise for—allegedly—not preventing members of the crew team from confronting university officials regarding their handling of the Nassar case: https://www.theonlycolors .com/2019/7/22/20706100/michigan-states-rowing-coach-just-got-fired; https://www.lansing statejournal.com/story/sports/2019/07/19/michiganstate-athletics-coach-firing/1778448001/. When I shared this with Tiffany, she expressed outrage at MSU's actions and shared that other MSU survivors were "pissed" about this decision.

Gregory,[11] a former tennis player for The Ohio State University, articulates the extent to which the perpetrator, Strauss, benefited from the complicity of the enabler, Coach John Daly. "I remember Coach smirking when Strauss's name came up—he knew what was going on," Gregory said. "In fact, if players didn't behave their punishment would be to go see Dr. Strauss." He called Daly's behavior "inappropriate" and "disgusting." "Shame on him," Gregory said. "And shame on the University for allowing this to go on with naïve 18-year-old kids. We were like lambs being led to the slaughter . . . I'm shocked at how widespread the abuse was. . . . All my teammates had similar experiences with Strauss and it makes me angry that nothing was done about it."

Gregory joined the class action lawsuit against Ohio State in hopes of changing a school culture that "enabled a really sick and dangerous guy." He added: "They need to take every complaint seriously. It's about believing people. As tennis players, we were isolated from the other teams, so I assumed we were the only ones being abused. My jaw dropped when I learned Strauss had abused guys on 13 other teams."[12]

My conversation with Gregory shed important light on the role of the enabler, particularly the notion of the institution as enabler.[13] Gregory was a walk-on (non-scholarship) member of the tennis team, who had to "earn" his place on the team. He emphasized that it was an honor to represent the team, and he was accordingly concerned that complaining would jeopardize his position. Gregory stated that the mandatory team physicals were referred to by his teammates as "fondling sessions with Strauss." That description was openly used in the presence of Coach Daly, who would "smirk, laughing off the comment." An athlete who refused to see Strauss would not be allowed to play. There was no choice but to be examined by him, even though the nature of the examination was common knowledge.

The important point made by Gregory is that enablers continued sending student athletes to Strauss in the face of incessant rumors. Moreover, after Strauss was terminated by The Ohio State University, he opened a private clinic, and student athletes were referred to him there. Besides, as Gregory noted, Strauss was granted emeritus status after

---

11. Gregory's identity is known to me.
12. https://rightsforohiostatevictims.com/coach-daly-knew-strauss-sex-abuse/.
13. Skype conversation, July 24, 2019.

his termination, and therefore continued to have access to OSU locker rooms. This represents institutional complicity at its most basic and blatant. Given the pervasive rumors regarding Strauss's conduct, Gregory is of the belief that there is "no way OSU can say they didn't know." After all, Strauss examined many athletes from many different sports in many different facilities. Similar to Mattie Larson and Tiffany Thomas-Lopez in their accounts of USA Gymnastics, Gregory reveals the essence of systemic, institutionalized complicity directly benefiting the perpetrator and harming survivors to whom a duty to protect was owed.

PV1 commented that "it took a parish" to molest him. This is not an empty metaphor; it was the reality confronting the survivor. Because of the number of enablers and their positions of authority, the predators were able to violate thousands of survivors. A criminal actor, whether a physician or priest, confident that his actions will go unpunished is, literally, an uncaged animal, free to prey on the innocent. Throughout the accounts of the assaults at Michigan State, Penn State, and Ohio State, and in USA Gymnastics and the Catholic Church, the sense of deliberate behavior in defining the enabler's actions is a powerful motif. It does not reach the level of conspiracy as defined by the law, but from the perspective of the survivor, it is clearly experienced as such. Wherever they turned, there was, in Tiffany's words, a "well-oiled institutionalized" mechanism of complicity that had one primary purpose: to protect the perpetrator.

According to the State of Michigan independent general counsel, William Forsyth:

> the fact remains that, according to nearly every survivor interviewed at MSU, the MSU employees who allegedly received reports of Nassar's sexual assault or improper medical treatment downplayed its seriousness or affirmatively discouraged the survivors from proceeding with their allegation. That so many survivors independently disclosed to so many different employees over so many years, each time with no success, reveals a problem that cannot be explained as mere isolated, individual failures; it is evidence of a larger cultural problem at the MSU Sports Medicine Clinic and MSU more broadly.[14]

14. Forsyth, p. 10.

When faced with serious allegations that amount to criminal wrong-doing, Michigan State employees discounted the young woman and deferred to Nassar, the world-renowned sports medicine doctor.[15]

Indeed, the perpetrators—Sandusky, Strauss, Nassar, the priests—were so emboldened by and confident in the complicity of their enablers that they committed their abuses in situations where they would foresee-ably be discovered. They knew they would not face any consequences. Their institutions' histories showed that no enabler would do anything other than continue to enable, regardless of the nature or depth of the complaints. The fact that predators were able to continue assaulting per-son after person, month after month, year after year, decade after decade is the clearest evidence of the depth of enabler complicity.

The Freeh Report on the abuse at Pennsylvania State University affirms this conclusion. It lays out in painstaking detail the environment and circumstances that enabled Jerry Sandusky. But for our purposes, it is the report's damning comments regarding the four most senior univer-sity officials that speak the loudest:

> These individuals [university president Spanier, vice president Schultz, athletic director Curley, and head football coach Paterno] unchecked by the Board of Trustees that did not perform its over-sight duties, empowered Sandusky to attract potential victims to the campus and football events by allowing him to have continued, unrestricted and unsupervised access to the University's facilities and affiliation with the University's prominent football program. Indeed, that continued access provided Sandusky with the very currency that enabled him to attract his victims. Some coaches, administrators and football program staff members ignored the red flags of Sandusky's behaviors and no one warned the public about him. . . .
>
> Once the Board was made aware of the investigations of San-dusky and the fact that senior University officials had testified before the Grand Jury in the investigations, it should have recog-

15. https://www.mlive.com/news/2018/04/msu_colleagues_initially_defen.html; https://www
.lansingstatejournal.com/story/news/local/2018/06/12/michigan-state-larry-nassar-jeffrey-kovan
-lara-investigation/694510002/;https://www.detroitnews.com/story/tech/2018/01/18/msu-president
-told-nassar-complaint-2014/1042071001/.

nized the potential risk to the University community and to the University's reputation. Instead, the Board, as a governing body failed to inquire reasonably and to demand information from Spanier. . . .

Spanier, Schultz, Paterno, and Curley gave the following reasons for taking no action to identify the February 9, 2001 child victim and for not reporting Sandusky to the authorities:

- Through counsel, Curley and Schultz stated that the "humane" thing to do in 2001 was to carefully and responsibly assess the best way to handle vague but troubling allegations. According to their counsel, these men were good people trying to do their best to make the right decisions.
- Paterno told a reporter that "I didn't know exactly how to handle it and I was afraid to do something that might jeopardize what the university procedure was. So I backed away and turned it over to some other people, people I thought would have a little more experience than I did. It didn't work out that way."
- Spanier said, in his interview with the Special Investigative Counsel, that he never heard a report from anyone that Sandusky was engaged in any sexual abuse of children. He also said that if had known or suspected that Sandusky was abusing children, he would have been the first to intervene.

Taking into account the available witness statements and evidence, the Special Investigative Counsel finds that it is more reasonable to conclude that in order to avoid the consequences of bad publicity, the most powerful leaders at the University—Spanier, Schultz, Paterno, and Curley—repeatedly concealed critical facts relating to Sandusky's child abuse from the authorities, the University's Board of Trustees, the Penn State community, and the public at large.[16]

The Freeh Report's plainly stated conclusion is equally applicable to the enabling that permeated the Catholic Church. The infrastructure of

---

16. Freeh Report, pp. 15–16.

the church was galvanized to guard against any consequences emanating from criminal actions by thousands of priests. Church officials' priority was to protect the institution, and as a result they abandoned the vulnerable victims: boys, girls, and nuns. The phrase that runs throughout the grand jury reports, indictments, and trials addressing priest abuse is "circling the wagons."

My understanding of how priest after priest was able to molest a seemingly endless list of victims over the course of hundreds of years was immeasurably enhanced by survivor PV1.[17] Our conversations were marked by his candor, self-reflection, and powerful insight. The complicity that enabled his assault reflected a power structure that protected his priest abuser. Not only did the abusing priest control PV1, but he also controlled those who might have intervened on his behalf. As priests themselves, their self-interest was best served by not protecting the victims. The resulting damage was profound. PV1 alludes to "soul murder," "spiritual rape," and "manipulation of religious commitments." He goes further, to suggest that priest abuse is in the "DNA of the priesthood," and that abuse is predicated on systematic mechanisms.

The 40th Statewide Investigating Grand Jury Report offers confirmation of these sentiments:

> A priest in the Diocese of Harrisburg abused five sisters in a single family, despite prior reports that were never acted on. In addition to sex acts, the priest collected samples of the girls' urine, pubic hair, and menstrual blood. Eventually, his house was searched and his collection was found. Without that kind of incontrovertible evidence, apparently, the diocese remained unwilling to err on the side of the children even in the face of multiple reports of abuse. . . . Elsewhere we saw the sort of disturbing disdain for victims. In the Diocese of Pittsburgh, church officials dismissed an incident of abuse on the ground that the 15-year-old had "pursued" the priest and "literally seduced" him into a relationship. After the priest was arrested, the church submitted an evaluation on his behalf to the court. The evaluation acknowledged that the

---

17. All notes of my conversations with PV1 are in my records. It goes without saying that I am greatly in PV1's debt for so openly engaging with me.

priest had admitted to "sado-masochistic" activities with several boys—but the sado-masochism was only "mild," and at least the priest was not "psychotic."[18]

The court records regarding priest abuse are ultimately mind-numbing: parish after parish, diocese after diocese, priest after priest, bishop after bishop, enabler after enabler, criminal after criminal, complicity after complicity. More from the Pennsylvania grand jury:

> The Grand Jury finds that the Diocese of Allentown and the Allentown Central Catholic High School knew full well the criminal conduct of Fromholzer [Father Francis J. Fromholzer]. Yet, knowing that Fromholzer was preying on young girls, the Diocese and School took no action. The victims were told to let it go. When these victims came forward again years later, they were met with disbelief and scorn. . . . Victims are reluctant to report to law enforcement or take any action for fear of retaliation from the Dioceses. That retaliation and intimidation takes many forms. . . . Action only began when Julianne (a victim who was abused when she was approximately 13–14 years old; at the time the GJ convened she was 68) began to speak to parties empowered to scrutinize the conduct of the Diocese; her own attorneys, law enforcement, and the press.[19]

When PV1 reported his assault to a priest, he expected that a "safe space" would be created in order to protect him and others. That was not forthcoming. Illustrating the depth of complicity and the unabated confidence that the perpetrator enjoyed as a result, PV1 explained that he was assaulted in the common room of the rectory; that is, an open space that other priests could walk through. There was no secret about the abuse being committed. The impunity with which the perpetrator acted required the complicity of others. But, these others were not random people who happened to be in the vicinity of the crime.

A distinctive element of the sexual abuse cases in the Catholic Church is that the relationships and positions of the parties are fluid: an enabling priest may himself be a perpetrator; a perpetrating priest may enable the

18. PA GJ, p. 5.
19. PA GJ, p. 29.

crimes of another priest. And these priests were all members of the Catholic Church, often of the same diocese or even parish. There is a certain incestuousness to the narrative. That is very different from the situations at Michigan State, Penn State, Ohio State, or in USA Gymnastics. There is no indication that those who were complicit in the crimes committed by Nassar, Sandusky, and Strauss committed sexual assault themselves.

The fact that enabling and perpetrating priests were effectively "interchangeable" heightened the danger to the vulnerable survivor. Whereas PV1 was hoping for safe space, the incestuousness of the situation implies that would not be practically possible. Safe spaces cannot be created when enablers and perpetrators could plausibly be one and the same. Protecting the vulnerable did not serve their interests. Indeed, protecting the survivor would suggest there was a problem that required a solution.

> On June 2, 2002, one of [Father Chester] Gawronski's 13 year old victims wrote a letter to [Bishop Donald] Trautman. Among other things, the victim requested the Church: 1) stop aiding and abetting priests; 2) ensure collections were not used to compensate priests; 3) publicize the names of pedophile priests; 4) identify any priest who has molested a child; and 5) establish a policy to ensure offending priests were reported to law enforcement. . . . The victim specifically cited that his dealings with his molestation recently resurfaced when learning of Trautman's "libelous" statement that there were no pedophiles in the Erie diocese. . . . Trautman responded to this victim by letter date June 21, 2002. Trautman stated that he was shocked the victim would "go to the press directly rather than to contact me regarding the past" and argued that the victim was 14 years old when the abuse occurred, not 11 as stated in the article. . . . Trautman's [subsequent] scorching indictment of Gawronski's decades of child sexual abuse was necessary to convince Rome to remove Gawronski from ministry. It was also the only full and fair accounting of Gawronski's crimes that either Trautman or the Diocese has provided to date. Unfortunately, it was contained within a private letter to Rome rather than through a public acknowledgment to Gawronski's victims or the public.[20]

---

20. PA GJ, pp. 78-79.

PV1 makes it clear that those who should have placed the victim above the perpetrator had a vested interest in protecting the perpetrator. The notion of "vested interests" is inherently important in assessing institutional complicity: the perceived cost (of being found out) to the institution is deemed to far outweigh the possible cost (of assault) to a victim, or even to a significant number of victims. Whether that calculation is explicit or implicit, it underlies the actions of the enablers and explains (without justifying) the multitudinous cases that populate the grand jury report.

The terms "systematic" and "institutionalized" lie at the heart of PV1's accounts. There was nothing happenstance in either the abuse or the complicity. His hope that he would be offered a "safe space" is a sad indication that nothing more could be expected. Protecting the institution was paramount, and practical assistance would not be forthcoming. The power dynamic was such that the enabling priests, who were in a position to assist PV1, had much to lose in acting on his complaints.

The grooming of potential victims was an integral part of the systematic abuse in the Catholic Church, and it highlights the deliberate manner in which victims were chosen. Its effects were compounded by institutionalized complicity. PV1 pointed out that priests told their fellow priests whom they were grooming. Who, then, could a survivor turn to? The perpetrator could systematically groom his selected target, secure in the complicity that enabled future attacks. He could prey on the weak and vulnerable, while simultaneously stroking the eager and tender egos of present survivors by showering them with attention and praise.

According to PV1, it was a source of pride to be singled out by a powerful priest. The attention, for all its perversity, was perceived as reflecting well on the victim. The grooming model was similarly utilized by Jerry Sandusky, who also carefully targeted vulnerable young people. These were predators honing in on their prey. Much like the priests, Sandusky took full advantage of the reverence in which he was held in the local community, buttressed by the complicity of the enablers. Both Sandusky and the priests felt sufficiently empowered to abuse the vulnerable in view of others, whether in the Penn State shower room or the church rectory. The clear similarities tragically reinforce the consequences of complicity.

The reliance on institutionalized complicity, whether deliberately invoked or not, is a theme that underpins the predators in all the cases discussed in this book. Without it, it would not be possible to explain their utter disregard for the risks of their recurring actions. Their full confidence and contemptuous disavowal of consequences are the direct results of their "knowing" their enablers.

Sarah Shiley was initially abused by her Catholic priest when she was 7 years old; the assaults continued until she was 14. When Shiley was 23 years old she shared details of the assaults with family members, who then sought to confront senior church officials. In the meantime, the abusing priest had been "assigned" to a parish in a different city for reasons that are unclear to Shiley. In addition to the reports of her family members, Shiley believes nine or ten additional reports were made regarding the abuse to which she was subjected.

Sarah emphasized to me the extent to which the church is a "well-oiled" institution with enormous power and resources, deeply intertwined with local officials.[21] When I asked her what she wanted from the enablers, her answer was twofold: "I wanted someone to listen" and "I wanted an expression of remorse." Neither has been forthcoming. In her opinion, this is a telling sign of the powerful spirit of institutional preservation in the Catholic Church.

The following excerpt (reproduced with Sarah's permission) from a complaining report she submitted is essential to understanding the consequences of institutional enabling and the perpetrator's perception that a child's body is his (or her) "playing field." Sarah was abused approximately 200 times over seven years at a variety of locations.

When Sarah was approximately 7 years old in approximately 1979, she attended Nativity of Our Lord for reconciliation. Fr. Sheehan instructed Sarah to sit on his lap in the confessional. He told Sarah that she was his "special Sarah". Sarah returned to school and told her classmates. She felt special having received such attention from a priest.

Sometimes, Sarah returned home from school to see Fr. Sheehan's car in her driveway. At least once a week, Fr. Sheehan lay on the couch in Sarah's living room and told Sarah to lay with him. Fr.

21. Skype conversation, July 23, 2019. In illustration of Shiley's description, see https://buffa lonews.com/2019/05/19/why-buffalos-child-molesting-priests-werent-arrested/.

Sheehan put Sarah's body on top of his, with her back against his stomach. Fr. Sheehan moved his body against Sarah's, simulating sex. On these occasions, Sarah felt Fr. Sheehan's erection against her buttocks. On some occasions, Fr. Sheehan took Sarah's hand and rubbed it on his genitals. Sarah tried to pull her hand away but was unable to resist his strength. Sometimes, Sarah tried to avoid Fr. Sheehan by running through the living room but Fr. Sheehan got mad if she did not come over to him. Other times, Sarah went to Fr. Sheehan right away, hoping for the abuse to end quickly.

As Sarah got older, Fr. Sheehan began kissing Sarah on the lips. He pushed his tongue into her mouth and told her that he loved her. Fr. Sheehan made Sarah tell him that she loved him as well. Fr. Sheehan pushed his hands underneath Sarah's clothing and manipulated her genitals. Fr. Sheehan told Sarah that he could feel her pubic hair.

On at least two occasions, Fr. Sheehan took Sarah's family to a cottage. During one of the trips, Fr. Sheehan got angry at Sarah because she was sick. Being ill meant that she was not able to cuddle with him. During the other trip, Fr. Sheehan kept Sarah back at the cottage while everyone else went swimming. Fr. Sheehan kissed Sarah and had her lay on top of him. He moved her body against his for his sexual pleasure.

On at least two other occasions, Sarah visited Fr. Sheehan at the rectory at Nativity of Our Lord. One Halloween, Sarah dressed up as Shirley Temple. Her mother took her to the rectory at Fr. Sheehan's request to see her costume. At the rectory, Sarah went to Fr. Sheehan's room upstairs, where she was alone with Fr. Sheehan. Sarah knows that something bad happened in the room, but does not recall the details. On another occasion, Sarah and another boy were stuffing envelopes at the rectory. Fr. Sheehan took them up to his living quarters where Sarah knows that something bad happened but does not recall the details.

In approximately 1983, Fr. Sheehan was transferred to St. John Bosco in Sheridan, NY. Sarah felt relieved that Fr. Sheehan was moving. However, Fr. Sheehan continued to be present in Sarah's life. On one occasion, Fr. Sheehan brought Sarah to the rectory at St. John Bosco where she spent the night with him. During the night, Sarah was with Fr. Sheehan in the kitchen. She recalls that he forced the back of her head towards his genitals. Sarah does not know whether she orally copulated Fr. Sheehan's penis.

The last incident of abuse occurred at Sarah's family home. Sarah was talking to her mother about not wanting to be in a swimsuit around the boys at school. Fr. Sheehan took Sarah to the living room and sat her on his lap. He touched Sarah's breasts and asked her if she was self-conscious about them. Sarah said no and left.

During the abuse, Fr. Sheehan gave Sarah gifts including jewelry, ornate boxes and silver coins. He called Sarah at home and insisted on speaking with her. On the phone, he asked Sarah incessantly if she loved him. After the abuse ended, Fr. Sheehan withdrew his attention towards Sarah but continued to socialize with Sarah's family. Sarah felt confused and ignored by Fr. Sheehan.[22]

Movement to Restore Trust—Buffalo Diocese "Listening Session"[23]

At the very young age of 7, I was sexually abused for the first time by a Buffalo priest. The horrific abuse continued until I was 14. I am here today with the intention to bring light to the reality of what many adult childhood sexual abuse survivors of the Diocese of Buffalo are facing.

In February 2018, I turned on the news and watched courageous Michael Whalen speak on a street in Buffalo. He was bravely telling of his abuse. I was frozen as I watched, feeling that familiar lump in my throat as I connected with his pain on a personal level. This was the shameful, embarrassing pain that I have repeatedly minimized, pushed aside, or swallowed deep in my gut. And here was this leather jacket clad man, full of strength, letting the world know of the injustices so many of us have faced.

22. Sarah Shiley submitted this complaint to the Independent Reconciliation Compensation Program (IRCP) on May 12, 2018. She provided me the document in full.
23. According to Shiley, "the document titled 'June 27th, Movement to Restore Trust' was written by me with the attention of sharing it verbally at a listening session on June 27th of 2019. Unfortunately the group (MRT) did not feel it was appropriate for me to share. At the very end of their meeting I walked over to the table where many of their board members were sitting or standing. I believe I handed the document over to John Hurley. This gentleman is the head of this Movement to Restore Trust. I told him that these were my words and if he could please read it and share it. To my knowledge it has not been published. My intention was that my voice was heard."

In March of 2018, the diocese called victims forward that had previously reported the abuse to them. (Family, counselors, my parent's friends and myself had all reported the abuse beginning in the mid-1990s several times.) What spurred me to call the diocese last year was that my abuser's name was NOT on their list. I was angry. All I could think of was "why?" Why wasn't his name there? So, after speaking with my husband and my brothers and sisters, I made the decision to pursue their call to come forward. I desperately wanted answers and knew that if I went through with this, I may finally get answers. Maybe, just maybe, his name would finally be in print. Then someone else could get help too. Someone else that was abused by him.

The diocese sent the packet directly to my house in a marked envelop. On a sunny, peaceful Sunday morning I began to fill in the large amount of paperwork. Simple enough I had thought. I would just write my shallow, clean and safe statement "I was abused by a priest as a child." I didn't think I'd have to dig any deeper than that. I could avoid the pain. But as I opened to the third page, that changed.

It asked, "What was the date and location that the abuse took place?" Five lines were included to write on underneath that question. About an inch of space to write.

I suddenly couldn't breathe. I went back. Back to it all that Sunday morning. Back to the left dark confessional at Nativity when it first began. Back to the striped velvet couch where it happened at least two times a week after school. Back to the cottages. Back to both rectories. Back to it all. There were not enough lines to cover every evil act.

Later that spring, my attorney and I estimated that my abuse occurred a minimum of 200 times.

200 times.

The realization that day as I sat attempting to fill in their IRCP form was that this was a very deep wound I had suffered. And now, through this process the wound was sliced open and profusely bleeding. The diocese offered no bandages in the form of support during this time. If not for my husband, family and counselor and my children counting on me, I don't think I would be here.

The diocese never called to check on me. No counseling was ever offered. No help as I was bleeding to death from the wound that they had inflicted on me and cut open again.

The past year has been very difficult for me. My abuser's name finally came out in print in November of last year partly due the tenacity of Charlie Specht and of brave Siobhan. I will always be grateful to them.

I made it through a very dark time last fall when a lingering deep memory came into focus. I had to accept it. I had to see it and heal. I had to accept that my abuse was horrific. I had to accept that the church was very much responsible. That my abuse could have been prevented had they not protected him. I had to accept that another child could have been saved after me when they moved him. Or that my first real kiss was at the age of 11 with a 40 something year old priest. I had to accept that my decades long nightly sleepwalking and choking in my sleep stemmed from that one night of a brutal abuse incident in his rectory kitchen in Sheridan. I had to accept who I am as a mother and teacher. That I'm hypervigilant because I feel the need to protect and save every child from harm. I had to accept that I greatly lack trust in men and authority figures. I had to accept this pain and the fact that this pain will never fully leave me.

The diocese DID NOT PROTECT ME. They did not protect the boy that was abused before me in South Buffalo. They did not protect the one abused after me when he was transferred yet again. My abuser was never removed from ministry. He died in 2006 still a practicing pastor of his church.

Bishop Malone has never reached out to me after all of this. None of the bishops or anyone else has after all these years. No counseling offered at any time. No empathy. No remorse. No personal apology. What does that say?

This will be lifelong pain. Pain caused by your indifference and an evil man.

My suggestions to the church:

- Offer list of counselors NOT affiliated with Catholic organizations. We don't want to go heal in the same place that we suffered.

- Consult with a team of professionals, well versed in the ramifications of CSA on adult survivors.
- CALL survivors directly! You honestly should be on your knees begging for forgiveness.
- Be transparent. Like see through transparency. I should not have to call media to get answers about my abuser.
- All victims/survivors should call the authorities and NOT the church to report abuse, no matter how long ago it was. Stop handling your issues internally. These are all criminal acts.
- Follow up with us . . . we are struggling and will for a lifetime.

We do not need a candle lit. We need to stop the bleeding and heal.

The deliberate and systemic, institutionalized inaction that Sarah Shiley and PV1 describe is hardly confined to the Catholic Church. Recall the case of Ohio State University tennis player Ron McDaniel, described in Chapter 4. McDaniel was abused by team doctor Richard Strauss. He was sent to Strauss by his coach, John Daly, who was fully cognizant of Strauss's pattern of behavior with student athletes. McDaniel reported his abuse to Daly, who dismissed his concerns as no big deal. When I asked McDaniel what he had expected of that conversation, McDaniel said he had thought Daly would ask more questions in order to better understand what had happened to his athlete, for whom he was responsible. Like PV1's safe space, this is a modest bar: nothing akin to demanding that the coach directly confront the abuser or aggressively protect the victim.

The full scope of the enabling infrastructure that facilitated Richard Strauss's sexual assaults is brought to light by the following material from the civil suit that Ron McDaniel filed against The Ohio State University. It illuminates, step-by-step, person-by-person, how student athletes fell prey to a predator. It makes a compelling case about what senior OSU officials knew, and how they failed to act on behalf of the individuals to whom they expressly owed a duty to protect.

236. Ronald McDaniel was a member of Defendant OSU's tennis team from 1981 through 1986, and had an athletic scholarship.
237. McDaniel relied on his scholarship to attend college.

238. McDaniel was treated by Dr. Strauss in the doctor's Larkins Hall office at OSU on at least two occasions.

239. The first occasion was during McDaniel's freshman year at OSU, in or about the winter of 1982, when McDaniel's coach, John Daly, told him to go to Larkins Hall to see one of the team doctors for cold-related symptoms. This is where he encountered Dr. Strauss for the first time.

240. During the winter 1982 examination, when McDaniel complained of swollen adenoids and a cold, Dr. Strauss told McDaniel that he needed conduct a full medical examination and instructed McDaniel to remove his pants.

241. McDaniel complied with Dr. Strauss's request. During the examination, under the guise of performing a needed medical evaluation to screen for hernias and structural damage, Dr. Strauss rubbed and massaged McDaniel's testicles and penis in what seemed like a sexual manner.

242. Dr. Strauss also asked personal questions about McDaniel's nationality and stared up and down at his body.

243. McDaniel felt very uncomfortable about how Dr. Strauss had conducted his examination, and he expressed his discomfort afterwards with more senior athletes and one of the head team trainers, named Jim.

244. The athletes and trainer laughed and told McDaniel that their nickname for Dr. Strauss was "Dr. Nuts" because, no matter what injury or illness an athlete had, Dr. Strauss would always examine their testicles.

245. Some athletes also told McDaniel that, during examinations, Dr. Strauss would try to rub them like a girlfriend does and sometimes stuck a finger up their rectums.

246. McDaniel soon learned that Dr. Strauss's seemingly inappropriate touching during medical examinations was well known and openly discussed among athletes, trainers, coaches, and the athletic director.

247. In McDaniel's experience, Dr. Strauss's genital examinations were a running joke among trainers, coaches, and administrators, including, but not limited to: athletic director Hugh Hindman; associate information director Steve Snapp; and co-head

athletic trainer Billy Hill. He often heard the trainers, coaches, and administrators joke and laugh about the athletes' complaints about Dr. Strauss's medical examinations.

248. In or about the fall of 1983, McDaniel sustained an ankle injury while running, and Coach Daly told him to go to Larkins Hall again to see a team doctor for medical treatment.

249. McDaniel did not want to go to Larkins Hall and risk seeing Dr. Strauss again, given his first experience, but felt that his athletic scholarship would be at risk if he disobeyed his coach's instruction.

250. McDaniel complied with his coach's instruction and went to Larkins Hall. He assumed that if he had to see Dr. Strauss again, the doctor would have no reason to conduct a testicular exam for an ankle injury.

251. During the fall 1983 examination, Dr. Strauss again instructed McDaniel to remove his shorts so that Dr. Strauss could perform a full medical examination.

252. McDaniel asked why he needed to "drop his shorts" for an ankle injury. Dr. Strauss grabbed the waistband of McDaniel's shorts to try to pull them down.

253. Dr. Strauss advised McDaniel that he had to check him for a hernia.

254. McDaniel refused to take his shorts off.

255. McDaniel then left Dr. Strauss's office. He decided he would never get examined by Dr. Strauss again because he felt violated.

256. McDaniel told Coach Daly about Dr. Strauss's medical examination and said he would never again get medical treatment from Dr. Strauss.

257. Coach Daly said, "Okay" and that was it.

258. Coach Daly did not follow up on McDaniel's complaint about Dr. Strauss. To McDaniel's knowledge, Coach Daly did not take any corrective action against Dr. Strauss or ensure that others did.

259. McDaniel was never informed or made aware of any OSU grievance procedure to complain about Dr. Strauss.

260. Until hearing media reports in early July, 2018, about an investigation into allegations that Dr. Strauss had sexually abused

OSU student-athletes, McDaniel did not know, or have reason to know, of OSU's role in Dr. Strauss's sexually abusive medical examinations of him or that other athletes had previously complained to OSU about Dr. Strauss's abuse.

261. Until hearing these media reports in early July, 2018, McDaniel had no reason to investigate whether OSU—in addition to Dr. Strauss—had harmed him.

262. This is because, in McDaniel's experience, Dr. Strauss's genital examinations were a running joke among trainers, coaches, and administrators. In addition, Coach Daly's unconcerned reaction to his complaint about Dr. Strauss, and his teammates' jokes about Dr. Strauss's examinations, did not give McDaniel any reason to investigate what OSU was doing or failing to do. Indeed, when McDaniel raised concerns about Dr. Strauss's examinations, Coach Daly's reaction served to reinforce McDaniel's reasonable belief that further inquiry would not be productive.

263. Even if, in 1983, McDaniel had tried to inquire further into OSU's role in permitting Dr. Strauss's abuse of him, the inquiry would have been futile, as OSU controlled access to that information, and, through its trainers, coaches, and administrators, treated complaints about Dr. Strauss's examinations as matters of no real concern.

264. If OSU had taken meaningful action to address prior reports of Dr. Strauss's sexual abuse, McDaniel would not have been abused by Dr. Strauss.

265. As a result of Dr. Strauss's abuse and OSU's failure to prevent it, McDaniel has suffered emotional and psychological damages. For example, McDaniel is plagued by a fear of medical examinations that ultimately resulted in delayed treatment of a testicular tumor. Because of the unchecked abuse by Dr. Strauss, McDaniel has avoided physical examinations involving his testicles and is extremely uncomfortable about seeing doctors for medical treatment that might involve a testicular exam. This had significant consequences for McDaniel, who had a bike accident in or around the spring of 1999 in which he suffered a blow to the area near his testicles. McDaniel chose to endure the pain rather than seek immediate medical attention, due to his experience with Dr. Strauss at

OSU. After six to eight months of continuing and increasing pain, McDaniel felt forced to obtain a medical consult and was, in turn, diagnosed with a benign testicular tumor. The tumor had grown to enormous proportions because of the delay in getting his testicle evaluated, and McDaniel suffered medical complications and pain as a result of the delay in getting treatment. Both medical providers who treated McDaniel were troubled by the fact that McDaniel had waited so long to get medical attention for this issue.[24]

The location of these assaults is significant. While Strauss and Nassar had private clinics and Sandusky took full advantage of his home's basement, all three also assaulted victims on university campuses. These blatant acts reflect the degree to which these perpetrators understood and took advantage of the institutionalized complicity surrounding them. The number of victims is unfathomable. Until law enforcement brought the proverbial hammer down on the predators, unimaginable harm was done to their young and vulnerable victims—harm that could have been prevented if those complicit had acted instead on the survivors' behalf.

Steve Snyder-Hill was a student at The Ohio State University from 1991 to 2000 and a student employee of the university while in graduate school from 1998 to 2000. He was examined by Strauss on or about January 5, 1995. The following material, as with McDaniel above, details Strauss's harassment and abuse of Snyder-Hill, and also reveals the profound misrepresentations made by the director of OSU's Student Health Services, Dr. Ted Grace. Grace's dishonesty in addition to his failure to act adds a new dimension to a narrative otherwise familiar from that involving John Daly, Hugh Hindman, and Andy Geiger.

195. Steve Snyder-Hill (then named Steve Hill) was a student at OSU from 1991 through 2000. He was also a student-employee in graduate school at OSU from 1998-2000.

196. Snyder-Hill was examined by Dr. Strauss once, on or about January 5, 1995, at OSU's student health center ("Student Health").

197. Snyder-Hill went to Student Health to have a lump in his chest checked.

24. Second Amended Complaint. Case: 2:18-cv-00736-MHW-EPD Doc #: 101-1 Filed: 11/07/19.

198. The triage nurse there recommended that Snyder-Hill see Dr. Strauss, which he did.

199. Snyder-Hill was alone in the room with Dr. Strauss.

200. Dr. Strauss told Snyder-Hill that he needed to remove all of his clothes, so that Dr. Strauss could perform a full medical exam.

201. Snyder-Hill complied with this request.

202. During the examination, Dr. Strauss made inappropriate comments to Snyder-Hill and asked inappropriate questions about Snyder-Hill's sexual and personal desires, which made Snyder-Hill very uncomfortable. These comments and questions included asking Snyder-Hill if he was gay, whether he had trouble sleeping with just one person, and whether he sexually desired to do something else; and telling Snyder-Hill that he worked with AIDS patients and was the doctor for the athletic department. Snyder-Hill felt as if Strauss was testing him to see how he would react to being in an uncomfortable position.

203. When Dr. Strauss told Snyder-Hill that he needed to check Snyder-Hill's testicles, Snyder-Hill felt very uncomfortable and said this was not necessary because his regular doctor had recently done this.

204. Dr. Strauss insisted on doing both testicular and rectal examinations, ignoring Snyder-Hill's statements that he did not need those exams, and Dr. Strauss performed both exams on Snyder-Hill before checking the lump in Snyder-Hill's chest.

205. Dr. Strauss fondled Snyder-Hill for an unnecessarily long period of time. Dr. Strauss put his face so uncomfortably close to Snyder-Hill's genital area during the prolonged examination that Snyder-Hill could feel Dr. Strauss breathing on his genitals. The rectal exam involved Dr. Strauss digitally penetrating Snyder-Hill's rectum with his finger. Dr. Strauss did not wear gloves at any point during the examination.

206. Snyder-Hill felt very uncomfortable and powerless throughout Dr. Strauss's examination. Snyder-Hill felt intimidated and became afraid to voice a concern.

207. This escalated when Dr. Strauss asked Snyder-Hill to lay down on the table, then leaned over to finally check the lump in

Snyder-Hill's chest—the only reason Snyder-Hill sought medical attention. Dr. Strauss massaged Snyder-Hill's chest for a prolonged time, initially brushing his groin against Snyder-Hill's side, but as he kept rubbing Snyder-Hill's chest, Dr. Strauss got much more aggressive, pushing his pelvic area up against Snyder-Hill's side and holding it there. Snyder-Hill could feel Dr. Strauss's erect penis pressed against him. Dr. Strauss kept himself pressed against Snyder-Hill for a prolonged time while rubbing and fondling his chest.

208. Snyder-Hill was shocked by this and felt that Dr. Strauss was trying to manipulate and intimidate him. As a result, Snyder-Hill could not look Dr. Strauss in the eyes during the exam or afterwards. Snyder-Hill felt very intimidated by Dr. Strauss.

209. The examination by Dr. Strauss weighed heavily on Snyder-Hill afterwards. He felt very uncomfortable and upset, and thought the examination was inappropriate. He also felt guilty that he had let Dr. Strauss touch him. He thought Dr. Strauss's topics of conversation were flirty and that, if Snyder-Hill had given Dr. Strauss a signal to proceed sexually, Dr. Strauss would have acted on it.

210. The next day, on January 6, 1995, Snyder-Hill called Student Health to lodge a complaint about Dr. Strauss. He spoke with the Assistant Director of Student Health, Judy Brady, who took notes on his oral complaint. The complaint is memorialized in a "Patient Comment" form dated January 6, 1995.

211. Brady told Snyder-Hill that someone would get back to him. Snyder-Hill said he wanted to speak with the top person at Student Health.

212. Dr. Ted Grace, Director of Student Health, called Snyder-Hill in response to the complaint

213. At some point between January 5 and January 24, 1995, Snyder-Hill, accompanied by his then-boyfriend, participated in a two-hour, in-person meeting with Dr. Grace, Dr. Strauss, and Dr. Louise Douce, OSU's Director of Counseling and Consulting Services. Snyder-Hill brought his boyfriend as a witness, which he felt was necessary because Dr. Strauss had denied any wrongdoing and Dr. Grace had supported Dr. Strauss's position during their prior telephone conversation. During the in-person meeting, Drs. Grace

and Douce required that Snyder-Hill recount his allegations about Dr. Strauss's inappropriate and abusive conduct during the January 5, 1996 examination. OSU's insistence that Snyder-Hill detail his abuse in the presence of his abuser was traumatic and psychologically harmful for Snyder-Hill.

214. After Snyder-Hill explained what Dr. Strauss had said and done in the examination, Dr. Strauss responded with pretextual and false explanations for his inappropriate statements and conduct. Snyder-Hill replied that he did not believe Dr. Strauss's explanations. As the meeting progressed, Dr. Strauss's demeanor escalated to anger, then rage. When Snyder-Hill explained that Dr. Strauss had pressed his erect penis into him, Dr. Strauss slammed his hand on the table and screamed directly at Snyder-Hill that Snyder-Hill was trying to destroy his reputation and career. Dr. Grace and Dr. Douce looked shocked by Dr. Strauss's outburst, but said nothing. At the end of the meeting, Dr. Douce said it appeared that the incident was just a misunderstanding, she was very confident that "Dr. Strauss was not guilty of any wrongdoing," and Snyder-Hill had just been confused and mistaken about Dr. Strauss's intentions. Id. at 129. Snyder-Hill told them that he didn't accept their conclusion, was unhappy with the result, and needed to go home and consult with his boyfriend on what to do next.

215. Dr. Grace called Snyder-Hill on January 24, 1995, as a follow-up to the meeting. Snyder-Hill told Dr. Grace that he still was not happy with the results of the meeting and did not accept it. Snyder-Hill also demanded that changes be made, so other students would not experience what he had experienced with Dr. Strauss. Snyder-Hill also voiced concern about where his complaint would go or be retained, in case Dr. Strauss acted this way with another patient. Snyder-Hill demanded that students be permitted to opt out of testicular and rectal examinations (or anything that might make them uncomfortable) and, at a minimum, have someone else present in the room during examinations (to avoid a situation where it would be the doctor's word against the student's). Snyder-Hill also demanded that he be notified if anyone else complained about Dr. Strauss's conduct. Dr. Grace agreed to

Snyder-Hill's demands, and then Snyder-Hill asked Dr. Grace to document their conversation in writing.

216. Per Snyder-Hill's request, Dr. Grace wrote a follow up letter to Snyder-Hill, dated January 26, 1995, in which he represented that "we had never received a complaint about Dr. Strauss before, although we have had several positive comments."

217. Dr. Grace's statement was false. In fact, "Student A" had complained about Dr. Strauss three days before Snyder-Hill's complaint, and many other students had complained about Dr. Strauss for many years before that to numerous OSU officials.

218. Dr. Grace's letter also assured Snyder-Hill that "[a]ny future complaints would include consideration of all prior complaints of a similar nature." This statement upset Snyder-Hill because it fell short of what Dr. Grace had agreed to during their phone conversation: Dr. Grace had told Snyder-Hill he would contact Snyder-Hill if OSU received another complaint about Dr. Strauss. As a result, Snyder-Hill felt slighted by this statement in Dr. Grace's letter. At the same time, Snyder-Hill believed this was probably the best he could get from OSU and Dr. Grace.

219. Dr. Grace also stated in the letter that "all patient comments—both positive and negative—are maintained in a quality assurance file that is available for review by the Joint Commission on Accreditation of Healthcare Organizations."

220. The letter also mentioned suggestions from Snyder-Hill about improvements to Student Health that resulted in a new form that "asks every patient if he or she would like to have a chaperone present during the office visit," and provides an opportunity for students to opt out of potential genital exams or touching in certain areas. This statement was also a misrepresentation because, "Student Health had already been developing an intake form to address Student A's concerns," before Snyder-Hill's conversation with Dr. Grace. Id. at 132.

221. Snyder-Hill felt that Dr. Grace had indirectly addressed some of his concerns and that the proposed changes to Student Health's protocols would prevent Dr. Strauss from abusing other students.

222. Neither Dr. Grace nor any other OSU administrator or employee informed Snyder-Hill of any OSU grievance procedure

to complain about Dr. Strauss. Nor did Dr. Grace, Dr. Douce, or any other OSU administrator or employee inform Snyder-Hill that he could report the incident with Dr. Strauss to law enforcement or other authorities.

223. Dr. Strauss's personnel file contains no mention of Snyder-Hill's complaint, or any disciplinary action or internal investigation stemming from the complaint. In fact, Dr. Grace's June 27, 1995 performance review of Dr. Strauss rated Dr. Strauss as excellent and did not mention Snyder-Hill's (or Student A's) complaint.

224. When OSU learned in 1996 from the Medical Board that its investigator had concluded that Dr. Strauss had been "performing inappropriate genital exams on male students" at OSU "for years," no one at OSU informed Snyder-Hill about this conclusion. Id. at 4.

225. Snyder-Hill heard nothing further about sexual abuse by Dr. Strauss until July 11, 2018, when he saw Dr. Strauss's photograph in media reports and recognized his face. Until seeing these media reports, Snyder-Hill did not know, or have reason to know, that Dr. Strauss had sexually abused other OSU students before abusing him or that others had previously complained to OSU about Dr. Strauss's abuse.

226. Until seeing these media reports on July 11, 2018, Snyder-Hill did not know, or have reason to know, of OSU's role in Dr. Strauss's sexually abusive medical examination of him in January of 1995.

227. Until seeing these media reports on July 11, 2018, Snyder-Hill had no reason to investigate whether OSU—in addition to Dr. Strauss—had harmed him.

228. This is because OSU, through Dr. Grace, falsely represented to Snyder-Hill that no one had previously complained about Dr. Strauss and/or concealed prior complaints about Dr.

229. Snyder-Hill reasonably relied on Dr. Grace's representations that Student Health had never received a complaint about Dr. Strauss before Snyder-Hill's and that Student Health had only received positive comments about Dr. Strauss.

230. Snyder-Hill believed, and had reason to believe, that OSU had responded adequately to his concerns about ensuring student safety in the future, because Dr. Grace informed him that his

complaint would be considered if there were any future complaints about Dr. Strauss, all patient comments about Dr. Strauss would be maintained in a quality assurance file subject to review, and Student Health had created a new form that would allow students to request a chaperone at office visits and an opportunity to opt out of potential genital exams or touching in other areas.

231. Even if, in 1995, Snyder-Hill had tried to inquire further into OSU's role in permitting Dr. Strauss's abuse of him, the inquiry would have been futile, as OSU controlled access to that information and, through Dr. Grace, had rebuffed Snyder-Hill's efforts by telling him that no one had previously complained about Dr. Strauss.

232. In short, based on Dr. Grace's false representations in 1995, Snyder-Hill reasonably believed that he was the first OSU student to complain about Dr. Strauss's medical examinations, no other students had been similarly abused, and OSU was taking reasonable action to ensure student safety in the future.

233. On July 11, 2018, Snyder-Hill was traumatized by learning the news about Dr. Strauss's serial sexual abuse, OSU's knowledge about it and failure to take appropriate action to stop it, and Dr. Strauss's death by suicide. He feels that OSU has robbed him of the ability to ever get closure on the sexual abuse he suffered at the hands of Dr. Strauss and to confront his abuser.

234. If OSU had taken meaningful action to address prior reports of Dr. Strauss's sexual abuse, Snyder-Hill would not have been abused by Dr. Strauss.

235. As a result of Dr. Strauss's abuse and OSU's failure to prevent it, Snyder-Hill has suffered emotional and psychological damages. To this day, he is extremely uncomfortable with physicians, particularly when getting testicular or rectal examinations. Snyder-Hill is in the military and, since his experience with Dr. Strauss, he has been uncomfortable using communal showers and therefore avoids going to the showers when other soldiers are there. In addition, learning about Dr. Strauss's sexual abuse, OSU's role in allowing it, and Dr. Strauss's death has re-traumatized Snyder-Hill, causing repressed memories of his painful experiences to resurface.

Snyder-Hill has been reliving those painful experiences, including the emotions he experienced during Dr. Strauss's exam and after he complained about Dr. Strauss to OSU. These experiences have also had a profound, devastating impact on Snyder-Hill's confidence and self-esteem as a gay man. When this abuse happened to him back in 1995, Snyder-Hill did not tell his parents about it because he was in the process of coming out of the closet as a gay man and was terrified that his parents might think all gay men acted like Dr. Strauss. So, Snyder-Hill lived with this secret of abuse to shelter his parents from the truth. The abuse also affected how he felt about himself being gay. Snyder-Hill attended seminars at OSU on how to change your sexuality and found it very difficult to accept his sexuality.[25]

It is instructive to compare and contrast the experiences of Steve Snyder-Hill and Ron McDaniel, because while they were both assaulted by the same perpetrator at the same institution, their enablers fit different paradigms. Snyder-Hill was not an athlete, but he was a student at Ohio State, and therefore the duty owed him cannot be distinguished from the duty owed McDaniel. In the aftermath of his assault by Strauss, Steve contacted the OSU Student Health Services and encountered Ted Grace. The complaint above makes clear that Grace falls into the category of deceitful enabler, as distinguished from a discouraging enabler (Kathy Klages at Michigan State) or a dismissive enabler (John Daly). As a deceitful enabler, Grace failed to honestly respond to Steve's reporting of an assault, thereby failing both to punish Strauss and to protect present and future students at Ohio State. In misleading Snyder-Hill by suggesting he was not aware of previous complaints against Strauss, Grace was deceitful toward the one person to whom he directly owed a duty to protect.

Ron McDaniel, by contrast, reported his abuse to his coach, who dismissed his complaint. That is the message McDaniel received from OSU athletic director Hindman, who laughed and walked away upon hearing what Strauss had just done *to one of his athletes*. Daly, the coach, and Hindman, a senior university official, had one duty and one duty only: to protect Ron McDaniel.

---

25. Second Amended Complaint. Case: 2:18-cv-00736-MHW-EPD Doc #: 101-1 Filed: 11/07/19.

By failing to take immediate action when Ron McDaniel and Steve Snyder-Hill shared their experiences with them, John Daly, Hugh Hindman, and Ted Grace missed opportunities to confront Strauss and protect vulnerable members of their community. They certainly *did not* owe a higher duty to Strauss or the university than to the students and athletes under their care. As a result of their inaction, McDaniel and Snyder-Hill were not only survivors of Strauss's assaults, but were forced to survive enablers whose complicity enhanced their peril and that of others.

In the face of horrific narratives like these, the stock responses of a well-meaning public are tragic but predictable:

"This must not happen again!"

"We must do something!"

"What is wrong with society?"

"How could no one have acted?"

"But [insert name of predator] is such a good guy."

"But [insert name of institution] is really committed to the safety of those in its care."

However well intentioned, these are empty phrases, mantras, and sloganeering. They serve to placate the speaker in particular, and society in general, but they are of no practical benefit to the survivor. What good is sympathy after the fact, when direct action would have had real impact and consequences? Indeed, empty words can have the opposite effect in the face of institutionalized complicity, because they reinforce the lack of consequences for the perpetrator's actions. From the survivors' perspective, they are akin to a "white flag." Society is surrendering before their plight.

It is not sufficient to merely state the obvious and reassure ourselves that this will not happen again. It has, and it will. Part of what makes reading the reports and grand jury findings so painful is the profound sense of déjà vu: the predator's sense of entitlement and confidence that survivors will not complain, bystanders will not intervene, and enablers will facilitate.

"God is fuming."

—Sarah Shiley, Skype conversation, July 23, 2019

"I feel disconnected from the world, alone, and in pain. I couldn't trust anyone to keep me safe back then, and I can't trust anyone to keep me safe today. I have lost my ability to be confident with myself and others. To those at MSU, USAG, and the USOC who knew about Larry Nassar but did not act, the sin of omission is just as bad as the sin itself. As if dealing with the intense publicity and pain around Nassar wasn't enough, you have added a heartless, depraved level of denial and victim shaming to the mix. You said terrible things, for example that victims didn't understand the nuanced difference between sexual abuse and medical treatment, and that it is virtually impossible to stop a determined sexual predator on your campus. This is disgusting. Do you know how these statements make us feel? Do you understand the impact of your words? Do you understand that these statements put other victims in a state of fear so deep that they may never come forward? Your actions are abusive in and of themselves. Your attitudes of apathy and dismissal have made the healing process particularly difficult, especially because you haven't taken action to produce legitimate investigations. This means that every day we still have to remind ourselves that it's okay that we came forward, what happened to us is very, very real, even though we so desperately tried to deny it for so long."

—Megan Halicek, victim impact statement

— 7 —

The Bystander Duty to Act

The cases discussed in this book have established the outlines of the bystander-enabler-victim relationship, a relationship tragically grounded in complicity. Despite the fundamental difference that the bystander is *present* at an event, whereas the enabler is *informed* of it, there is a critical similarity between the two roles: both are guilty of a *crime of omission*. And in their failure to act, they are complicit in the harm suffered by the victim.

Looking at the relationship from the other side, survivor expectations regarding the enabler are not met. Tiffany Thomas-Lopez could not have been clearer: "I wanted someone to do something; to shut Larry the fuck down." Survivors harbor hopes, but too often are met with resounding silence.

Indeed, Tiffany's case goes to the heart of the matter. She found that her decision to report Nassar's assaults had punitive consequences—not to the perpetrator, Nassar, but to Tiffany herself. Tiffany Thomas-Lopez was assaulted 150 times by Larry Nassar. She graphically demonstrated to a Michigan State University trainer, Liana Hadden, how Nassar assaulted her by digitally penetrating her with his bare hand. Hadden told her to share this with another MSU trainer, Destiny Teachnor-Hauk. Tiffany did so. And as a result, she received increasingly painful "treatments" by

Nassar, and was ultimately dropped from the Michigan State softball team. That cost was imposed on Tiffany by Nassar's colleagues.

The evil of the perpetrator is greatly facilitated and enhanced by the *conscious decision* of the bystander or enabler not to intervene on behalf of the survivor. This is an essential element of the act of complicity, manifested in moving away from the individual in distress. It has profound physical and emotional consequences for the survivor.

The sense of being abandoned was a constant refrain in all my interactions with the survivors. This goes beyond the basic feeling of being deserted to a sense that the bystander-enabler *actively facilitated* the harm. There is a gnawing sense of "if only." But in the cases before us here, no one stepped into that breach.

The enablers' responses to the survivors leave little room for doubt about enabler complicity, whether dismissive, discouraging, deceitful, or punitive. Kathy Klages discouraged Lindsey Lemke; USA Gymnastics turned its back on Mattie Larson;[1] MSU's trainers failed Tiffany Thomas-Lopez; Coach John Daly "smirked"; Catholic bishops and priests protected the church at all costs; Penn State senior officials similarly put the Nittany Lion brand above all else. All these enablers, uniquely positioned in their institutions to act decisively against the perpetrators, chose not to act when informed of crimes committed against the vulnerable survivors, *to whom they owed a duty.*

The all-encompassing institutional and moral power of these individuals is of prime importance when considering the complicity of the bystander-enabler. There was no danger posed to the enabler in any of the situations examined here. The only individual at risk was the survivor, whose suffering was enhanced by enabler complicity.

To turn a blind eye to that suffering is to condemn future survivors to the same fate. Therefore, the question of how to minimize the possibility that future bystanders and enablers will turn away is of the utmost importance. To facilitate the argument regarding criminalizing the enabler, it is necessary to engage in a detailed discussion regarding the criminalization of the bystander. There is a logical progression in the sequencing of the two proposed crimes.

---

1. https://officialmissval.com/times-up-usag/.

As outlined in my previous book, *The Crime of Complicity*, there is social benefit in criminalizing the bystander who fails to act on behalf of the person in peril. I reached that conclusion by applying lessons learned from the Holocaust to the contemporary context. I do not presume to equate the events of 1939–1945 to those today, but it is my conviction that it is imperative to protect the vulnerable individual—even if that means imposing a fine and/or incarceration on another individual who does not have a preexisting relationship with the victim or does not even know his or her name. That is, stripped to its core, the essence of the bystander-victim relationship.

The discussion that follows in this chapter is based on my active engagement with Representative Brian King of the Utah State Legislature in crafting bystander legislation; my prior research, conducted over the years; and a law review article co-authored with my research assistant, Jessie Dyer. I include Rep. King's legislative proposal in full, in order to give the reader insight into bystander legislative language as it has been developed, and thus lead the way to possible enabler legislative language. I also analyze the arguments brought against Rep. King's proposal in the Utah Legislature. These arguments provide a deeper understanding of the duty to care as it applies both to the bystander and the enabler.

There are important differences between the bystander and the enabler: One is physically present when the vulnerable individual is in peril and needs assistance; the other hears of the peril or is in a clear position to know of the distress. The bystander, in most instances, is a random observer of a potential tragedy; the enabler is a direct participant in a terrible crime. The victim may see the bystander, but the victim-bystander relationship is generally fleeting, at best. More likely than not, neither knows the other's name. By contrast, the survivors of Nassar's, Strauss' and the priests' assaults knew their enablers, even though these individuals were not present at the time of the assaults. The survivors were well aware of their identity.

The recommendation to codify both bystander and enabler duty to act is predicated on the principle that both owe a *duty*. The bystander duty is specifically to dial 9-1-1. An exception is allowed if doing so would endanger the bystander. The enabler duty is to directly intervene to protect individuals for whom they are responsible. In the overwhelming majority of cases, a self-endangerment exception is not justified for an enabler, because a decision not to act would have consequences for the vulnerable *that far outweigh potential harm to the enabler*. The person in peril must always be kept in the forefront of any discussion about legislating the duty to act.

Codification in a criminal code clearly does not guarantee individual action, but criminal sanction, in conjunction with significant public attention, can be a most effective deterrent. The effort to criminalize bystander duty to act has had mixed results. Ten U.S. states and a number of foreign countries have passed such legislation, but the efforts in Utah have yet to succeed.[2] The voices of opposition raise important and valid points that demand serious consideration, in particular, qualms about the idea of "legislating morality."

Given the similarities in their underlying philosophical and jurisprudential natures, it is fair to assume that enabler legislation will arouse the same objections as bystander legislation. In both cases, the premise for the proposed legislation is a crime of *omission*. In both cases, the proposed legislation has one primary purpose: to provide assistance to an individual who is not in a position to protect themselves.

In this book, I use sexual assault as the locus for a broader examination of bystander and enabler complicity. Sexual assault is understood as an egregious crime, and it is a focus of public discussion today. It is a useful starting point, because the issues are clear. But it must be remembered that every day, everywhere, in all sorts of circumstances and conditions, people suffer because others turn away rather than offering them assistance.

In addressing complicity, the actors whom we single out are the victim and bystander-enabler. Duty to Act legislation is predicated on victim protection and victim rights. In the bystander paradigm, we focus on two categories of victim: (1) those injured by a perpetrator, and (2) those in distress for a reason not caused by a third party, for example, a fall, a medical emergency, or a natural disaster. The recommendation to impose an obligation to provide assistance is based on the ability to act on behalf

---

2. The ten states are California, Florida, Hawaii, Massachusetts, Minnesota, Ohio, Rhode Island, Vermont, Washington, and Wisconsin. Their provisions are discussed later in this chapter.

of an individual facing harm, however it is caused. In recommending the imposition of a criminal penalty on the bystander or enabler who fails to provide assistance, the proposed legislation has a twofold purpose: to punish the individual who failed to act and to serve as a clear warning to potential bystanders and enablers in the future.

We have all been bystanders at some point in our lives. I myself have sometimes done the right thing, other times, not. I have no satisfactory explanation for my conduct other than the basic clichés: "I was in a hurry"; "I didn't want to get involved"; "the circumstances were not clear." Not particularly compelling or dramatic, but they reflect the common reality.

Two instances come to mind, both fairly typical of human interactions in day-to-day life. In one, I saw something; in the other, I heard something. I was fully in control of my faculties, aware that another person was in distress, yet I chose to ignore a college student overturning a shopping cart filled with beer cans and bottles pushed by a homeless individual; I was hurrying to a football game. I ignored a neighbor's eight-year-old child who was crying hysterically all night outside their house; I went back to sleep.

A simple phone call to law enforcement would have intervened in the assault and alleviated the suffering of the child. The proposed legislation would not impose a requirement on me to exchange a word with the college student or interact with my neighbors, as there is no intent to impose on the bystander an obligation to engage the perpetrator. In that regard the bystander's responsibility contrasts with that of the enabler, who is in a position of authority and therefore fully qualified to engage or confront the perpetrator.

In assessing the bystander, two criteria must be met before penalty can be assigned: (1) knowledge of the danger, and (2) capacity to act. In the instance with the homeless individual, I met both tests, because the assault occurred two feet from me in broad daylight. I certainly could not argue, "I didn't see it. I didn't hear it." I had no defense for my decision not to act.

The other situation was not so clear-cut. I was in my house at night, the child lived across the street. But I did sense that the crying was not normal, that the child was outside despite the late hour. And the crying went on for a very long time. It was obvious this situation was different; pretending otherwise was convenient and easy. I later learned the child's parents had locked him out of the house. My decision not to act on behalf of the child was not as egregious as in the case of the homeless individual, which was a clear failure on my part.

In both situations, I was clearly a bystander. I did not personally know the people involved. Even though I had seen the child and his parents, I do not recall ever exchanging a word with them. And in both situations, there was undoubtedly a victim. The perpetrators—the college student and the child's parents—are not of interest in the context of bystander Duty to Act legislation. The only relationship under consideration is that between the bystander and the victim. The sole question before us is what the former did to assist the latter.

In both cases, I failed to call the authorities. There is no defense available to me, the more so because no danger was posed to me. Therefore, bystander legislation would correctly punish me for my failure to act. All I had to do was dial 9-1-1.

With these situations in mind, we turn to concrete efforts to enact bystander legislation. Over the past few years, my research assistant, Jessie Dyer, and I have been actively engaged with Utah State Representative Brian King in his efforts to enact a Bystander Duty to Act bill. In 2018, 2019, and again in 2020, the Utah House Judiciary Committee voted Rep. King's legislation favorably for a full floor debate and vote. The bill was defeated each time.

Rep. King's legislation can be perceived as an "add-on" to duty requirements that the Utah Legislature previously codified. The duty to assist laws enacted by the legislature in 1953, however, are limited in application to vulnerable children and the elderly.[3] The logical extension of this duty requirement to other individuals in peril, incapable of the simple act of dialing 9-1-1, is the sole obligation King's legislation imposes on the bystander.

---

3. Utah Code Ann. § 62A-4a-403 and Utah Code Ann. § 62A-3-305.

The text of the proposed legislation is as follows: [4]

911 RESPONSIBILITIES IN AN EMERGENCY

2020 GENERAL SESSION

STATE OF UTAH

Chief Sponsor: Brian S. King

Senate Sponsor: _____

LONG TITLE

General Description:

This bill creates a duty to contact emergency services in an emergency.

Highlighted Provisions:

This bill:

- defines terms;
- makes it a class B misdemeanor to fail to contact emergency services in the event of a crime or another emergency subject to certain exceptions;
- prohibits a prosecutor from basing charges for commission of an offense other than the offense created in this bill on an individual's failure to contact emergency services;
- amends provisions of the Good Samaritan Act to provide immunity from liability to an individual who contacts emergency services in accordance with the requirements of this bill;
- addresses civil liability issues related to this bill; and
- makes technical changes.

Money Appropriated in this Bill:

None

Other Special Clauses:

None

Utah Code Sections Affected:

---

4. H.B. 104, 2020 Leg., 63rd Sess. (Utah 2019).

AMENDS:

78B-4-501, as last amended by Laws of Utah 2018, Chapter 62

ENACTS:

76-9-1101, Utah Code Annotated 1953

Be it enacted by the Legislature of the state of Utah:

Section 1. Section 76-9-1101 is enacted to read:

76-9-1101. Failure to provide assistance.

(1) As used in this section:

(a) (i) "Assistance" means making reasonable effort to contact paramedics, fire protection, law enforcement, or other appropriate emergency services.

(ii) "Assistance" does not include action that places the individual taking the action, or another individual, in danger.

(b) "Emergency" means that an individual is suffering from serious bodily injury and is in need of assistance.

(c) "Legal privilege" means any privilege designated by common law, statute, or rule of evidence.

(d) "Serious bodily injury" means injury that involves a substantial risk of death, unconsciousness, extreme physical pain, protracted and obvious disfigurement, or protracted loss or impairment of the function of a bodily member, organ, or mental faculty.

(2) An individual is guilty of a class B misdemeanor if the individual:

(a) observes that a crime has occurred or is occurring or that an emergency is occurring;

(b) has personal knowledge that another individual is suffering serious bodily injury resulting from a crime or emergency;

(c) is able to provide reasonable assistance to the individual described in Subsection (2)(b); and

(d) willfully fails to provide reasonable assistance to the individual described in Subsection (2)(b).

(3) An individual is not guilty of violating Subsection (2) if the individual reasonably believes another individual has, or likely has, already provided or is providing reasonable assistance to the individual described in Subsection (2)(b).

(4) Notwithstanding any contrary provision of law, a prosecutor may not use an individual's violation of Subsection (2) as the basis for charging the individual with another offense.

(5) This section does not create an independent basis for civil liability for failure to provide the assistance described in this section.

(6) The fact that an individual is charged with or convicted of a crime under this section may not be used to establish that the individual violated a duty on which a claim for personal injuries may be based.

(7) Subsection (2) does not apply to the extent that an individual is prohibited from providing assistance by a legal privilege.

Section 2. Section 78B-4-501 is amended to read:

78B-4-501. Good Samaritan Law.

(1) As used in this section:

(a) "Child" means an individual of such an age that a reasonable person would perceive the individual as unable to open the door of a locked motor vehicle, but in any case younger than 18 years of age.

(b) "Emergency" means an unexpected occurrence involving injury, threat of injury, or illness to a person or the public, including motor vehicle accidents, disasters, actual or threatened discharges, removal or disposal of hazardous materials, and other accidents or events of a similar nature.

(c) "Emergency care" includes actual assistance or advice offered to avoid, mitigate, or attempt to mitigate the effects of an emergency.

(d) "First responder" means a state or local:

(i) law enforcement officer, as defined in Section 53-13-103;

(ii) firefighter, as defined in Section 34A-3-113; or

(iii) emergency medical service provider, as defined in Section 26-8a-102.

(e) "Motor vehicle" means the same as that term is defined in Section 41-1a-102.

(2) A person who renders emergency care at or near the scene of, or during, an emergency, gratuitously and in good faith, or as required under Section 76-9-1101, is not liable for any civil damages or penalties as a result of any act or omission by the person

rendering the emergency care, unless the person is grossly negligent or caused the emergency.

(3) (a) A person who gratuitously, and in good faith, assists a governmental agency or political subdivision in an activity described in Subsections (3)(a)(i) through (iii) is not liable for any civil damages or penalties as a result of any act or omission, unless the person rendering assistance is grossly negligent in:

(i) implementing measures to control the causes of epidemic and communicable diseases and other conditions significantly affecting the public health, or necessary to protect the public health as set out in Title 26A, Chapter 1, Local Health Departments;

(ii) investigating and controlling suspected bioterrorism and disease as set out in Title 26, Chapter 23b, Detection of Public Health Emergencies Act; and

(iii) responding to a national, state, or local emergency, a public health emergency as defined in Section 26-23b-102, or a declaration by the president of the United States or other federal official requesting public health-related activities.

(b) The immunity in this Subsection (3) is in addition to any immunity or protection in state or federal law that may apply.

(4) (a) A person who uses reasonable force to enter a locked and unattended motor vehicle to remove a confined child is not liable for damages in a civil action if all of the following apply:

(i) the person has a good faith belief that the confined child is in imminent danger of suffering physical injury or death unless the confined child is removed from the motor vehicle;

(ii) the person determines that the motor vehicle is locked and there is no reasonable manner in which the person can remove the confined child from the motor vehicle;

(iii) before entering the motor vehicle, the person notifies a first responder of the confined child;

(iv) the person does not use more force than is necessary under the circumstances to enter the motor vehicle and remove the confined child from the vehicle; and

(v) the person remains with the child until a first responder arrives at the motor vehicle.

(b) A person is not immune from civil liability under this Subsection (4) if the person fails to abide by any of the provisions of Subsection (4)(a) or commits any unnecessary or malicious damage to the motor vehicle.

Current Legislation:

§ 62A-4a-403. Reporting requirements

(1)(a) Except as provided in Subsection (2), when any individual, including an individual licensed under Title 58, Chapter 31b, Nurse Practice Act, or Title 58, Chapter 67, Utah Medical Practice Act, has reason to believe that a child has been subjected to abuse or neglect, or observes a child being subjected to conditions or circumstances that would reasonably result in abuse or neglect, that individual shall immediately report the alleged abuse or neglect to the nearest peace officer, law enforcement agency, or office of the division.

(b) Upon receipt of a report described in Subsection (1)(a), the peace officer or law enforcement agency shall immediately notify the nearest office of the division. If an initial report of abuse or neglect is made to the division, the division shall immediately notify the appropriate local law enforcement agency.

(c) The division shall, in addition to its own investigation, comply with and lend support to investigations by law enforcement undertaken to investigate a report described in Subsection (1)(a).

(2) Subject to Subsection (3), the notification requirement described in Subsection (1)(a) does not apply to a member of the clergy, with regard to any confession made to the member of the clergy while functioning in the ministerial capacity of the member of the clergy and without the consent of the individual making the confession, if:

(a) the perpetrator made the confession directly to the member of the clergy; and

(b) the member of the clergy is, under canon law or church doctrine or practice, bound to maintain the confidentiality of that confession.

(3)(a) When a member of the clergy receives information about abuse or neglect from any source other than confession of the perpetrator, the member of the clergy is required to report that information even though the member of the clergy may have also received information about abuse or neglect from the confession of the perpetrator.

(b) Exemption of the reporting requirement for a member of the clergy does not exempt the member of the clergy from any other efforts required by law to prevent further abuse or neglect by the perpetrator.

§ 62A-3-305. Reporting requirements—Investigation—Immunity—Violation—Penalty—Nonmedical healing

(1) A person who has reason to believe that a vulnerable adult has been the subject of abuse, neglect, or exploitation shall immediately notify Adult Protective Services intake or the nearest law enforcement agency. When the initial report is made to law enforcement, law enforcement shall immediately notify Adult Protective Services intake. Adult Protective Services and law enforcement shall coordinate, as appropriate, their efforts to provide protection to the vulnerable adult.

(2) When the initial report or subsequent investigation by Adult Protective Services indicates that a criminal offense may have occurred against a vulnerable adult:

(a) Adult Protective Services shall notify the nearest local law enforcement agency regarding the potential offense; and

(b) the law enforcement agency may initiate an investigation in cooperation with Adult Protective Services.

(3) A person who in good faith makes a report or otherwise notifies a law enforcement agency or Adult Protective Services of suspected abuse, neglect, or exploitation is immune from civil and criminal liability in connection with the report or other notification.

(4)(a) A person who willfully fails to report suspected abuse, neglect, or exploitation of a vulnerable adult is guilty of a class B misdemeanor.

(b) A covered provider or covered contractor, as defined in Section 26-21-201, that knowingly fails to report suspected abuse or neglect, as required by this section, is subject to a private right of action and liability for the abuse or neglect of another person that is committed by the individual who was not reported to Adult Protective Services in accordance with this section.

(5) Under circumstances not amounting to a violation of Section 76-8-508, a person who threatens, intimidates, or attempts to intimidate a vulnerable adult who is the subject of a report, a witness, the person who made the report, or any other person cooperating with an investigation conducted pursuant to this chapter is guilty of a class B misdemeanor.

(6) An adult is not considered abused, neglected, or a vulnerable adult for the reason that the adult has chosen to rely solely upon religious, nonmedical forms of healing in lieu of medical care.

While the Utah Legislature has yet to ratify Representative King's "911 Responsibilities in an Emergency" legislation, our experience in working with his office in this endeavor sheds invaluable light on the complexity of the legislative process in matters where morality and legality intersect. It is this complicated space that the question of bystander duty occupies. For some legislators, there is a sense of "crossing a line" that casts doubt on the viability of legislating what some refer to as "the right thing to do." While other arguments were voiced in opposition to the proposed legislation, this is the issue that raises the greatest concern for legislators. We need to ask, why? And, what do we learn from this?

In focusing on the area where morality and legality come together, a preliminary question is how to frame the duty owed by person A to person B when there is no preexisting relationship or otherwise legislated duty. This requires the creation of a duty between two individuals who do not know each other—in the case of Utah, when the person in peril is neither a child nor elderly. The protection offered by Rep. King's legislation falls outside specially designated protected zones. It is this extra step of extending existing obligations that has proven particularly vexing.

Legislators have found it especially challenging to recognize this "middle category" of individuals, without special characteristics or unique qualities that would necessarily cause them to require assistance, as vulnerable in a particular moment of peril. The legislature has shown itself unwilling to impose a requirement on the bystander to intervene on such an individual's behalf when circumstances clearly dictate that help is needed.

While legislators acknowledge there are instances when individuals in distress require assistance, they tend to reference the "right thing to do" argument. This assessment that the bystander will be sufficiently morally grounded to act positively on behalf of the vulnerable victim seemingly soothes the soul of those who voice it, for it reflects a belief in the basic goodness of humanity. Similarly, those that subscribe to this precept reject the notion of punishment and deterrence in such situations, for they perceive the requirement as solely moral. The absence of a mechanism whereby the bystander who chooses not to intervene is punished fails both the immediate victim and victims in the future.

The resistance over the past three years from a majority of Utah legislators highlights a crucial question: Who is deserving of protection? If it is the victim, then the most obvious way to ensure protection is to impose a legal requirement with criminal penalty. If it is the bystander, then failure to ratify Rep. King's legislation ensures the adoption of a bystander protection model. It is unclear why members of the legislature would prefer protecting the bystander rather than the vulnerable.

The Utah State Legislature has made plain its stand: The "moral" bystander will "know what to do," and if he or she does not act on this knowledge, then the victim will not be relieved of peril. There will be no consequences for walking away. This seems to be a sense of duty turned on its head. Should not the primary focus of legislation in a democracy be to extend protections to the weak, rather than the strong? In the moment of peril, it is the *victim* who is weak and the *bystander* who is strong.

In debate before the House Judiciary Committee on January 21, 2018, one representative focused on the idea that this legislation was a "180-degree turn" from a legal standard that seemingly has been in place "since the beginning of time":

> So, my question is, what is the compelling policy argument for changing a law that has essentially existed forever? You had suggested maybe so that we could mitigate the likelihood of crime or loss of life, but we're becoming a safer, less violent, nation all the time, it seems those arguments would fit more 100 years ago, or

200 years ago, or back in old England, in places and times where people were literally dying in the street and others walked by. We didn't do it then; we've resisted it until now.[5]

Another representative echoed similar concerns:

The challenge we have as legislators, as lawmakers, is do we take the moral imperative that most of us feel and now do we make it a legal imperative that has legal consequences? I'm not arguing with you about the fact that it is good, and it is the right thing, but we also try to be careful, and we recognize that words have meaning, and we also recognize as we sit here, that it's very difficult to anticipate all of the consequences as a result of passage.[6]

This same representative also voiced concern over the type and weight of the liability that such legislation may present:

I do believe it also does set a standard, because we're saying to the people of the state, "if you fail to act in these situations, you're criminally liable." Well clearly if I'm criminally liable I have a civil duty as well.[7]

During the House floor debate on February 19, 2019, a third representative brought up a second issue that has been a significant source of concern among legislators: criminalizing the failure to act, and thereby legislating a "crime of omission":

Traditionally under criminal law, as the prior speaker noted, the criminal law requires a criminal act, and criminal intent. Here we are criminalizing doing nothing, we are criminalizing inaction. Now references made to our current law where we have a duty to report abuse of children or abuse of the elderly, we make those exceptions in the law because of the distinct and unique

5. *Duty to Assist in an Emergency: Hearing on H.B. 125 before the H. Judiciary Comm.*, 2018 Leg., 62nd Sess. (Utah 2018) (statement of Rep. Brian Greene, Member, H. Judiciary Comm.). https://le.utah.gov/av/committeeArchive.jsp?timelineID=105983.
6. *Duty to Assist in an Emergency: Hearing on H.B. 125 before the H. Judiciary Comm.*, 2018 Leg., 62nd Sess. (Utah 2018) (statement of Rep. Lowry Snow, Member, H. Judiciary Comm.). https://le.utah.gov/av/committeeArchive.jsp?timelineID=105983.
7. *Id.*

vulnerability of children and elderly. This bill, and this law, would open up that liability to society at large, to everyone, not just children and elderly but anyone who is in distress. That is a big leap, it is a big leap for us to take in our law.[8]

This representative then referenced the murder of Sherrice Iverson, noting how it aroused his interest in terms of Cash's liability under Utah law:

I did locate under Utah law, under existing law, section 76-2-202 it is our accomplice liability statute that says anyone who "intentionally aids another person to engage in conduct which constitutes an offense shall be criminally liable as a party for such conduct." Intentionally aids, the case law in Utah, I read a few of the cases, aiding [sic] you're considered aiding if you aid in a crime, if you stand by and do nothing. And so, for example, in the case of *State v. Cheney*, a man was held liable under the accomplice liability statute for standing by and allowing his child to be raped. In the case of *Beltron v. Felix*, it was a case of a sexual assault where two men entered into a store, one of the men raped one of the women who was there while the other one watched, waited for the crime to occur without intervention, and the observing friend was charged with aiding in his friend of the commission of a crime.[9]

Despite his stated concern that criminalizing acts of omission would be a drastic departure from current legislation, the representative nevertheless showed how current Utah law does just that:

We have an existing law that allows those who do nothing in these situations where a crime is being occurred, where someone is in need, we allow them to be prosecuted as an accomplice.[10]

---

8. *Responsibilities in an Emergency: Deb. on H.B. 170 before the H.R.*, 2019 Leg., 63rd Sess. (Utah 2019) (statement of Rep. Merrill Nelson). https://le.utah.gov/av/floorArchive.jsp?marker ID=106198.
9. *Id.*
10. *Id.*

Another representative, in the floor debate of February 2018, having said that he appreciated the idea of sending a message that everyone should step up and be a Good Samaritan, commented as follows:

> I don't like the idea of legislating goodness. I think it's been mentioned before but the good people of Utah do reach out and I don't see that there's a problem. Maybe it'll require a few more, maybe we'll get a few more reports, but I worry more about the chilling effect that it might have.[11]

Like several other opponents to the bill, this representative was apprehensive about deviating from the status quo:

> it's just such a departure from our criminal code and our law, without any mens rea or action on your part, you can become a criminal by your inaction. While I recognize the need for vulnerable adults and our youth, I don't think we should take it to the extent that this law does.[12]

In the statements quoted here, these four representatives articulate principled reservations about the legislation. In essence, they are expressing two separate, but perhaps related, concerns regarding (1) imposing a legal duty to act on the bystander, and (2) penalizing a crime of omission. These issues were voiced throughout discussion of the legislation and represent the most compelling reasons to vote against it. We need to examine the sources of these concerns, and how best to overcome them.

Expanding the duty to act necessarily focuses attention on the consequences of imposing a relationship between individuals where none would otherwise exist. This is distinct from the relationship between an individual and the state, in which the duty question is predicated on a contractual relationship. The discomfort lawmakers expressed regarding the transient or fleeting relationship that Rep. King discusses is based on their assessment of the risks of creating an obligation between two otherwise unrelated individuals.

---

11. *Duty to Assist in an Emergency: Deb. on H.B. 125 before the H.R.*, 2018 Leg., 62nd Sess. (Utah 2018) (statement of Rep. Kelly Miles). https://le.utah.gov/av/floorArchive.jsp?markerID=102313.
12. *Id.*

Members of the legislature prefer that this duty be contained within the boundaries of morality, rather than extended to the terrain of the law. That is, although they acknowledge that the person in distress would benefit from bystander intervention, they believe that criminalizing the failure (omission) of such intervention would represent government overreach in demanding particular actions. This argument is, frankly, focused on the bystander, not on the victim.

By limiting discussion of the existential issue of duty to an inquiry concerning moral values, predicated on the comforting idea that "we know to do the right thing," we are leaving an individual in peril to the presumed good graces of another. In the inherently limited paradigm, should the bystander not intervene (that is, dial 9-1-1), there will be three, or perhaps four, results: (1) no assistance to a victim, (2) no punishment to the bystander for failing to provide assistance, and (3) no deterrence to future bystanders, thereby arguably (4) no assistance to future victims. From the perspective of present and future victims, this represents abandonment, compounded by a knowing and deliberate determination not to punish the bystander who was in a position to act.

While it can be assumed that these legislators do not wish ill on the victim, the practical result of their opposition to bystander Duty to Act legislation leads to that very result. Their aversion to legislating a crime of omission has similar consequences. Why do these four representatives find the creation of a crime of omission so objectionable, when the sole purpose of Rep. King's legislation is to minimize harm to a vulnerable member of society? In general, criminal codes, including that of the State of Utah, do include crimes of omission; two obvious examples are driving through a stop sign and not paying taxes, both of which incur criminal penalty. Crimes of omission are defined in order to punish a failure. Is walking away from a person in peril not a failure?

In the spirit of the age-old question, "Am I my brother's keeper?"[13] we must ask whom do we protect, and what are the consequences of failing to acknowledge accountability? While bystander legislation has been enacted in some jurisdictions, efforts to create similar measures

---

13. Genesis 4:9.

elsewhere has been met with resistance by lawmakers. In general, their reservations fall into the following categories:

A. Prosecutorial discretion
B. Legislating morality
C. Creation of a nanny state
D. Greater burden on emergency personnel
E. Possibility of additional criminal liability
F. Possibility of civil liability
G. Distrust of law enforcement

Prosecutorial Discretion

Prosecutors are given a generous amount of discretion when it comes to deciding whether to prosecute. It has been well established that so long as a prosecutor does not base his or her decision on an impermissible factor, there is no violation of due process.[14]

> Although a prosecutor obviously cannot base charging decisions on a defendant's race, sex, religion, or exercise of a statutory or constitutional right, so long as the prosecutor has probable cause to believe that the accused committed an offense defined by statute, the decision whether or not to prosecute, and what charge to file . . . generally rests entirely in his discretion.[15]

When facing criminal charges, a defendant may justifiably feel uneasy that their case rests largely with an individual who can decide to bring charges based upon a wide variety of factors. The system allows prosecutors to operate without judicial interference, and review of a prosecutor's exercise of discretion is narrow in scope.[16]

---

14. U.S.C.A. Const. Amend. 14. *Pugach v. Klein*, 193 F. Supp. 630 (S.D.N.Y.1961). See also *United States v. Andersen*, 940 F.2d 593 (10th Cir.1991); *United States v. Morehead*, 959 F.2d 1489, 1499 (10th Cir.1992).

15. *United States v. Curtis*, 344 F.3d 1057, 1064 (10th Cir. 2003) (internal quotation marks and citations omitted).

16. § 3513. Role of the court, 13 Wash. Prac., Criminal Practice & Procedure § 3513 (3d ed.) citing: *United States v. Smith*, 354 A.2d 510 (D.C.1976).

Concern over prosecutorial misconduct has risen over the past few decades. However, this is less likely due to a rise in prosecutorial misconduct than to increased media coverage.[17] The growing public concern about prosecutorial misconduct has been met with a shift in regulations that are aimed toward greater legal and political accountability for prosecutors.[18]

Prosecutors already must consider legal, administrative, and equitable reasons when deciding whether to decline or pursue charges.[19] Data from the ten states that have some form of bystander legislation show no evidence that crimes that arose under these statutes were overzealously prosecuted. This may be because factual findings to support the allegation that an individual willfully declined to assist an individual in crisis are difficult to establish.

The prosecutor's office likely thinks that a successful prosecutor is one who "works quickly, disposing of as many cases as possible through plea bargains."[20] In most states that impose a criminal penalty for failure to assist, the penalty only amounts to a misdemeanor. Absent a clear path to conviction, it would appear that prosecutors are inclined to move quickly on to more pressing matters.

Legislating Morality

In the discussions on proposed bystander legislation in the Utah State Legislature, the notion that this was simply an attempt to "legislate morality" was commonly voiced by state representatives. This is a long-standing concern that has been stated many times in various ways:

> It is indeed, most highly desirable that [people] should not merely abstain from doing harm to their neighbors, but should render active services to their neighbors. In general however the penal

---

17. Bruce Green (FNa1) & Ellen Yaroshefsky (FNaa1), *Prosecutorial Accountability 2.0*, 92 Notre Dame L. Rev. 51, 87 (2016).
18. *Id.*
19. Josh Bowers, *Legal Guilt, Normative Innocence, and the Equitable Decision Not to Prosecute*, 110 Colum. L. Rev. 1655 (2010).
20. Janet C. Hoeffel, *Prosecutorial Discretion at the Core: The Good Prosecutor Meets Brady*, 109 Penn St. L. Rev. 1133, 1136 (2005).

law must content itself with keeping [individuals] from doing positive harm and must leave to public opinion, and to the teachers of morality and religion, the office of furnishing [people] with motives for doing positive good.[21]

While some balk at the idea of legislating morality, it should not be forgotten that for the first hundred years after the establishment of the United States, courts consistently upheld morals legislation against constitutional challenges.[22] Even in the 21st century congressional legislation has been upheld by the U.S. Supreme Court primarily for its moral implications.[23]

The overlap between morality and law is undeniable. Law does have added pressures and is backed by force, but it seems a reasonable assumption that law is derived from moral considerations. One might well argue that any proposed change to any legislation could be understood as "legislating morality." This criticism should rightly be ignored so that legislators can move on to discussing and vetting bystander legislation on its own merits.

Creation of a Nanny State

"Nanny state" is a pejorative term referring to "a government that overregulates its citizens by interfering with individual choice."[24] The term has been used to describe former New York City Mayor Michael Bloomberg's efforts to increase levels of health and standards of living by restricting the sale of large soft drinks, along with regulating sodium and trans fats.[25]

While the term is typically used as a criticism, a nanny state is not necessarily an adverse system. Regulations are meant to reduce the negative impact of "externalities"; that is, "if those imposing costs on others

---

21. T. B. Macauley, A Penal Code Prepared by the Indian Law Commissioners 55–56 (1837).
22. Daniel F. Piar, *Morality As A Legitimate Government Interest*, 117 Penn St. L. Rev. 139 (2012).
23. *Gonzales v. Carhart*, 550 U.S. 124, 130 (2007).
24. Nanny State, Black's Law Dictionary (10th ed. 2014).
25. Karen Harned, "The Michael Bloomberg Nanny State in New York: A Cautionary Tale," *Forbes* (May 10, 2013), https://www.forbes.com/sites/realspin/2013/05/10/the-michael -bloomberg-nanny-state-in-new-york-a-cautionary-tale/#4cc7c5f07109.

are forced to pay for these costs, society will get the socially optimal amount of the activity generating the costs."[26] Problems arise when regulators create legislation with the intent of improving the life of an individual, but disregard any costs that others may experience.[27] This type of regulation has been described as "the interference with another person, against their will, and justified by a claim that the person interfered with will be better off."[28]

Greater Burden on Emergency Service Personnel

It has been argued that a potential unintended side effect of bystander legislation might be that it places an inordinate burden on emergency services. This issue probably cannot be addressed universally, because each jurisdiction and municipality has different resources available to provide such public necessities.

During the legislative process for Rep. King's bystander proposal, an active fire fighter and president of the Professional Fire Fighters of Utah (an organization composed of fire fighters throughout the state) testified in favor of the legislation. He acknowledged that it would mean an increase in calls but contended that fire fighters are not afraid of work. As a fire fighter who, by his estimation, responds to thousands of emergency calls a year, he stated that there had been numerous times when he arrived at a scene only to wish that someone had called 9-1-1 sooner.

Possibility of Additional Criminal Liability

Those already hesitant about creating criminal liability for inaction become even more alarmed at the idea that such a law could become a basis for heightening criminal liability. Many criminal statutes consider as a general rule that "a person is guilty of involuntary manslaughter when as a direct result of the doing of an unlawful act in a reckless or grossly

---

26. M. Todd Henderson, *The Nanny Corporation,* 76 U. Chi. L. Rev. 1517, 1523 (2009).
27. *Id.*
28. *Id.*

negligent manner, or the doing of a lawful act in a reckless or grossly negligent manner, he causes the death of another person."[29] If there is a legally required duty to assist, then it could become an "unlawful act" not to assist. And if an individual were to die due to another person's inaction, that other person could be guilty of involuntary manslaughter.

Concern over heightened criminal liability has not been overlooked by legislators. In 2019, Rep. King introduced Duty to Assist legislation that addressed this issue with the following language:

> Notwithstanding any contrary provision of state law, a prosecutor may not use an individual's violation of Subsection (2) as the basis for charging the individual with another offense.[30]

Possibility of Civil Liability

Some have expressed concern that the civil liability attached to bystander legislation is too great to justify its potential benefits. This concern can easily be addressed by including a provision such as: "Nothing contained in this section shall alter existing law with respect to civil liability."

Absent a provision exculpating an individual from civil liability, there are in any case barriers to bringing a civil action based upon bystander legislation. In Wisconsin, the parents of a sixteen-year-old whose life was tragically cut short attempted to bring a wrongful death suit with its basis in the state's bystander legislation.[31] The complaint alleged that defendant's inactions negligently lead to their son's death.[32] This claim was dismissed because the plaintiffs were unable to establish that the defendant's inactions were the proximate cause of their son's death.[33]

Bringing a civil suit based upon bystander legislation requires the plaintiff to show that if the defendant had acted, then the injury or alleged damages would not have occurred or would have been lessened. Bystander legislation applies to individuals who have nothing to do with

---

29. 18 Pa. Stat. and Cons. Stat. Ann. § 2504 (West).
30. H.B. 170, 2019 Leg., 63rd Sess. (Utah 2019).
31. *Logarta v. Gustafson*, 998 F. Supp. 998, 999 (E.D. Wis. 199.8).
32. *Id.* at 1001.
33. *Id.* at 1007.

the original source of peril to an individual. The obligation to assist or call for help is triggered only once an individual is *already* suffering a serious physical injury that the bystander did not contribute to in any way. Proving in civil litigation that "but for" the bystander's inactions the injury could not have taken place, or that the injury was causally aggravated by those inactions, is a difficult burden to meet. Every civil suit predicated on bystander legislation and listed on the legal databases Lexis and Westlaw failed because the plaintiffs were not able to establish that the bystander proximately caused or aggravated any damages.

Nevertheless, the fact that it is even a remote possibility that civil suits could be brought on the basis of Duty to Assist legislation remains a sticking point for some. Rep. King attempted to allay all such fears with language in his proposed bill:

> This section does not create an independent basis for civil liability for failure to provide the assistance described in this section. The fact that an individual is charged or convicted with a crime under this section may not be used to establish that the individual violated a duty on which a claim for personal injuries may be based.[34]

Distrust of Law Enforcement

Research suggests that fear of police involvement is one of the most prevalent reasons that individuals do not call, or delay calling, for help in an emergency.[35] This is particularly so in situations that involve drug overdoses.[36] In an attempt to encourage individuals to call 9-1-1, 40 states (as of July 25, 2017) have passed laws that provide protection from prosecution for certain drug offenses for both the person calling for medical assistance and the person who overdosed.[37]

34. H.B. 104, 2020 Leg., 63d Sess. (Utah 2020) (internal subdivisions omitted).
35. Tracy, M., Piper, T. M., Ompad, D., Bucciarelli, A., Coffin, P. O., Vlahov, D. & Galea, S., *Circumstances of witnessed drug overdose in New York City: Implications for intervention,* 79(2) Drug and Alcohol Dependence, 181–190 (2005) https://doi.org/10.1016/j.drugalcdep.2005.01.010.
36. *Id.*
37. Drug Policy Alliance, *Good Samaritan Fatal Overdose Prevention Laws* (2019) http://www.drugpolicy.org/issues/good-samaritan-fatal-overdose-prevention-laws.

Fear of law enforcement is also very real in minority communities. According to the American Psychological Association (APA), "the probability of being black, unarmed and shot by police is about 3.5 times the probability of being white, unarmed and shot by police."[38] The APA states that "[r]educing and circumventing bias is one way to chip away at the disparities in how police treat black civilians."[39] There are many ways to approach racially disparate treatment by law enforcement, but it is a systemic problem that will take years, if not decades, to solve. There is no evidence to suggest that the passage of Duty to Assist legislation will have a positive or negative effect on the issues that minorities face with law enforcement.

Human Rights Watch (HRW), an international nongovernmental organization, stated that public safety is undermined because immigrant communities in the United States are afraid of calling law enforcement.[40] Crimes such as rape go unreported because victims fear that calling law enforcement will result in their deportation. HRW suggests that this problem is difficult to fix on a community or state level, and the best approach would be for the U.S. Congress to pass comprehensive immigration reform.[41]

It has also been shown that those with family members who are mentally ill may resist calling law enforcement out of fear that the encounter could turn deadly.[42] In 2017, a mother in Brooklyn called 9-1-1 when her 32-year-old son with schizophrenia was acting erratically. Police were unable to calm the man and opened fire after he lunged at them with a knife. This was not an uncommon incident. Efforts have been made in New York and other cities to provide police officers with crisis intervention training, and to deploy teams consisting of an officer plus a social worker to calls involving the mentally ill. While distrust of law

---

38. Kirsten Weir, *Policing in black & white*, 47(11) American Psychological Association, 36 (December 2016) https://www.apa.org/monitor/2016/12/cover-policing.
39. *Id.*
40. Human Rights Watch, *US: Immigrants "Afraid to Call 911"* (May 14, 2014) https://www.hrw.org/news/2014/05/14/us-immigrants-afraid-call-911.
41. *Id.*
42. This paragraph relies on Rich Schapiro, "Families of mentally ill fear calling police may turn into deadly encounter," *New York Daily News* (Apr. 05, 2018) https://www.nydailynews.com/new-york/families-mentally-ill-fear-calling-police-turn-deadly-article-1.3917552.

enforcement is an issue, the benefits of bystander legislation outweigh these costs.

The law reflects societal norms, mores, and morals. Sometimes, the law is ahead of society; other times, the law is a step behind. Regardless, the law must be understood as codifying what society seeks to be, how it perceives itself, how the relationship between the state and individual is defined, and how interactions among individuals are regulated. The law is not a replacement for morals and morality, but rather their articulation and manifestation. The two are not in conflict with each other, nor is one superior to the other. On the contrary, law and morality can be viewed as complementing one another. The importance of the law, perhaps the *essence* of the law, is that it reflects society's belief that when an act is sufficiently harmful, it demands punishment and sanction. It represents the demand for accountability for wrongful deeds. It is the culmination of a process whereby the state, through the legislative process, has reached the conclusion that an action is sufficiently harmful that it warrants criminal prosecution. Criminalizing an action is the codification of those beliefs.

Criminalizing the bystander's failure to act reflects society's belief that the consequences of not providing assistance to the person in peril is so significant that punishment is warranted. For the state not to impose a penalty on the bystander for failing to dial 9-1-1 is to abandon the person in danger. It is for that reason that whatever punishment is meted to the perpetrator, it is essential also to send a strong message to the broader community regarding the penalty for not assisting the victim.

Imposing a criminal obligation on the bystander articulates a clear position: protecting the vulnerable victim is of the utmost importance, and failure to do so will result in criminal punishment. The punishment is directed both at the specific actor (the bystander) and the general public.

In contrast to specific deterrence, which focuses exclusively on the wrongdoer, general deterrence takes a broader, societal perspective in assessing the importance and power of punishment. General deterrence requires undertaking a broad effort to disseminate knowledge of the law, and to educate the public regarding its legal obligation to act on behalf of the victim.

The crime of omission is, in fact, acknowledged in criminal law in several U.S. states, as reflected in the following chart.[43]

State	Mandatory Reporting	Crime	Penalty
California	Only victims of rape and murder that are 14-years-old or younger	Misdemeanor	Up to 6 months in prison, $1,500 fine, or both
Florida	Only victims of sexual battery	1st Degree Misdemeanor	Up to 1 year in jail
Hawaii	Only victims of crimes	Petty Misdemeanor	Up to 30 days in jail and a fine up to $1000
Massachusetts	Only victims of rape, murder, manslaughter, armed robbery, or hazing	Misdemeanor	$500–$2,500 fine (or up to $1,000 fine as to hazing)
Minnesota	Any crime and any victim	Petty Misdemeanor	Up to $300 fine
Ohio	Only if a felony has been or will be committed	4th Degree Misdemeanor	Up to 30 days in jail and a fine up to $250
Rhode Island	Any crime and any victim	Misdemeanor	Up to 6 months in prison, $500 fine, or both
Vermont	Any crime and any victim	Infraction	Up to $100 fine
Washington	Only victims of violent offenses, sexual abuse, or assault of a child	Gross Misdemeanor	Up to 364 days in jail and a fine up to $5,000
Wisconsin	Any crime and any victim	Class C Misdemeanor	Up to 30 days in jail and a fine up to $500

---

43. Chart created by Jessie Dyer, S. J. Quinney College of Law, University of Utah (JD expected 2020).

The following chart presents a timeline of the creation of Duty to Assist legislation in these states:

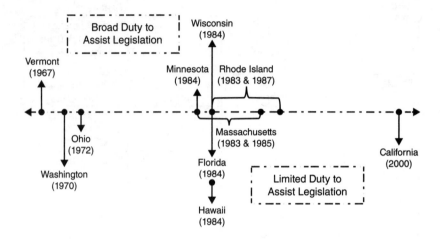

Of these ten states that have imposed an affirmative duty upon bystanders who have no relation to the victim, only four require action by any person at the scene of an emergency, regardless of the crime or the victim (broad duty to assist). The remaining six states have bystander legislation that is limited to either a specific category of victim or a specific type of crime (limited duty to assist).

All states in the U.S. have created a list of professionals who are legally mandated to report the neglect or abuse of a child. States differ with regard to the action of bystanders who know that a child is being abused or neglected. Some state legislation includes language stating that such individuals may report child abuse, while other states stipulate that such individuals must report child abuse.

States with a "*may* report" requirement are shown on the following map: [44]

---

44. Mandatory Reporters of Child Abuse and Neglect (current as of 2015) https://www.childwelfare.gov/pubPDFs/manda.pdf.

In these states there is no legal requirement for an individual to report the neglect or abuse of a child if that individual has no identifiable relationship to the child. Another way of looking at the map would be to say, if the events leading to Sherrice Iverson's death were repeated, David Cash would not be subject to criminal punishment in the states marked in gray.

In some jurisdictions, the duty is restricted to particular contractual, professional, or family contexts, perhaps involving a lifeguard, a teacher, or a parent. These reflect commonly understood notions of duty, responsibility, and accountability and are largely uncontroversial. Failure to fulfill the required duty results in financial and criminal penalties. This paradigm is indicative of sociocultural realities that impose greater responsibility. Obligations imposed on teachers to report suspected family abuse of their students, on pain of penalty, are one example.

Greater sensitivity to racial, gender, ethnic, and age discrimination has similarly led to reporting requirements in the workplace, institutions of higher learning, and other settings where injury may be caused to an individual. The injury need not be physical; emotional distress is sufficient to impose a reporting requirement. Failure to meet this obligation may result in consequences for the individual accountable to report, as well as for the offender.

In these restricted settings, then, the state has imposed penalties on the bystander who fails to alert the authorities in the face of an individual in distress. Is opposition muted by the assumption that this duty is limited to a very *specific circumstance*, confined to *particular actors* on whom the duty can be imposed? In other words, are we, as a society, willing to tolerate this imposition in *particular environments*, when those tasked with the obligation to act are clearly defined and their duties are specifically delineated? The answer appears to be yes. The next question must be, why? And further, is not the extension of this obligation to a broader duty to act an obvious next step? Indeed, such an extension would seem even more plausible given development of modern technology that makes it so easy for the bystander to act.

The commonly understood reason for imposing a duty to act in these limited settings is predicated on a preexisting relationship in which a person in a position of authority assumes responsibility for a vulnerable individual, whether the infirm, a student, or a child. These duties impose liability and punishment on the bystander who fails to provide assistance. Parent-child, teacher-student: in our society these are all contractual relationships. Perhaps this explains our willingness to consent to the imposition of a legal duty in these limited contexts. The hesitation to make the leap to extending the obligation to a noncontractual relationship such as the random and transitory interaction between a bystander and the person in peril requires us to reexamine the notions of relationship and obligation.

Precisely because the danger faced by the person in peril may be acute and immediate, not to impose a duty on the bystander will exacerbate the harm. The objections of those who shy away from codifying that duty would perhaps be understandable if history demonstrated the veracity of the statement that "good people know to do the right thing." The reality is that even good people do not always know to do the right thing (for a variety of reasons), and not all people are good people. History unfortunately proves both statements. The innumerable examples of the bystander who acts by deciding not to act highlight the requirement to impose a *legal* duty to act, with legal consequences for failing to do so.

Ultimately, the only relevant question is how to effect societal change so that the person in peril will be provided assistance when it is needed most. There is no expectation that codifying the duty as a criminal act will *guarantee* that a bystander will dial 9-1-1. But it does significantly move the needle by setting up criminal implications of failure to act, and thus serve as a warning (deterrence) to society that failure to act has direct consequences. The impetus for forcefully recommending this fundamental shift, throughout the United States and internationally, is the understanding that criminal penalty and deterrence, in conjunction with educational outreach, will provide a person in peril with needed assistance.

It is important to distinguish between bystander legislation and Good Samaritan laws. The latter grant immunity to the bystander whose good faith attempts to alleviate another person's distress fail, leading instead to unintended harm to that individual. The emphasis is on the *unintended* consequences of the bystander's efforts. Good Samaritan laws protect the well-intentioned bystander. Bystander legislation imposes a duty to act on a bystander who might otherwise choose not to act.

Bystander legislation carries no expectation or demand that the bystander provide detailed information, wait for the authorities, identify him- or herself, engage in heroic measures, or intervene in a physical encounter. To impose such duties on the bystander would be both unreasonable and dangerous: unreasonable, because an obligation beyond dialing 9-1-1 would constitute an unfair burden on an individual who is randomly present at the time; dangerous, because the situation might escalate as a result of the intervention.

There are endless reasons why a person could find themselves in peril: tripping on a crack in the sidewalk, a heart attack, a car accident, belonging to the "wrong" ethnic group, being in the wrong place at the wrong time. But there they are, incapable of helping themselves. And you, the bystander, are there. Or the person in peril could be you. Sometimes it really is nothing more than good fortune that distinguishes the victim from the bystander. In other words, this is you, me, and the person next to both of us.

Being a bystander is a status. The bystander does not intend to come into that status but falls into it a result of particular circumstances.

Whether they were walking by or driving by or just happened to be there at that moment, they find themselves present at a critical moment in the life of another human being. Neither party intended this relationship. A critical aspect of the duty created by bystander legislation is that even though there is no prior or ongoing relationship between the two individuals, the bystander is obligated to take positive action on behalf of the victim.

The bystander owes a duty regardless of who the person in peril is, or to what group, however defined, that individual belongs. To create exceptions, to demarcate classes of groups and individuals to whom a bystander does or does not owe a duty exacerbates the vulnerability of all victims. Unfortunately, denigration, humiliation, and the mocking of the "other" have seeped into much of contemporary political and social culture. Creating categories or tolerating the labeling of someone as the "other" has critical ramifications in the bystander-victim context.

To pursue such an argument would violate both the letter and spirit of the proposed legislation. Even if the bystander obligation were to be viewed exclusively as a moral, rather than legal, duty, it must be all encompassing. Imposing a legal obligation ensures that no exceptions or exclusions predicated on victim identity, broadly defined, will be tolerated. The victim is in distress, and the bystander is positioned to provide the minimal assistance that the proposed legislation requires.

The notion of "tagging" a bystander as complicit in a victim's distress has been of concern to many people. The sole intent of the proposed legislation is to impose on the bystander a positive duty to act on behalf of the victim, albeit in a limited manner. There is no intention, either in law or in spirit, of blaming the bystander for the initial cause of the victim's distress, whether it is the result of a perpetrator's actions or an unfortunate circumstance.

The complicity is unrelated to what caused the event or to any criminal liability of a perpetrator; rather, it attaches in the aftermath of an event, when the bystander is in a position to assist. In describing failure to assist as complicity, the intent is to frame the act as a crime. This is not to suggest that the bystander is equivalent to the perpetrator, but to point to the fact that failure to act *exacerbates the harm*. That is how complicity is to be understood from the perspective of the victim: Did the bystander act to mitigate the harm? The question of complicity, then, is narrowly viewed. To conflate it with a broader understanding of the term is misguided.

Complicity is the second step in a process begun when the injury occurred. The first step, whether caused by a perpetrator or an unfortunate event, is unrelated to the bystander, whose role comes into play after the initial injury or harm. In cases that involve a perpetrator, it is crucial to realize that the perpetrator and the bystander are two distinct actors, with no commonality between them. They are not co-conspirators; they are not collaborators. The bystander did not commit the crime of aiding and abetting. They did not have common purpose. There was no previous interaction between them that resulted in harm to the victim.

In my earlier book on the crime of complicity in the context of the Holocaust, I described my father's death march from Nisch, Yugoslavia, to Sophia, Bulgaria. Along the way, villagers taunted him and his fellow prisoners by offering them water to drink, and then denying it to them. On a number of occasions, I have been asked whether those villagers were thereby transformed from bystanders into perpetrators, or at least into accomplices. This is a legitimate question and worthy of reflection, for it raises the important issue of how an individual's status can change within the same situation.[45]

In this case, it would be an unimaginable stretch to suggest the act of taunting is commensurate to that of a perpetrator. Recall my own experience as a bystander with the student and the homeless person. If I had cheered the student on, encouraging him to assault the homeless individual, would my status have changed from bystander to something else? If I had said to the homeless individual, "You deserve it," would I have incurred greater liability?

Given the negative impact from the perspective of the victim (our sole source of concern), one might reasonably construct a legal argument whereby the taunting, cheering, or mocking bystander would carry greater guilt than the bystander who merely looked on. But however tempting, this path would likely create even more complications in what

---

45. I would note that my father disagreed with my thesis regarding bystander obligation. From his perspective, the bystander (here, the Yugoslav gentile) does not owe a duty to the "other" (here, the Jewish prisoner of German guards).

is already a complex undertaking. Although the taunting and cheering of bystanders should not be condoned, enhancing the degree of their criminal liability on that basis would doubtless create roadblocks to the adoption of bystander legislation. Our singular purpose must be to convince legislators and the public that bystander complicity is not to be tolerated, and anything that blunts that central argument is to be avoided.

Bystander and victim are connected only by a tenuous link. The bystander knows that an individual is in distress and incapable of acting on their own behalf. In other words, they are helpless. Because the bystander can either see or hear the victim in distress, he or she cannot claim ignorance of the situation. But they can make a deliberate decision not to act. In choosing not to act, not to offer assistance, the bystander becomes complicit. The bystander is not responsible for the cause of the injury but is directly in a position to alleviate the situation. What you do in *that* critical moment determines whether you are complicit or not. There is no middle ground: it is a black and white dilemma. Call, and you have acted positively by alerting authorities. Choose not to call, and you have enhanced the peril, making you complicit.

Three examples, drawn at random from real life, illustrate the duty to act and costs of not doing so. These decisions speak to the essence of being a member of society. The failure to provide minimal assistance— the recommended requirement is a very low bar—can make the difference between life and death.

In Michigan, a child is drowning. His mother has lost control of him and is unable to find him in the water. Her male companion is searching frantically, even though he does not know how to swim. Mere feet away, a group of people is watching this drama unfold. They take out their smartphones. But instead of calling for assistance, they take pictures of the drowning child. Fortunately, a recently paroled individual, who also cannot swim, jumps into the water and saves the child. Tragically, the mother's friend drowns. And what of those who filmed? Because the State of Michigan does not have a bystander obligation law, no criminal prosecution is initiated.

In Florida, an adult is drowning. He is screaming for help. He clearly understands he is in extreme peril. His screams are heard by a group of teens standing within reach, on a bridge. They take out their smartphones. Do they call for immediate assistance? No. Instead, they film the flailing man, laughing as they watch him drown. Florida does not have a bystander obligation law either.

In both these cases, the individuals watching the drowning victims were complicit. They did not cause the initial tragedy. But they were present, aware of the situation, and capable of acting on behalf of the victims. And in both cases, they chose not to do so. These were deliberate decisions. They abandoned these individuals. However, they did not physically walk away, but callously filmed them in their distress. This fact adds to the outrage surrounding their conduct and character.

In a bank in Germany, an elderly man suffers a heart attack. Three other customers see him on the floor. All recognize he is in distress. All walk around him. None alerts bank officials or law enforcement. The man dies. In accordance with German law, the three are fined heavily for failing to act on his behalf.

While it cannot be known whether calling 9-1-1 (or the German equivalent) would actually have saved the lives of any of the victims in the scenarios described here, it is clear that it would have enhanced their chances of survival. Moreover, calling for assistance would in no way have endangered the bystanders. This point is of great relevance for the proposed legislation when we consider mitigating circumstances. The concern that harm could befall a bystander who attempts to provide assistance has been raised on a number of occasions in the context of unintended consequences. As has been stated before, there is absolutely no intention to put the bystander in harm's way. But we also must not create an unwieldy loophole, giving the bystander an easy "out" from providing assistance.

It has been argued, for example, that bystanders to the sexual assaults of film mogul Harvey Weinstein and other celebrities feared that if they spoke out, they would face financial recriminations and jeopardize their careers. Those concerns are not to be dismissed. Weinstein and his like are undeniably powerful and influential. Whether they would actually punish someone for alerting the authorities cannot be known, but the mere fear of retaliation would, for some, be sufficient justification not to act. However, some of the biggest names in the entertainment industry did know, or had sufficient cause to know, and decided to turn a blind eye, acting in their own best financial interests. These individuals form a distinct category from the vulnerable coterie of neophytes that inevitably surrounds the strong and powerful, hoping to benefit from their business affiliations.

While one might, perhaps, summon up a modicum of sympathy for those fearful of the potential loss of position and earnings, these consequences do not equate to the actual harm caused to the target of a sexual assault. In such a situation, an "equivalency" argument falls short. That said, there are circumstances that do justify mitigating the obligation to act. The phrase "snitches get stiches" captures a particular mindset that I have heard frequently in the context of gang members or minority communities, where the level of trust in law enforcement is very low.

In contrast to punishment for crimes such as murder, rape, or robbery, the idea of punishment for failing to act is not a given. Thus, while punishment for failure to pay taxes or heed a red light is generally accepted as necessary for proper functioning of government and society, legislation punishing failure to provide minimal assistance is deemed controversial. To fully appreciate the disconnect, we must view the consequences from the perspective of the person in peril. *That person* is the basis of the effort to criminalize bystander, and subsequently enabler, complicity.

Indeed, there is a natural sequencing from criminalizing bystander complicity to addressing enabler complicity. The enabler is an authority figure, directly positioned to address specific complaints. Furthermore, the enabler has the authority to act decisively to prevent future harm. The bystander is an individual with a happenstance relationship to the victim, whose decision to act has an immediate effect on a specific crisis point. By contrast, the enabler, by virtue of his or her position, has a duty toward the individual in distress; the enabler's decisions have an impact *both* on a particular survivor and on the *continued ability* of the predator to commit crimes. Therefore, we cannot lump the two in the same category of guilt and responsibility.

In the cases discussed in the preceding chapters, the enablers— trainers, coaches, USA Gymnastics officials, members of the Catholic Church hierarchy, university officials—chose not to act when informed of crimes committed against vulnerable survivors. These are the individuals who were best positioned to act. Their decision to protect predator and institution alike is sufficient justification for the proposal to criminalize enabler conduct. As the survivors made clear to me, they have no doubt regarding the duty owed them by the enablers. And they believe that duty reached out from themselves to future targets.

The bystander was present, the enabler was informed, but there is one critical similarity: both actors are complicit. Both are guilty of a crime of omission: the failure to act.

We now return to the enabler.

"If over these many years, just one adult listened and had the courage and character to act, this tragedy could have been avoided. I and so many others would have never, ever met you. Larry, you should have been locked up a long, long time ago. The fact is, we have no idea how many people you victimized, or what was done, or not done that allowed you to keep doing it, and to get away with it for so long. Over those thirty years when survivors came forward, adult after adult, many in positions of authority, protected you, telling each survivor it was okay, that you weren't abusing them. In fact, many adults had you convince the survivors that they were being dramatic or had been mistaken. This is like being violated all over again."

—*Aly Raisman, victim impact statement*

"If our program, our head coach, if anyone in our athletic department felt like we were a danger. . . . we would have been removed."

—*Keith Appling MSU basketball player, named in a 2010 report of sexual assault, according to a 2018 Outside the Lines report. No charges were filed; the case drew local media coverage and prompted campus protests.*[1]

---

1. https://www.espn.com/mens-college-basketball/story/_/id/28708436/ex-michigan-state-star-keith-appling-facing-heroin-charges; https://www.espn.com/espn/story/_/id/22214566/pattern-denial-inaction-information-suppression-michigan-state-goes-larry-nassar-case-espn.

— 8 —

Criminalize the Enabler

This chapter presents a roadmap for criminalizing the enabler. To that end it focuses primarily, but not exclusively, on Cardinal Bernard Law, archbishop of Boston from 1984 until his resignation in 2002.[2] For the crimes he enabled, the actions he tolerated, the abuses he ignored, and the extraordinary harm that resulted from his deliberately ignoring warning after warning, Cardinal Law has been referred to as the "godfather" of sexual crimes against children in the Catholic Church.[3] Had laws criminalizing the enabler been in effect, it is all but certain that he would have been prosecuted. But in fact, he never faced criminal charges.

Tragically, the same is true of the other enablers discussed here, including some of the biggest, most highly recognized names in college athletics. In addition to Cardinal Law's actions, this chapter will analyze the systemic rape culture among football and basketball players at Michigan State University. These assaults and rapes are described in the outstanding ESPN documentary *Spartan Silence: Crisis at Michigan State*, which makes clear how Michigan State prioritized protecting its image and

---

2. https://www.cnn.com/2017/12/20/world/former-boston-cardinal-bernard-law-dead/index.html.
3. https://www.bostonherald.com/2017/12/21/michael-dowd-cardinal-should-have-faced-criminal-charges/.

reputation over protecting the lives of those who were attacked.[4,5] Rather than address a disturbing pattern of conduct among its star athletes, the institution brusquely told the survivors, "Get on with your lives."

The problem extends beyond the manner in which football and basketball players conducted themselves. Interviews with survivors, attorneys, and sexual assault counselors, and review of police reports and official correspondence give the strong impression that their coaches acted as enablers by failing to aggressively address the issue, either proactively or reactively. How else to explain the systemic pattern of sexual assaults by the athletes whom the coaches themselves had brought to the campus?

Indeed, on at least one occasion, significant alarm was expressed over a highly regarded potential football recruit whose high school record suggested he would not be a suitable candidate.[6] The concerns were ignored, the individual enrolled at the university, he played on the football team, and today he is in jail, having been convicted of assault with intent to commit criminal sexual penetration.[7]

That enablers such as the athletic staff at Michigan State or Cardinal Law have consistently been able to avoid prosecution is, for the survivors, akin to a twofold betrayal: they were attacked by someone they knew and subsequently abandoned by an institution they loved. In recommending criminalization of the enabler, our intent is to put an end to the recurrence of the trauma caused by the enabler's decision to turn away, ignore obvious pain, and make the decision to favor the institution over the individual.

While there are legal avenues available for imposing penalties on enablers—civil suits and Title IX actions, in particular—the means are

4. https://player.vimeo.com/video/310658133.
5. Indeed, at the time of writing, it has been reported that a team physician at the University of Michigan assaulted student athletes in the early 1970s. https://www.detroitnews.com/story/news/local/michigan/2020/02/19/university-michigan-investigates-sex-complaints-against-former-football-doctor/4712724002/. In full disclosure, my late father was on the faculty of the University of Michigan Medical School in those years.
6. https://www.detroitnews.com/story/sports/college/michigan-state-university/2020/01/12/auston-robertson-sex-assault-record-lengthy-before-msu-then-raped-again/2735431001/.
7. https://statenews.com/article/2018/12/ex-msu-football-player-auston-robertson-sentenced-to-up-to-10-years.

limited and, as we have seen, rarely bear fruit. Some predators are successfully punished, but enablers have fairly consistently been shielded from prosecution and have thus avoided consequences for their actions. Legislation that would criminalize enablers would necessarily require exercise of prosecutorial discretion, yet that does not obviate the need for their robust prosecution. Along with balancing competing interests, the deterrence of future enablers is a crucial component of such statutes.

In the pages that follow, we will hear the voice of the enabler through Cardinal Law's deposition. Such a document provides invaluable insight into the enabler's mindset, particularly how the enabler rationalizes and justifies his or her behavior with one goal in mind: to protect the institution; and one inevitable consequence: to abandon the survivor. The extensive excerpts from Law's deposition bear close reading not only for the light they shed on his own conduct, but equally for the insights they provide regarding other enablers.

Cardinal Law was chosen as a case in point because he highlights so starkly the manner in which enablers bob, dodge, and weave in their conscious effort to protect their institution, and perhaps themselves. Arguably, many enablers identify so powerfully with their institution that they believe they are one and the same: a unity that allows no room for anyone else. It is inevitable, then, that survivors come in a distant second, and their abandonment is the painful and obvious consequence. This theme defines the enabler–survivor relationship and explains why even the most minimal of survivor expectations are not met. The survivors' one hope is that they will be protected, but as we have come to see, the enablers' priorities are so overwhelmingly fixed that the survivors stand no chance.

The failure to prosecute Cardinal Law reflects limitations in the current legal system, including shortcomings in mandatory reporting laws. As a powerful member of the Catholic Church's hierarchy, Cardinal Law was uniquely positioned to affect the lives of thousands. For precisely this reason, his actions exemplify the rationale for the proposal discussed in this chapter. The rationale for recommending criminalization of the enabler, similar to efforts to legislate bystander obligation, reflects the costly reality consistently expressed by survivors: those who were able to provide assistance failed those in need.

The discussion of Cardinal Law is readily applicable to the late Joe Paterno, the iconic football coach at Pennsylvania State University. Although for some, Paterno's protection of Jerry Sandusky cast a dark cloud over his reputation, others continue to hold "Joe Pa" in high esteem years after his death. By all objective measurements, Paterno turned a sleepy backwater in the middle of Pennsylvania into a football mecca, building a national powerhouse that was highly respected. However, that undeniable achievement came at a terrible price.

We cannot—*must not*—accept that Paterno's on-field successes be used to rationalize, justify, or defend Penn State's actions when faced with Jerry Sandusky's criminal behavior. The obvious response should have been to protect the boys assaulted in the university's locker room by directly confronting Sandusky. However, similar to Cardinal Law, senior Penn State officials made a conscious decision to protect the institution rather than the vulnerable human beings in their care. We have seen it time and again: Penn State versus a fourteen-year-old child; the Catholic Church versus Peter Pollard; Michigan State University versus Tiffany Thomas-Lopez.

Knowledge is an essential component in the recommendation to criminalize the enabler. In September 1984, shortly after Law had been installed as archbishop of Boston, he received a letter from the aunt of seven young boys who claimed that each boy had been abused by Father John Geoghan. Indeed, Law received numerous, similar letters informing him of concerns about ongoing abuse by priests under his authority. The boys' aunt was worried Geoghan had not been removed from his ecclesiastical role. Rather, he had been transferred from one parish to another, repeatedly occupying positions in which he supervised young boys. For a period, he was placed on "sick leave," and later was provided funds to study in Rome. When he returned from Rome, Geoghan declared he was "cured" of his attraction to young boys, and thereafter reinstated in a leadership role under Cardinal Law.

The letter written to Cardinal Law expressly conveyed Geoghan's history of abusing young boys and the effect the abuse had on the community. The cardinal's response was once again to transfer Geoghan to another parish within Boston and inform a parish leader of his history. In Geoghan's new position, he was again assigned to oversee groups of young boys and began preying on several of those under his care.

Years later, Cardinal Law removed Geoghan from his position and had him sent to a program for priest sex offenders. Geoghan was initially labeled a "high-risk homosexual pedophile," and subsequently classified as an "atypical pedophile in remission." After just a few months in the program, Geoghan was again assigned to join the parish in a leadership role. Predictably, he resumed his abuse of young boys.

Eventually, Cardinal Law removed Geoghan from this position. Geoghan was placed on leave and ultimately asked to retire. The cardinal wrote him a conciliatory letter: "I realize this is a difficult time for you and for those close to you. If I can be of help to you in some way, please contact me. Be assured you are remembered in my prayers." These astounding words speak for themselves.

In investigating Cardinal Law's actions, the Massachusetts attorney general stated, "We have an obligation to look and see if any criminal statutes apply." But at the same time, he cautioned that criminal law might be ineffective in this case, specifically citing the lack of a mandatory reporting requirement for priests.[8]

Michael Dowd, a lawyer representing plaintiffs in civil actions related to priest abuse in the Catholic Church, believed Cardinal Law should have been held criminally liable for his actions. Law's criminal intent could easily have been proven before a court by his orchestration of cover-ups in the face of new crimes and his decades of secret settlements to keep these tragedies out of the public eye. His guilty knowledge could have served as additional proof that he knew his acts were criminal.

The counterargument is that Law could not have known in advance that any priest would in fact sexually abuse a child. That might be a successful argument in a first trial, but not the second, the third, the fourth, or the hundredth.[9]

Nevertheless, Cardinal Law was not held criminally liable as an enabler of child sex abuse. Such a blatant example of the limitations of the current system justifies dramatic change to both penalize enablers and actively deter the abuse of children. Because children are often unable to protect themselves in such situations, the legal system must be

---

8. https://www.bostonherald.com/2017/12/21/michael-dowd-cardinal-should-have-faced-criminal-charges/.
9. *Id.*

an avenue for protection. That must be its primary obligation and duty. Criminalization of the enabler would reflect that absolute requirement.

The facts and circumstances surrounding Law's tenure as cardinal indicate he was aware of the ongoing abuse committed by perpetrators under his authority. Yet, the state attorney general was unable to find a legal basis for establishing criminal liability. It is telling that he cited a limitation of the state's mandatory reporting law, specifically the fact that state law created a carve-out for priests. Mandatory reporting laws can potentially be used as an effective hook for criminal behavior, but this was not possible in Cardinal Law's situation.

The inherent difficulty in holding enablers liable under civil law is apparent from Cardinal Law's deposition in the civil cases filed against him. The multiple days of testimony make for frustrating reading, because he was singularly adept at obfuscation, denying responsibility, involvement, and knowledge. His words are an insult to the survivors to whom he ostensibly owed a duty. The determined effort to brush off any recollection of easily ascertainable facts shows Bernard Law for who he was: an unrepentant enabler, whose sole purpose was to protect the Catholic Church, regardless of the costs and consequences to the individuals who had been harmed.

Law's words vividly illustrate the manner in which an enabler articulates his or her positions and frames arguments.

Q: We put in front of you Exhibit 43, a letter from Mr. Nash to you, that in detail set out allegations that you, yourself, acknowledged were serious allegations—

A: That's correct.

Q: —of gross misconduct by Father Rebeiro; is that correct?

A: That's correct.

Q: And he wrote this letter to you and he gave you details about other parishes where Father Rebeiro had served, with other allegations of sexual misconduct, and you wrote back to Mr. Nash, and you said to him, "After some consultation, I find that this matter is something that is personal to Father Rebeiro and must be considered such." Is that correct?

A: That's correct.

Q: So there was no investigation of these serious allegations. There was simply a letter from you indicating that this was a matter that was personal to Father Rebeiro, correct?

A: My response in seeing Mr. Nash's letter, which remains my response, is that I have no recollection of seeing that letter. My presumption is that this matter was handled for me by someone assisting me, and that this letter was prepared for my signature.

Q: Cardinal Law, do you read your letters before you sign them as a general practice? Did you in 1984?

A: You know, did I on April the 3rd, 1984, three days into the job, read every letter that was put before me? Probably not. Is it my—is it my custom now to read every letter carefully? It depends. Some are matters of routine, and I would not. But I cannot recall this letter. I cannot recall Mr. Nash's letter, and so it's really not possible for me to go into that matter further. I think you need to ask those who were handling this case for me. In this instance, I would imagine it would have been Bishop Daily.

Q: Well, we don't—should Bishop Daily have brought Mr. Nash's letter to your attention prior—we're conjecturing here, because we really don't know who sent out your letter—

A: We are conjecturing.

Q: We don't know—we really don't know whether you saw Mr. Nash's letter, and we really don't know whether you read the letter of April 3, 1984 before you put your signature on it, correct?

A: That's correct.

Q: So if, in fact, as you conjecture it was Bishop Daily that got this complaint about a priest exposing himself, masturbating in front of a woman and then taking advantage of her when her husband is dealing with one of his parents' funeral arrangements, if, in fact, Bishop Daily had received a letter such as that and drafted a response such as Exhibit 44, would he have been acting in accordance with the policy that you describe in Exhibit No. 12 and what you would have done had you been aware of the Shanley allegations?

A: What would have to be done, Mr. MacLeish, is to ask Bishop Daily what, in fact, he did, and I'm not going to conjecture at this point what he did or didn't do. I can simply answer that I do not recall seeing this letter, I do not recall seeing this letter, that I consider these to be very serious allegations, and that I would have wanted them investigated, and acted upon if they—if that was warranted. What happened, I cannot conjecture. I cannot conjecture at this point. I would need to—one would need to talk to Bishop Daily about that.

Q: Well, we don't know whether we'd need to talk to Bishop Daily because we don't even know if it was Bishop Daily that drafted this letter of April 3, 1984, correct?

A: That's correct.

Q: All we know is that it's your signature on the letter.

A: That's correct.[10]

This exchange is typical of the overall tone of Cardinal Law's deposition. As is common among enablers, Cardinal Law denies direct knowledge of abuse and shifts blame away from himself, despite the fact he was the person ultimately in charge of the priests who were abusing children.

Cardinal Law was not the neighborhood priest, entrusted with a small parish. He was the archbishop of Boston.

We move ahead to other exchanges in the deposition that underscore the scope of his role as an enabler of abuse by priests under his authority. In one case, a priest who had abused young boys remained in his position from 1984 to 2002, even when it was quite clear that his conduct warranted taking action against him:

---

10. https://www.bishop-accountability.org/resources/resource-files/courtdocs/LawDeposition-2002-08-13.htm.

Q: You testified earlier that if you had been aware of the 1966 report about Paul Shanley, you would have undertaken a series of actions including assessments and possibly even removal from active ministry; correct?

A: That's correct.

Q: But now I put in front of you Father Rebeiro's case and the complaint made by Mr. Nash in 1984, the same year in which you state you wish you had known about the 1966 allegation of Paul Shanley, correct?

A: That's correct.

Q: And we know that Father Rebeiro continued in ministry from 1984 up until the time he was removed just this past weekend [in 2002], correct?

A: That's correct.[11]

Yet another exchange exemplifies the way in which enablers frequently shift blame to others and deny any knowledge or accountability:

Q: But I'm not attempting to point my finger at you. If I did, I apologize. I will ask you, Cardinal Law, were there any other instances where you can recall, between 1984 and 1990, which is the time period that we're focusing on in the Ford, Busa and Driscoll cases, that you can recall, where there was an allegation of sexual misconduct, and the matter was not dealt with in accordance with the policy that you described earlier in the day?

Go ahead.

A: The way in which these matters were handled was through delegation. My expectation was and is that allegations would be looked at, would be examined, and that credible allegations would be acted upon, and that would include getting some kind of a medical assessment, if it seemed that there was substance to the allegation.

---

11. *Id.*

Now, were there cases that came that were not looked at? I rely on those working with me, and if I had in my head a case that hadn't been adequately looked at, I would ask that it be looked at. As you know, and I realize it's—well, it's not totally out of the time frame, but one of the things that we did after we committed our policy— developed it and committed it to writing in 1993, sometime after that, I asked that all previous cases be reviewed in the light of that policy, and if it was felt that they were not adequately dealt with in accord with that policy, that those cases be opened again.

Do I know of—as I sit here, do I know of cases that were not dealt with adequately? No, I don't. And if there are any, I would hope that they would now be dealt with adequately.[12]

In an exchange referencing Peter Pollard, Cardinal Law further demonstrated his evasiveness and ability to shirk all responsibility for abuse that occurred under his authority. While the excerpt below is admittedly lengthy, it enables us to fully appreciate the manner in which a skilled enabler evades, and avoids, any and all responsibility.

Q: Do you remember receiving this letter, which set forth allegations of sexual misconduct involving a minor by one Peter Pollard involving Father George Rosenkranz. Do you remember receiving that communication?

A: I do not recall receiving this communication.

Q: Well, during this period of time, as you've stated, your intention was to have as your first priority the protection of children; is that correct?

A: That's correct.

Q: So wouldn't it seem likely, in view of that being your first priority in the 1984 to 1990 time period, that any allegation about a priest being involved in sexual misconduct with minors would have been something that would have come to your attention?

---

12. *Id.*

A: Not necessarily. It would have been—it would have come to the attention of those responsible for following up on this type of matter, and that would have been, as I've indicated, at an earlier time frame, the moderator of the Curia, at a later time frame, the secretary for ministerial personnel, and yet at a later time frame the person holding the responsibility of delegate. A number of things come to your attention every single day, and if they're going to be handled well and expeditiously, delegation is a good way for that to happen.

Q: Sure. But the protection of children, you've stated, was your first priority?

A: In the hand—

Q: May I finish the question, please, Cardinal Law. You've testified that the protection of children was your first priority. Understanding that you have many other responsibilities in the '84 to 1990 time period, wouldn't a letter making allegations of sexual misconduct involving a child for a priest who is currently in service, wouldn't that be the type of matter that would go to the top of the list that would come before you, Cardinal Law?

A: I believe I answered your question earlier, Mr. MacLeish, by indicating that in order to handle these cases effectively, expeditiously and well, I had persons delegated to deal with these cases. And so this matter would go to the person who was responsible for following up to be sure that it was handled in an appropriate way.

Q: Cardinal Law, there's been testimony by Bishop McCormack that after he received this letter, he did not have Father Rosenkranz evaluated. He stated as much in his deposition, and we can mark a copy of the transcript if you'd like to see it during the break, but that he did not have Father Rosenkranz assessed, and that Father Rosenkranz was removed from active ministry following another allegation in 1990.

A: I know that he is removed from active ministry. I wasn't sure of the date of that removal.

Q: . . . My question is, is that since the protection of children is the number one priority and since your policy is, as you've described it earlier, is to generally accept the credibility of the person making the report, did Bishop McCormack act in accordance with the policy by not sending Father Rosenkranz in for an assessment?

. . .

A: Certainly it would have been my understanding of—and it would have been my intent that someone against whom a credible allegation had been made would indeed be assessed.

Q: Okay. And as you sit here today, can you think of any reason why Mr. Pollard's allegations were not deemed to be credible, that you know of, that anybody might have told you?

A: No, I cannot.

Q: So accepting my representations as true—and, again, we do have the deposition transcript of Bishop McCormack, and we do know that Father Rosenkranz was not removed, nor was he assessed. Can you now state that if the 1966 allegations involving Paul Shanley had been brought to your attention, that in light of what happened in the Pollard/Rosenkranz case and the earlier exhibit involving Father Rebeiro and his allegation—the allegations made by Mr. Nash, can you state with certainty, Cardinal Law, that if you would have received the 1966 allegation in 1984, that you would have acted upon it?

. . .

A: That I would have acted upon it—

Q: Yes.

A: —yes. And I would presume that those who were delegated to act in my name would have acted upon it. That would be my presumption, and that is my presumption, and if you—if your recital of what occurred in the instance of Father Rosenkranz is as it is, and I have no reason to doubt what you're reporting, then I would hope that this is an aberration rather than a rule.

. . .

A: Again, I wouldn't know what extenuating circumstances may underlie that decision of not having him assessed. I would also say, Mr. MacLeish, that while I have acknowledged and do acknowledge that the action of Father Rebeiro, the allegations against him, both the earlier and the current, are of totally unacceptable behavior, I find the evil of sexual abuse of a minor really qualitatively quite different and much more intense than that. Both are wrong.

Q: Than what? I'm sorry.

A: But in the one case you're talking about a minor. In the other case you're talking about an adult. I think that the abuse done to a minor is particularly heinous, and you seem to move from one to the other as though they're sort of the same thing. I would think that the action against the minor is particularly heinous.

Q: Well, Cardinal Law, Mr. Nash reports to you in Exhibit No. 43 that one of the allegations involving Father Rebeiro involved blocking the only exit door—

A: I—

Q: Excuse me. If I could, please—exposing himself and masturbating in front of her. You state there's a qualitative difference between that allegation and the allegation of Mr. Pollard involving a sexual assault when he was a minor? Is that your testimony?

A: What I'm saying is that sexual abuse of a minor has an added quality of heinousness about it, and that's why our focus is so clearly on the protection of children. That is not to say that other acts of aggressive sexual behavior toward adults are not also deplorable and are not also to be dealt with. They are. The only point I'm making is that you seem to move from the one to the other as though they're sort of the same thing. I would think that the evil of child abuse is a far, far worse evil that has to be dealt with.

Q: Than sexual assault on women?

A: That both—no, no, that's not what I'm saying, Mr. MacLeish.

. . .

A: That's not what I'm saying.

Q: I'm confused by what you are saying, Cardinal Law.

A: Well—

Q: Are you stating there is no qualitative difference, because I think that was the word you used, between the allegations of sexual assault, masturbation by Father Rebeiro, and the allegations that are set forth in Mr. Pollard's letter which involve sexual assault on a minor?

. . .

Q: Okay. Now, Cardinal Law, let's mark Bishop McCormack's deposition on what happened in the—if we could, please, on what happened in the Pollard allegation. I can read you a section of it.

(Law Exhibit No. 46, excerpt of Bishop McCormack's Deposition, marked for identification.)

A: This is the Pollard allegation? This is Pollard here?

Q: Yes.

A: Because the name is crossed out.

Q: Yes. It is the Pollard allegation, and he's comfortable with his name being used.

Again, this is an allegation, as you'll see, on the first page, Cardinal Law, where it's stated by Mr. Pollard that under the guise of teaching him about sexuality, Father Rosenkranz kissed him, had him lie on top of him and he kissed him. He had him expose himself and discuss sex with him. Do you see that? That's the allegation against Father Rosenkranz.

A: Yes.

Q: Now, we have in front of you Exhibit No. 46, which is Bishop McCormack's deposition. I'd like to read you a section and then ask you a question about it, if I could. I'm referring, starting on page 268, line 13. You can follow along with me if you'd like. Do you have it there, Cardinal Law?

A: Yes, I do.

[The following is read from Bishop McCormack's deposition]

Q: After you spoke with Father Rosenkranz and he admitted to some horsing around, did you have another meeting with Mr. Pollard?

A: Yes.

Q: And you told Mr. Pollard that you were not going to remove Mr. Rosenkranz from active ministry; is that correct?

A: Yes.

Q: And Father Rosenkranz remained in active ministry for several more years; is that correct?

A: I'm not clear for how long, but I knew that we didn't take him out at that time, correct.

Q: And then you became aware later on of other allegations of sexual abuse against Father Rosenkranz—

A: Yes.

Q: —is that correct?

A: Yes.

Q: Did you make a mistake in not removing Father Rosenkranz in 1987 when his sexual molestation of Mr. Pollard was reported to you, did you make a mistake?

A: What I want to say is that I don't recall these allegations—

Q: This was the letter—

A: —but I could be—my memory probably isn't working well and—but I do remember Pollard coming to me, and I do remember him being angry because I had come to the—you know, I couldn't—I didn't know who was saying—who was telling the truth and I was very logical about the whole thing. And so that he says that, "I wonder whether you believed me," and I feel very badly now that I didn't believe him more, but I was taking one person's word against another and it was very difficult. And so having gone through the assessment and then the assessment not showing up anything that was deviant, I then had to decide, you know, which was the—how do you handle Father Rosenkranz and how do you handle Mr. Pollard? So I told him that. As I look back at that, I regret that terribly.

Q: Well, you see actually the attachment is the actual letter—a copy of the letter that he sent to Cardinal Law in which he reports this is not horsing around. I think I read you the paragraph earlier.

A: Right.

Q: And if you take a look at the next page—and, again, you're welcome to read this; we're going to be getting together again, but it says, "but be on notice," at the bottom of the second page, last full paragraph, "If you take no significant action to find appropriate and effective treatment for him and to locate his other victims, I will make every effort to make this information public, even at my own expense." Do you see that?

A: Yes.

Q: And so you know, also, do you not, Father McCormack, that after you decided to keep Father Rosenkranz in active ministry in the '90s, there surfaced more allegations against Father Rosenkranz, at which point he was removed; is that correct?

A: At some time after this he was removed. I notice that the Department of Social Services [DSS] and the Essex DA [district attorney] was also notified by Mr. Pollard.

Q: Right. Not by you, but by the—

A: No, by Mr. Pollard. We would encourage them to do that.

Q: I'm not asking about DSS; I'm asking about what you did, and what you did after Mr. Pollard came and complained to you after writing to Cardinal Law you decided that Mr. Rosenkranz should go into active ministry and then there were further complaints later on about Father Rosenkranz and he was removed?

A: That's right.

Q: And you said you feel terribly about that right now, is that correct?

A: Yes, correct.

[Reading from McCormack's deposition ends here]

Q: Do you see that, Cardinal Law?

A: Yes, I do.

Q: When Bishop McCormack was undertaking the action which he's testified to with respect to Father Rosenkranz, was he acting in accordance with the unwritten policy that was in effect between 1984 and 1990?

A: My presumption is he was attempting to implement the policy. The implication on page 270 is that there was the assessment, and this assessment did not show anything that was deviant. My presumption is that Father McCormack at that time was attempting to implement that policy, yes.

Q: Between 1984, Cardinal Law, and 1990, can you think of any priest that went for an assessment that was not returned to active ministry following the assessment?

A: It would be necessary for me, Mr. MacLeish, to check the records on that as to how many allegations were made, how each of them—and I don't have that in my mind at this moment.

Q: I asked you that question—I'll get the reference for you during the break—at I think the first day of your deposition, and you indicated you wanted the opportunity to look back at the records. Have you done that, Cardinal Law?

A: I will ask that I be helped in doing that.

Q: You have not done it as of today, though; is that correct?

A: Well, you know, Mr. MacLeish we've been asked to provide a lot of records to you and a lot of other people, and I have a limited number of folks who are working on this, and we're trying to get things done in as orderly as fashion as we can, and the more things we're asked to bring forward like this, the more impeded we are in moving forward in implementing a very effective policy, but we're doing the best we can, and we will get that information to you.

Q: As you sit here today, though, without the benefit of that information, can you identify in your own mind any one priest in that period of time when my clients allege they were being sexually assaulted by Father Shanley, any one case where a priest was assessed and was not returned to active ministry?

. . .

A: I would have to check the records, Mr. MacLeish, in order to give you an answer to that question.[13]

In each of the preceding extracts, Cardinal Law demonstrates the classic enabler's mindset: deny direct knowledge, shift blame to others, and preserve the reputations of self and the institution. The systemic nature of his enabling behavior comes across loud and clear.

This phenomenon resounded like thunder on January 31 and February 1, 2020, when I met in Lansing, Michigan, with three women who have a deep understanding of Michigan State University: Lauren Allswede and Liz Abdnour are former employees of the university, and Karen Truszkowski is an attorney litigating against MSU. My purpose was to gain a deeper understanding of the culture at Michigan State. They were beyond gracious, patiently answering my endless questions. Some questions I asked repeatedly, primarily because I found it hard to take in the disturbing implications to the institution. While I had read many articles about Michigan State, spent significant time with its victims of Larry Nassar (Lindsay Lemke, Tiffany Thomas-Lopez, Jane Doe 1), and watched numerous victim impact statements of other such

---

13. *Id.*

survivors, none of this prepared me for what I was to learn over the six hours we spent together and the interactions that followed.

When I arrived in Lauren Allswede's office, I already had an inkling, as a devoted reader of MGOBLOG (a website dedicated to University of Michigan sports), of various rumors, intimations, suggestions, and innuendo regarding the sports culture at Michigan State University.[14] Perhaps I took anything negative about MSU with a grain of salt, given the website's obvious leanings. Even when reading articles in mainstream media, I was hesitant to jump to conclusions; "Didn't Sparty learn anything after Penn State?" As much as I "bleed maize and blue" (University of Michigan's school colors), I did not want my passion for all things Michigan to color my perspective and conclusions. While I had made clear to Allswede that I am "true blue," I promised to be open-minded regarding Michigan State University. I had made a similar commitment to Thomas-Lopez, Lemke, and JD1.

When I set out to write this book, my intent was to examine how someone like Larry Nassar was so enabled that he was able to perpetrate serial abuse on such an overwhelming scale. Over the course of the two days I spent listening to Allswede, Abdnour, and Truszkowski it became apparent that the culture that enabled Nassar reaches far beyond the worlds of women's gymnastics (in the case of Lindsay Lemke) and women's softball (in the case of Tiffany Thomas-Lopez).

As horrendous as Nassar was—one cannot underestimate the evil he perpetrated over decades—to explain the culture at Michigan State University solely through the lens of his actions, and the actions of his enablers, is to miss important and disturbing issues that extend well beyond this one individual. This realization was a great surprise to me. It is relevant to the present purposes because it highlights dramatically how deeply the enabler culture is embedded at Michigan State and the degree to which the systemic turning-the-back to the survivor is institutionalized: Sports culture creates rape culture. Priority given to athletes is priority taken from victims.

It is in this context that the following discussion of Michigan State is framed. Granted, only certain members of these teams have been involved. However, the sheer number of alleged assaults and the manner in which they were handled strongly suggests a systemic pattern that makes it

14. https://mgoblog.com.

imperative to criminalize the enabler. Otherwise, the pattern will continue with no consequences for those who failed the survivors after the attacks.

Allegations of sexual assault and rape have been made against Michigan State's basketball and football players for years, seemingly without any accountability demanded by head basketball coach Tom Izzo or (now former) head football coach Mark Dantonio.[15] That in spite of the latter's insistence that Michigan State is a "safe campus." That claim, made with the unctuous and sanctimonious self-confidence that came to define Dantonio, is so patently ridiculous that one wonders whether he understood what he was saying. When confronted with the rapes committed by three of his players in 2018, he blatantly stated this was new territory. Lauren Allswede correctly called him out on this. The incidents detailed below bear her out.

In 2007 four football players allegedly raped a woman named Ashley Dowser. Ashley died by overdose in 2012.[16] A diary revealing the details of the rape and her subsequent intent to harm herself was found by her brother after her death. When the incident was reported to Michigan State University police in 2014, a police interview revealed that the four players "ran a train" on Ashley. Furthermore, it was suggested that this practice was not uncommon among MSU football players.[17] Scott Becker, associate director of the MSU Counseling Center, inaccurately and inappropriately concluded that it was unlikely that Ashley was raped because there were inconsistencies in her diary entries. The Ingham County Prosecutor's Office (ICPO), citing Becker's statement, declined charges.

In 2009, Travis Walton, a former MSU basketball player and student assistant coach, punched a woman at a bar in East Lansing. The survivor, Ashley Thompson, was taken to a hospital, where she was diagnosed with a concussion. Walton pled guilty to littering.

In 2009 a gang rape was allegedly committed by a number of Michigan State football players. Though the survivor (Jane Doe) filed a police report, no charges were filed by the prosecutor.

---

15. Dantonio unexpectedly announced his resignation on February 4, 2020: https://www.thebig lead.com/posts/mark-dantonio-resignation-timing-lawsuit-bonus-recruits-01e08xahhvay.
16. https://www.desmondfuneralhome.com/obituary/Ashley-Elizabeth-Dowser/Waterford -MI/1136997.
17. An unnamed football player discussed this when questioned by the police; https://player .vimeo.com/video/310658133.

The same year, two additional domestic assaults were alleged to have been committed by MSU football players against two separate women (Jane Does). In both cases, no charges were filed.

In 2010 a woman (Jane Doe) was allegedly raped by two players on the Michigan State men's basketball team and one former player. The woman and her parents reported the incident to athletic director Mark Hollis, who performed his own investigation with the help of Alan Haller, Deputy Director of the MSU Athletics Department.[18] Hollis later met with the woman's parents and said that no action could be taken, but that if something similar were to happen in the future, action would be taken.

Just a few months later, Carolyn Schaner was allegedly raped by two other members of MSU's men's basketball team, Keith Appling and Adreian Payne. Carolyn went to the hospital the same night and reported the incident to police. The university's General Counsel's Office and upper administration removed the players from their dorm, and Kristine Zayko, deputy general university counsel, coordinated with other administrators to rearrange the players' school schedules in order to keep them apart from Carolyn. These scheduling changes were not made in collaboration with Carolyn, nor were the changes even communicated to her. Carolyn met with Deb Martinez from the ICPO several days after the alleged rape and was told charges would be declined.

Instead of performing its own Title IX investigation, Michigan State University hired an outside law firm to investigate the incident. When this firm had completed its investigation, the team met with Carolyn to deliver its findings. Before the meeting, Carolyn was told that she would not be permitted to have her counselor with her. During the meeting, Carolyn was asked why, when she was being assaulted and raped, she did not choose to leave from one of the building's exits. Finally, she was told that the team could not determine by a preponderance of the evidence that the university's policy had been violated.

In 2013 a rape was reported against an MSU football player, but no criminal charges were filed. The same year, another woman was physically assaulted by an MSU football player. The victim stated that she only wanted an apology. The player apologized, and no criminal charges were filed.

---

18. https://msuspartans.com/staff-directory/alan-haller/9.

In 2015, an MSU football player named Keith Mumphery allegedly raped a woman. After two investigations, he was found responsible of violating the university's sexual misconduct policy, though no criminal charges were filed.

Also in 2015, Bailey Kowalski was allegedly raped by three MSU basketball players (who are not publicly named at this time; this case is described in greater detail in the following chapter). The MSU Counseling Center discouraged Bailey from reporting because she had been "swimming with big fish." Bailey did file a police report in 2019, and the investigation is ongoing.

In 2017, a woman (Jane Doe) was allegedly raped by three Michigan State football players, Josh King, Demetric Vance, and Donnie Corley. The MSU Counseling Center discouraged the survivor from filing a police report, telling her instead to "focus on healing."

King, Vance, Corley, and their teammate Auston Robertson are part of a much larger narrative that raises profoundly important questions regarding Mark Dantonio and Michigan State University. To adequately convey the scope of the issue, below is an excerpt from Tony Paul's excellent article in the Detroit News:

> In early 2016, Dantonio gathered his coaching staff in his office at the Skandalaris Football Center to discuss recruiting.
>
> Dantonio asked each of them their thoughts on Robertson. "I have a daughter on that campus, and I wouldn't feel comfortable with Auston Robertson being on campus with my daughter," said Burton (Ron Burton, Defensive Line Coach, ANG)
>
> There was cause for alarm.
>
> Robertson had a checkered history, according to Blackwell's testimony. Ledo did not return multiple messages from The News.
>
> MSU was aware of these measures and the reasons behind them, Fort Wayne Community Schools spokeswoman Krista J. Stockman confirmed to The News.
>
> In fact, sexually disturbing behavior by Robertson had been documented by police. When Robertson was just 11 years old, a neighborhood woman told police Robertson threatened to rape her daughter, according to court records obtained by The Detroit News.

From July 2009 through October 2015, Robertson was accused of at least 11 instances of sexually assaulting, threatening, grabbing, dragging, tackling or disrobing five girls or women, according to police and court records obtained by The News.

The question: Would Robertson's behavior bar him from MSU?

Dantonio wanted him on the team. Hollis, the athletic director, did not.

It's also not clear what exactly MSU knew about Robertson's past. What is clear, however, is that he was admitted to attend Michigan State.

On April 9, Dantonio received a call from one of his players: Robertson had raped someone again.

Another victim

Robertson had been out with a buddy around 11 p.m. the night before when he met the girlfriend of a teammate.

The three had pizza, according to police testimony, before Robertson's girlfriend picked them up and gave the woman a ride home.

Robertson "wanted to make sure she got there safely," according to Meridian Township Police, so he offered to walk her up to her second-floor apartment.

There, he followed her to the bedroom and raped her while his girlfriend waited outside, according to police.

Robertson fled to Indiana, but less than two weeks later he was charged with third-degree criminal sexual conduct and was kicked off the team.

Robertson "broke our trust," Dantonio told reporters.

"Obviously, we took a risk," he added. "We vetted the young man." [19]

NO.

Robertson did not "break our trust" as Dantonio self-righteously claimed in a wave of sanctimoniousness, quite the opposite. It was Dantonio—and Dantonio alone—who violated the trust of the MSU community by allowing, onto a major college campus, a student—yes, a

19. https://www.detroitnews.com/story/sports/college/michigan-state-university/2020/01/12/recruiting-trouble-msu-sex-assaults-throw-football-program-loss/4232804002/.

student who happened to be particularly skilled on football Saturdays—whose previous behavior was documented and known. In playing the role of the victim, Dantonio did the unimaginable: he knowingly endangered a community and then claimed to have HIS trust violated. THAT is the epitome of the enabler who purports to take the high road but, in essence, creates the atmosphere that tolerated the behavior of Robertson.

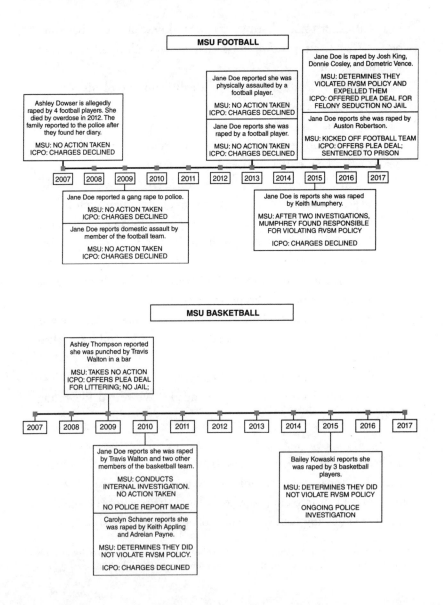

Tom Izzo is a very successful men's college basketball coach. Like him or dislike him, he wins big.[20] He has been richly rewarded by Michigan State University with countless awards and accolades and was elected to the extremely prestigious Naismith Memorial Basketball Hall of Fame. By all accounts, Izzo is one of the most respected members of the coaching fraternity, both in the Big 10 conference and nationally. A number of NBA teams have expressed great interest in hiring him—but he has rebuffed all offers, stating that he is a Spartan for life.

Izzo's players, however, as we have seen, have been involved in numerous off-court incidents, primarily violence against women, including sexual assaults. These episodes suggest a disturbing systemic pattern, but there is an additional aspect to them that demands our attention in the context of the enabler. To understand the world of big-time college athletics, and our focus in this context on coaches such as Dantonio and Izzo, it is important to recognize that these men, no different from other Division I coaches are—perhaps inevitably—"control freaks."

Division I sports is big business, and the expectations and demands on the coach are profound.[21] The average fan of a Division I team most likely could not name a Nobel Prize winner on the faculty, yet has detailed knowledge of the defensive coordinator of the football team and whom the basketball coach is recruiting. A loss on a Saturday inevitably means that the university president will be inundated with phone calls, text messages, emails, and visits from irate fans, alums, and donors. The stakes are so high, the money so significant, the pressure so relentless, that maybe it should not be surprising if coaches commit recruiting and other violations. Recruiting is the life-blood of a major sports program. And as shown in the case of Auston Robertson, coaches will make allowances and assume risks with particular individuals who promise great potential, even against the advice of colleagues and outside experts.

Perhaps the coach assumes that a player's unwanted behavior will fade away in a new environment, or hopes that the player will develop some newfound maturity. Regardless, coaches will make controversial

20. http://www.hoophall.com/hall-of-famers/tom-izzo; https://msuspartans.com/sports/mens-basketball/roster/coaches/tom-izzo/616.
21. https://www.cleveland.com/osu/2020/02/topped-by-ohio-state-big-ten-sports-approaches-2-billion-a-year-in-spending.html.

decisions regarding "at risk" recruits because a potential game-breaker, a player who can become a mainstay and help a program make the leap into top tier level, is justifiable from a cost-benefit perspective.

The pressures on coaches is so enormous that the life cycle of a college head football coach at a particular institution is brief:

> Keep this in mind when you review college football coaching carousel grades: about a third of these guys will be fired within four years.
>
> That's based on the results of every FBS [Football Bowl Subdivision] hire made from 2005 through 2014. I chose that span because it's a full decade, but happened long enough ago that we can say those hires all played out one way or another.
>
> Roughly another quarter of them will leave the school on their own terms within four years, which could mean they did such a great job for you, they got an even bigger job, which would be good for you. Or it could mean they just left.
>
> Either way, your currently redshirting freshmen will probably play for a totally different coaching staff as seniors.[22]

In reality, most fans care only about wins and losses. That fact encourages tolerating behavior that borders on the unacceptable, or maybe is subject to disciplinary action by the coaches, if it does not fully morph into the criminal. Football coaches may lament the practicality of monitoring everyone on their teams of 100 or more players, but that argument cannot be used of basketball teams, whose members number between 15 and 20. Coaches, in fact, invest significant time, resources, and energy in ensuring that their players maintain adequate GPAs and stay out of trouble so that they are not ruled ineligible or suspended. As the late Vince Lombardi made clear: "Winning isn't everything, it's the only thing."

At Michigan State, Tom Izzo is not only the face of Spartan basketball, but he is seen by many as the face of the university. His reputation regarding recruiting violations may be untarnished, but that is certainly not reflected in the conduct and behavior of his players, on or off campus. The

---

22. https://www.bannersociety.com/2020/2/20/21145985/college-football-coaches-average-years?mc_cid=cc5a9cbc6c&mc_eid=4277862d6c.

list of Michigan State basketball players who have committed crimes, are alleged to have committed crimes, or have been investigated on suspicion of committing crimes is long and disturbing. We need to ask whether Izzo demanded accountability from his players, suspended them in the face of serious allegations, and concretely addressed their misbehavior.

Basketball playing rotations are fairly small—eight to ten players in a game—so each player is critical. Systems are in place to ensure players' availability, and it is widely assumed that very little escapes the coaches' attention, directly or indirectly. Otherwise it would not be possible to impose the discipline required to check egos and guarantee that the team will be ready to play. The team needs each player; the fan base is counting on each one. But does the head coach so need a player that he is willing to overlook conduct that warrants sanction?

The numbers, and the cases detailed previously, suggest that coach Tom Izzo was willing to accept behavior that resulted in direct harm to Michigan State's students. His failure to aggressively, publicly, and consistently address these acts over several years cannot be ignored. Izzo is the head basketball coach, but he is also a university employee. As such, he has a duty of care to all MSU students, no less to Bailey Kowalski, Ashley Thompson, Carolyn Schaner, or the Jane Does mentioned previously, than to the athletes.

Tom Izzo, like Mark Dantonio, must be recognized as an enabler. Both men actively developed coach–player relationships, recruiting impressionable young people, bringing them to campus, convincing them of the power of the team, and then turned a blind eye when they committed heinous crimes. They sought to protect the perpetrators at the expense of vulnerable young people to whom they owed an equal duty of care. The successes enjoyed by Izzo and Dantonio, and the renown they have brought the university, cannot be used to wave away the disturbing conduct of their student athletes. Indeed, as these lines were written, a lawsuit was brought by former MSU football recruiting coordinator Curtis Blackwell against "a wrongful termination and unlawful arrest lawsuit he filed against Dantonio, former athletic director Mark Hollis, former university president Lou Anna Simon and two university police officers."[23]

---

23. https://bleacherreport.com/articles/2854480-ex-michigan-st-staffer-mark-dantonio-ignored-warning-signs-on-auston-robertson.

College football is big business at institutions such as Michigan State and Penn State:

> Michigan State football coach Mark Dantonio had 4.3 million reasons to be happy Thursday. Dantonio's longevity bonus vested Thursday, meaning coach received a $4.3 million bonus, according to the Detroit Free Press.
>
> With that bonus added to his $4.4 million salary, the 63-year-old Dantonio will make about $8.7 million next season. That makes Dantonio the second-highest paid college football coach for 2020. Only Alabama's Nick Saban makes more.
>
> That bonus comes at a less-than-optimal time for Michigan State. While Dantonio has experienced plenty of success with the school, the Spartans have struggled lately. Over the past two seasons, the Michigan State football team has gone 14-12 and has had one of the worst offenses in the Big Ten. There were legitimate questions about whether Dantonio should return for another season.[24]

Bonuses on such a scale, commonly offered to university presidents, athletic directors, and other high-level administrators, cultivate a win-at-all-costs attitude, because so many people, at different levels in the institution, have a vested interest in the success of the teams.

The desire to win, protect an institution, and achieve corporate or political success is understandable. But at some point, a line is crossed. As we have seen throughout this book, harm results directly from the enabler's decision to abandon those to whom he or she owes a duty of protection: Mark Dantonio, Tom Izzo, Joe Paterno, and innumerable administrators, coaches, presidents, cardinals, popes, CEOs, and others in positions of power made the decision to enable the wrongdoer, thereby creating possible harm for others. It is for that reason that criminalizing the enabler is vitally important, for otherwise not only will a specific enabler go unpunished, but there will be no deterrence model for future enablers.

---

24. https://sports.yahoo.com/mike-dantonio-becomes-secondhighest-paid-college-football-coach-after-43-million-bonus-hits-212633101.html.

The following discussion of mandatory reporting laws must be approached with the survivor's expectation of the enabler foremost in mind.

Mandatory Reporting

As evidenced by the example of Cardinal Law, inherent shortcomings in state mandatory reporting laws are a serious limitation to enforcing enabler liability. Mandatory reporting laws punish inaction. Specifically, they define individuals, or in some instances professional positions in society, who must report instances of abuse—including sexual abuse—or else risk legal punishment. Intuitively, this legal avenue seems to be an option for holding enablers accountable under the criminal law system. However, while mandatory reporting laws punish enablers by penalizing inaction, their effectiveness is dependent upon the language used in state legislation. A survey of ten states' mandatory reporting laws—including each of the states in which the survivors discussed in this book were abused—illustrates the wide range of mandatory reporting provisions across the country.[25]

Mandatory reporting laws were first crafted as early as 1963 in an effort by states to protect children from child abuse. Within five years, all 50 states had passed laws requiring mandatory reporting in one form or another. The hastiness with which states enacted mandatory reporting legislation is indicative of their commitment to the goal of protecting the vulnerable, yet it also suggests that these laws should be examined closely because they were enacted quickly and without a rigorous understanding of the nature of abuse and its interplay with such a reporting requirement. No federal law requires mandated reporting, but the Child Abuse Prevention and Treatment Act requires states to enact mandatory reporting legislation as a condition of receiving certain forms of federal funding.[26]

---

25. The states are California, Florida, Massachusetts, Michigan, New York, Ohio, Pennsylvania, Texas, Utah, and Washington.
26. See 42 U.S.C. §§ 5101–5119 (2006).

Initially, state mandatory reporting laws were centered on medical staff, due to their perceived experience and being in a unique position to identify abuse. However, a few states created a broader scope of liability: universal application of mandatory reporting; i.e., placing the duty to report upon *all* individuals. By creating universal application of mandatory reporting, states could ensure "appropriate protection of the maximum number of children."[27] Despite the sound logic behind universal mandatory reporting, most states' laws do not create such a provision, but instead create a list of positions in society required to report suspected abuse.

Mandatory reporting laws can be tools to hold enablers accountable. As described, oftentimes a victim of sexual assault has a simple request of enablers: to put an end to the abuse by reporting it to someone in authority. While this goal can be furthered by mandatory reporting laws, the current laws of many states should be amended to address certain gaps in effectiveness.

Mandatory reporting laws differ from bystander legislation, which requires that the individual be present at the scene when a victim is being accosted or assaulted by a perpetrator. Mandatory reporting laws require individuals to report instances of abuse *whether or not* the individual is present when the abuse occurs, so long as the individual has sufficient *knowledge* of the abuse.

Generally, mandatory reporting laws deal with five main issues:

1. Liability: who is liable for failing to report abuse?
2. Protection: who is the state protecting?
3. Reporting requirements: what kind of report is required?
4. Exceptions: who, if anyone, is exempt from liability?
5. Degree of criminality: what type of crime is involved in failing to report abuse and what are the civil and criminal consequences?

States deal with each of these issues in various ways and with varying effectiveness. The following pages describe how the ten states under consideration address the main issues, with a view to recommending

---

27. *See* Vincent De Francis, *Child Abuse—The Legislative Response*, 44 Denv. L.J. 3, 20 (1967).

new or amended legislation that would more effectively address enabler complicity.

As the table demonstrates, most state mandatory reporting laws provide a list of certain societal positions (i.e., positions, titles, or offices held by an individual), for example, "school counselor." Further, most states focus such laws on the protection of minors and the elderly. Most states require immediate reporting, though most allow exceptions for certain societal positions, most commonly for priests in the setting of a confessional and for attorneys and doctors under their respective professional privileges of confidentiality. Punishments for failure to report range from fines and imprisonment to civil damages.

State	Liability	Protection	Reporting	Exceptions	Punishment
CA	Specific list: 46 positions	Children	Initial and follow-up reports	Yes	Fine Imprisonment
FL	Universal applicability	Children	Immediate report	Yes	Fine Imprisonment
MA	Specific list: 47	Children	Written report	Yes	Fine
MI	Specific list: 30	Children	Immediate report	Yes	Fine Imprisonment
NY	Specific list: 45	Children	Immediate report	Yes	Civil damages Misdemeanor
OH	Specific list: 34	Children and individuals with disabilities	Immediate report	Yes	Misdemeanor
PA	Specific list: 32	Children	Immediate report	Yes	Fine Imprisonment Civil Damages
TX	Universal applicability	Children	Immediate report	No	Misdemeanor
UT	Universal applicability	Children	Immediate report	Yes	Misdemeanor
WA	Specific list: 19	All victims of sexual assault	Immediate report	Yes	Misdemeanor

Liability

Liability is the issue in mandatory reporting laws that varies most widely from state to state. Generally speaking, states take one of two approaches in deciding who is liable for failing to report abuse. Either they create a specific list of the various societal positions for which reporting is mandatory; for example, a state law will declare that "the following positions are mandatory reporters" and then present a comprehensive list of societal positions, such as "school counselor, teacher, social worker." Alternatively, states simply declare that "any individual" must report abuse when that individual is made aware of it.

Of the states surveyed, seven take the first approach. Washington lists 19 types of societal positions for which reporting are mandatory, whereas Massachusetts lists 47. Such a wide variation in the number of positions covered clearly makes the schemes of liability in some states more effective than those in others. The types of listed positions vary, though most states focus on those in which professionals interact with children, such as social workers, school employees, and medical staff. This strategy creates an inherent limitation in holding enablers accountable, because individuals occupying positions not listed are not required to report abuse even when they are made aware of it. As such, these types of laws are effective in holding enablers legally accountable only to the extent that they expressly list positions within the statute.

Three of the states surveyed take the second approach. Though this approach is less common, it seems to be more effective in holding enablers legally accountable because it avoids the inherent limitation of defining, in advance, the positions that are liable.

As public awareness of abuse has grown, some states have sought to improve legislation in order to expand the scope of liability under mandatory reporting laws. Specifically, in response to increased public attention to abuse by clergymen, Massachusetts passed Senate Bill 2230 in 2003, which included faith leaders in the scope of its mandatory reporting law:

[P]riests, rabbi[s], ordained or licensed minister[s] of any church, religious society, or faith, or an accredited Christian Science practitioner, or any person or layperson in any church, religious society or faith acting in a capacity as a leader, official, delegate or other designated function on behalf of any church, religious society or faith.[28]

A study by Leonard G. Brown III and Kevin Gallagher, published in the *Villanova Law Review*, found that "twelve states directly reacted to a high-profile child abuse event and changed their mandatory reporting laws to ensure that such a situation did not happen again."[29] Such change is warranted and welcomed.

A related issue, relevant to events discussed in this book, is whether athletic coaches are included as mandatory reporters. Of the states that provide a specific list of mandatory reporters, only New York mentions the position of "coach" within its state statute. And the New York statute limits the requirement to "compensated school employee[s] required to hold a temporary coaching license or professional coaching certificate."

With regard to the institutional nature of the sexual abuse and enabler problem at universities, universal liability is likely preferable to a specific list system because the former helps to hold the entire institution accountable, rather than just a few expressly identified upper-level mandatory reporters. If fans, employees, and students cannot avoid liability by concluding that it is someone else's duty to report abuse, there is a chance that the culture of enabling at such institutions could change. A universal liability system might also force institutions to engage in more public awareness efforts about what to do when individuals become aware of assault. Indeed, if we ultimately want the enabling institution to be accountable, it is imperative to hold members at every level of the institution accountable.

As is shown in the preceding table, of the ten states surveyed, California, Massachusetts, Michigan, New York, Ohio, Pennsylvania, and Washington provide a specific list of societal positions to which liability attaches. From the perspective of the survivor, this approach is too narrow because it fails to attach liability when the enabler does not hold a certain position expressly listed in the state's law. The better approach is that taken by Florida, Texas, and Utah, whose laws provide that "any individual" who becomes aware of abuse is required to report that abuse.

---

28. *State Child Welfare Legislation 2002–2003*, Nat'l Conf. of St. Legs. 1, 16 (2004).
29. Leonard G. Brown III & Kevin Gallagher, Mandatory Reporting of Abuse: A Historical Perspective on the Evolution of States' Current Mandatory Reporting Laws with a Review of the Laws in the Commonwealth of Pennsylvania, Villanova L.R.: Tolle Lege, Vol. 59 (2014).

This approach protects survivors and holds enablers accountable, no matter the position held by the potential enabler.

Protection

Generally, mandatory reporting laws focus on protecting those who are vulnerable in society: children, those with intellectual disabilities, and the elderly. While it is, of course, appropriate to seek to protect the vulnerable, limiting that protection to certain groups while ignoring others who may suffer abuse is shortsighted.

As described in detail in this book, individuals from many walks of life and of many different ages are subjected to sexual abuse. Only one state of the ten surveyed takes this fact into account: Washington's statute declares that it aims to protect all victims of sexual assault.

The next table details the persons whom the mandatory reporting laws of the ten states protect. All but Washington limit protection to certain groups of survivors—most commonly children who are victims of abuse or neglect. From the survivor's perspective, this approach is restrictive because it fails to acknowledge scenarios, such as the numerous examples described in this book, in which the survivor is not a child but, say, a 20-year-old national or collegiate athlete. This limitation can be remedied through a change in approach toward that of Washington, where all survivors of assault are protected by the law.

State	Who is the state protecting?
CA	Child victims of abuse or neglect
FL	Child victims of abuse
MA	Children suffering physical or emotional injury resulting from abuse, neglect, or exploitation
MI	Child victims of abuse or neglect
NY	Children who are abused or maltreated
OH	Children and individuals with developmental disabilities who are suffering or facing a substantial risk of suffering abuse or neglect
PA	Victims of child abuse or neglect
TX	Children whose physical or mental health or welfare have been adversely affected by abuse or neglect
UT	Child victims of abuse or neglect
WA	All victims of sexual assault

Reporting Requirements

Virtually every state surveyed required the immediate reporting of abuse. This is sensible given the seriousness of sexual abuse and assault. An immediacy requirement incentivizes individuals to end the abuse as soon as possible. As the next table shows, states are fairly uniform in their approach to reporting requirements. Essentially, all states require that a prompt report be made to law enforcement or another agency when an individual who falls under a mandatory reporting law becomes aware of abuse.

State	What kind of report is required?
CA	An initial report by telephone to the agency and a written follow-up report within 36 hours
FL	An immediate report to the central abuse hotline
MA	A written report filed with the department
MI	An immediate report by telephone and an oral report within 72 hours
NY	An immediate report to the person in charge of the institution, school, facility, or agency
OH	An immediate report
PA	An immediate report to centralized intake
TX	An immediate report to any state law enforcement agency, the department, or the state agency that operates, licenses, certifies, or registers the facility in which the alleged abuse or neglect occurred
UT	An immediate report to a law enforcement agency
WA	An immediate report to a law enforcement agency

Exceptions

All states that take the specific list approach implicitly exempt from liability those positions that are not specified (i.e., "non-mandated reporters"). Additionally, many states create other specific exemptions: for example, members of clergy who are made aware of abuse in the confessional, attorneys who receive information under the attorney-client privilege, and medical professionals who receive information under similar privileges. Presumably, such exemptions are created in order to incentivize individuals to communicate instances of abuse in settings that they feel are confidential. The rationale underlying these exemptions is that they do not create the risk of benefitting enablers because those in such positions are held to professional ethical standards that should lead them to make prudent decisions and ultimately persuade parishioners, clients, or patients, to communicate their knowledge of ongoing abuse to others who can report it.

Notably, however, a few states do limit these types of exemptions. Among the ten states surveyed here, Texas is the only one that does not allow for any exemptions: all mandated reporters must report abuse, notwithstanding professional privileges.

Clearly, the most effective mandatory reporting law would (1) state that any person must report abuse when he or she becomes aware of the abuse, and (2) create as *few exemptions* as possible. In this way, a mandatory reporting law would encompass the maximum number of enablers possible and create legal liability for them if they failed to report the abuse.

The next table details specific exemptions that states have carved out of their mandatory reporting laws; most common are exemptions for clergymen and attorneys.

State	Who, if anyone, is exempt from liability?
CA	Non-mandated reporters; members of clergy in the confessional setting
FL	Attorney-client and members of clergy in the confessional setting—but not any others
MA	Non-mandated reporters, mandated reporters in non-professional capacities, members of clergy in the confessional setting
MI	Non-mandated reporters; attorney-client and members of clergy in the confessional setting
NY	Non-mandated reporters
OH	Non-mandated reporters; attorney-client, members of clergy in the confessional setting, and physician-patient privileges
PA	Non-mandated reporters; attorney-client and members of clergy in the confessional setting
TX	No exemptions
UT	Members of clergy in the confessional setting
WA	Non-mandated reporters

Degree of Criminality

The legal consequences for those who fail to report abuse under mandatory reporting laws generally include some combination of civil damages, fines, and imprisonment. These penalties affect the accountability that survivors demand of enablers for their failure to act to prevent or stop abuse.

The next table lists the specific penalties for failure to report under mandatory reporter laws in the ten states surveyed. As is shown, many states create a misdemeanor for a failure to report; specific penalties are assessed, including fines and imprisonment.

State	Degree of Criminality and Primary Criminal Penalties
CA	Misdemeanor: fine of up to $1,000; imprisonment for up to 6 months
FL	Misdemeanor: fine of up to $1,000; imprisonment for up to 1 year
MA	Fine of up to $1,000
MI	Fine of up to $500; imprisonment for up to 93 days; civil damages
NY	Misdemeanor; civil damages
OH	Misdemeanor
PA	Misdemeanor
TX	Misdemeanor
UT	Misdemeanor
WA	Misdemeanor

The following chart, taken from the *Villanova Law Review* article cited earlier, outlines penalties provided by all 50 states under their mandatory reporting laws.[30]

State	Primary Penalty	Additional Penalty
Alabama	Misdemeanor (6 months, $500)	
Alaska	Class A misdemeanor	
Arizona	Class 1 misdemeanor	Class 6 felony (reportable offense)
Arkansas	Class C misdemeanor (reckless)	Class A misdemeanor (knowing)
California	6 months, $1,000 (mandated reporter)	1 year, $5,000 (willful failure)
Colorado	Class 3 misdemeanor	

---

30. Leonard G. Brown III & Kevin Gallagher, Mandatory Reporting of Abuse: A Historical Perspective on the Evolution of States' Current Mandatory Reporting Laws with a Review of the Laws in the Commonwealth of Pennsylvania, Villanova L.R.: Tolle Lege, Vol. 59 (2014).

State	Primary Penalty	Additional Penalty
Connecticut	$500–$2,500 fine, education/ training	
Delaware	$10,000	$50,000 (subsequent)
Florida	1st degree misdemeanor (1 year, $1,000)	3rd degree felony (live with child)
Georgia	Misdemeanor	
Hawaii	Petty misdemeanor	
Idaho	Misdemeanor	
Illinois	Class A misdemeanor	Class 4 felony (subsequent)
Indiana	Class B misdemeanor	
Iowa	Simple misdemeanor	
Kansas	Class B misdemeanor	
Kentucky	Class B misdemeanor	
Louisiana	$10,000, 5 years	
Maine	$500	
Maryland	NOT ADDRESSED IN STATUTE	
Massachusetts	$1,000	
Michigan	Misdemeanor (93 days, $500)	
Minnesota	Misdemeanor	Felony (if child dies)
Mississippi	1 year, $5,000	
Missouri	Class A misdemeanor	
Montana	Misdemeanor	
Nebraska	Class III misdemeanor	
Nevada	Misdemeanor	
New Hampshire	Misdemeanor	
New Jersey	Disorderly person	
New Mexico	Misdemeanor (1 year, $1,000)	
New York	Class A misdemeanor	
North Carolina	NOT ADDRESSED IN STATUTE	
North Dakota	Class B misdemeanor	
Ohio	4th degree misdemeanor	1st degree misdemeanor (clergy)
Oklahoma	Misdemeanor	
Oregon	Class A violation	

State	Primary Penalty	Additional Penalty
Pennsylvania	3rd degree misdemeanor	Misdemeanor 2 (subsequent)
Rhode Island	Misdemeanor (1 year, $500)	
South Carolina	Misdemeanor (6 months, $500)	
South Dakota	Class 1 misdemeanor	
Tennessee	Class A misdemeanor ($2,500)	
Texas	Class A misdemeanor	State jail felony (intellectually disabled child)
Utah	Class B misdemeanor	
Vermont	$500	6 months, $1,000 (cover up)
Virginia	$500	$100–$1,000 (subsequent)
Washington	Gross misdemeanor (1 year, $5,000)	
West Virginia	Misdemeanor (10 days, $100)	
Wisconsin	6 months, $1,000	
Wyoming	NOT ADDRESSED IN STATUTE	

Recommendations

Our discussion of the ten-state survey of mandatory reporting laws offers a path toward effectively holding enablers liable for failing to report instances of abuse. First, liability should apply to all individuals, not simply to a list of predetermined societal positions. Applying liability to all would ensure that enablers could not evade accountability just because they do not happen to occupy a position expressly stated in the statute.

Second, all victims of sexual assault or abuse should be protected, not only those who are traditionally perceived to be the "most" vulnerable. Abuse unfortunately is not constrained by common perceptions; protection should not be either.

Third, the requirement of an immediate report would help to ensure that abuse is terminated as quickly as possible and would prevent enablers from continuing to look the other way.

Fourth, a mandatory reporting law should create as few exemptions as necessary. While public policy might favor certain exemptions for clerical confessions and professional confidentiality, other exemptions should be avoided.

Fifth, civil liability, fines, and imprisonment can all be used to deter enablers by punishing them for failure to report abuse. By holding enablers legally accountable for failure to report abuse and assault, survivors' pleas for action would be honored and further abuse could be avoided.

We close this chapter with some voices from the ESPN documentary *Spartan Silence*, because they speak so powerfully, compellingly, and directly to the role of the enabler.

Lauren Allswede:

They want to protect the integrity of the programs; don't want scandal, don't want sexual assault allegations or domestic violence allegations.

Most of the time when it involved athletes, it would be dealt with in-house. None of it was transparent, it was very insulated, and people were, a lot of times, discouraged from seeking resources outside of the athletic department.

I think that the athletic department wanted to keep control over that information.

A lot of the statements that are coming out now from administration claiming there's no rape culture is misleading.

It was more about the image and the reputation and the success of the program than it was about ending violence and making it a priority.

Like I said, MSU wanted to protect their image, not wanting a scandal, not wanting a crisis. Part of it, too, just has to do with culturally and socially how we deal with trauma, and a lot of times people don't care about the crimes.

[In response to the football coach claiming an episode was "new grounds" that "have not happened previously."] That's just factually not true because we know there are players who were accused of rape, people that we saw within our program who had been victimized by several of his players throughout the years. So him saying that it wasn't a problem isn't true.

I don't know how he couldn't know, and if he didn't know that's another failure because he should be aware of it. He should be doing something. MSU administration has really been trying to convince everybody that things are getting better without addressing what's still wrong.

A lot of good staff left because nothing was changing. It wasn't getting better and the concerns weren't being taken seriously. Survivors are silenced and not believed.

John Manley, attorney-at-law:

When institutions minimize and lie about something this serious, it's not an accident. There is a reason. The reason Michigan State didn't come clean on this much earlier was because they knew they had a massive problem on their hands.

Tiffany Thomas-Lopez:

She [Destiny Teachnor-Hauk] brushed me off and made it seem like I was crazy. She made me feel like I was crazy.

And once I wasn't able to play anymore, and having to go through what I went through and no one believing me and no one listening to me, I couldn't look at them. I couldn't, like, face, you know, what had happened. I felt like they thought I was a liar, that this really didn't happen to me, and I detached myself from everything.

I allowed the athletic trainers to silence me, to not allow me to share the truth. And I'm sure until the day I die I'll have this guilt.

"I knew that he had abused me. I reported it. Michigan State University, the school I loved and trusted, had the audacity to tell me that I did not understand the difference between sexual assault and a medical procedure. That master manipulator took advantage of his title, he abused me, and when I found the strength to talk about what had happened, I was ignored and my voice was silenced. I spent years trying to get over what happened that day, and the damage the investigation did to my life. Years of not being able to trust anyone, and messy relationships, and feeling so alone every single day. You're scared of doctors and men and figures of authority."

—*Amanda Thomashow, victim impact statement*

"They had an opportunity to listen, to do something, to act, and they chose to stay quiet."

—*Tiffany Thomas Lopez*[1]

---

1. "Spartan Silence: Crisis at Michigan State," https://player.vimeo.com/video/310658133.

— 9 —

Sexual Assault and Enabling at Universities: Title IX

As a freshman at Michigan State University, Bailey Kowalski was confident, joyful, and trusting.[2] Her robust interest in sports and athletics led her to major in sports journalism in pursuit of her lifelong ambition to become a sports journalist.[3] In April 2015, at age eighteen, she was assaulted. Bailey's experiences in the aftermath of being violated bring much to bear on this chapter's discussion of Title IX and those who enable sexual assaults on college campuses.

Bailey and I were introduced by her attorney, Karen Truszkowski, after my meetings in Lansing with Truszkowski, Lauren Allswede, and

---

2. "Bailey Kowalski discusses her alleged rape at Michigan State," April 11, 2019, https://www .youtube.com/watch?v=8mUBCGp8kvA. Much of Bailey's story is taken from my interview with her. Numerous other sources were also consulted, including First Amended Complaint and Jury Demand, Case 1:18-cv-00390-PLM-RSK, Docket No. 23. (11 Dec. 2018); Kyle Austin, MLive, "Judge refuses to dismiss lawsuit against MSU over handling of sexual assault cases involving athletes" (updated August 21, 2019), https://www.mlive.com/spartans/2019/08/judge-believes -msu-had-different-process-for-sexual-assault-cases-involving-athletes-allows-lawsuit-to-proceed .html. Where Bailey's case is ongoing, discussion of her story relies on the allegations she has made against Michigan State University.
3. First Amended Complaint and Jury Demand, Case 1:18-cv-00390-PLM-RSK, Docket No. 23, 3:14 (11 Dec. 2018).

177

Liz Abdnour (see Chapter 8). Bailey was gracious and generous with her time, describing her travails with painful honesty mixed with humor. As with the other survivors described in this book, our discussion focused on the aftermath of the assault and the expectations she had from those best positioned to provide assistance. Bailey, like all the other survivors I interviewed, was abandoned by those in positions of authority.

This chapter emphasizes legal issues, as did Chapter 8. Some of the language is necessarily technical, but we must not lose sight of the fact that our primary focus is to provide assistance to future survivors, while recommending measures to enforce punishment and sanctions on the enablers. We cannot allow the legal issues to hide the fact that real people have suffered terrible harm; for that reason, Bailey's story will be recounted in detail. If we view the question of the enabler exclusively through the narrow lens of the law, we will forget the purpose of our endeavor.

The beginning of April 2015 in East Lansing, Michigan, was a delirious, exciting time: the MSU Spartan basketball team had recently advanced to the March Madness Final Four tournament. The community was buzzing with the possibility not only that the Spartans might advance to the championship game, but that they might win the whole tournament. But on April 4, 2015, the Spartans were defeated by Duke in a 20-point loss.[4] Elation was dashed by disappointment.

On April 11, a week after Michigan State's loss, Bailey Kowalski and her roommate went to a local bar.[5] Later, sometime after midnight, the MSU basketball team entered the bar.[6] Bailey was shortly approached by one of the team members, who offered to buy her a drink and asked if she would like to meet the "other guys."[7]

Being a sports journalism major, Bailey naturally was interested in interacting with a basketball team fresh from the NCAA March Madness tournament, and she accepted the drink and the offer.[8] At no time

4. Michigan State vs. Duke Box Score, April 4, 2015, https://www.sports-reference.com/cbb /boxscores/2015-04-04-duke.html.
5. First Amended Complaint and Jury Demand, Case 1:18-cv-00390-PLM-RSK, Docket No. 23, 4:15 (11 Dec. 2018).
6. Id. at 4:17.
7. Id. at 4:18.
8. Id. at 4:19.

during her interaction with the team did Bailey indicate she had a romantic interest in any of its members.[9]

Sometime later, while they were conversing, one of the players invited Bailey to a party at the apartment of some of the others.[10] One team member said that the roommate, with whom she had come to the bar, was already there.[11] As it turned out, that was a lie.

By this time, Bailey was having a hard time holding onto her glass, even though she had not had much to drink.[12] She accepted a ride to the party from two of the players.[13] They ended up at the off-campus apartment of one of the team members.[14] Strangely, though, there was no party going on when Bailey arrived.[15] And she soon realized that her roommate was not in fact at the apartment, as she had been led to expect.[16] Bailey felt out of sorts: she was extremely hungry and thirsty[17] and felt "discombobulated."[18] When she tried to send a text message, she could not control her thumbs to type.[19]

Then, one of the team members pulled Bailey into a bedroom and told her, "You are mine for the night."[20] She immediately became uncomfortable, for she had no intention of having physical contact with any of the people at the "party."[21] She was able to get out of the bedroom and make her way back to the living room, where music was playing from a laptop.[22] She tried to change the music, but found she was unable to use her hands properly.[23] At this point, Bailey realized something was wrong; she thought she might have been drugged.[24]

---

9. *Id.*
10. *Id.* at 4:20.
11. *Id.*
12. *Id.*
13. *Id.* at 4:21.
14. *Id.*
15. *Id.* at 4:22.
16. *Id.* at 5:23.
17. *Id.* at 4:22.
18. *Id.*
19. *Id.* at 5:24.
20. *Id.* at 5:25.
21. *Id.*
22. *Id.* at 5:25-26.
23. *Id.* at 5:26.
24. *Id.*

Then, Bailey was gang raped.[25]

At some point, she blacked out.[26] She woke up a few hours later on a couch in the apartment.[27] Bailey called a taxi and went back to her campus dorm, where she saw her roommate.[28] Her roommate did not know anything about a party the night before.[29] In fact, she told Bailey that she had been looking for her but had not been able to find her.[30]

Bailey was distraught and traumatized.[31] Later, she confided to one of her friends in her dorm that she had been raped by three Michigan State basketball players on the morning of April 12.[32] It took her a week to build up the courage to go with her friend to the Michigan State University Counseling Center (MSUCC) to report the incident.[33]

At the MSUCC, Bailey completed an initial intake and assessment, filling out a questionnaire on which she reported the rape.[34] She was then interviewed, in private, by a female counselor who asked her additional questions. When asked if she knew who her attackers were, Bailey disclosed that they were three "notable MSU basketball players."[35]

The counselor's demeanor suddenly changed.[36] She abruptly told Bailey that another person needed to be in the room. Bailey was not sure why this was the case.[37] Even after the counselor returned with the additional MSUCC staff person, it was not made clear to her. The first counselor asked Bailey to repeat what she had previously said in front of the staff person. Bailey complied.

The two then asked if she had gone to the police. Bailey said that she had not, because she used a fake ID to get into the bar with her roommate and was afraid of getting in trouble. They said they understood and asked if she had taken a rape test kit. Bailey responded that she had not,

---

25. *Id.* at 5:27-30
26. *Id.* at 6:31.
27. *Id.*
28. *Id.* at 6:31-32.
29. *Id.* at 6:32.
30. *Id.*
31. *Id.* at 6:33.
32. *Id.*
33. *Id.*
34. *Id.*
35. *Id.* at 6:34.
36. *Id.*
37. *Id.* at 6:36.

because she did not want her parents to receive a bill for the kit. Finally, they asked if she had gone "elsewhere," to which she answered no.

At this point, the MSUCC personnel proceeded to discuss with Bailey her options. And they were few: Bailey was told she could report the rapes to the police or deal with the aftermath of the rapes on her own.[38]

The additional staff member told Bailey that if she notified the police, she would face an uphill battle that would create anxiety and unwanted media attention and publicity.[39] The staff member added this had been the experience of many other female students sexually assaulted by well-known athletes.[40] Bailey was informed that the staff had seen many cases concerning "guys with big names," and that the best thing for her would be to "just get [her]self better."[41] When she discussed pressing charges, the staff responded, "If you pursue this, you are going to be swimming with some really big fish."[42]

The conversation continued, but Bailey was not informed she had a right to have a no-contact order put in place, preventing the three attackers from running into her at her dorm.[43] Similarly, she was not advised she could report the rapes to the Office of Institutional Equity, nor of her Title IX rights, protections, and accommodations.[44] The MSUCC did, however, refer Bailey to the Michigan State University Sexual Assault Program.[45]

Bailey left the MSUCC frightened and convinced that she should not report the rapes to law enforcement.[46] In her mind, there was nothing to be done but push on with her education. And for a while, she tried doing just that.

However, in October 2015, Bailey was forced to withdraw from Michigan State University after being admitted to the Sparrow Hospital outpatient psychiatric day program for intensive treatment.[47] When she

---

38. *Id.* at 6:37.
39. *Id.* at 8:48.
40. *Id.* at 7:38-39.
41. *Id.* at 7:40.
42. *Id.* at 7:41.
43. *Id.* at 7:42.
44. *Id.* at 7:44.
45. *Id.* at 7:45.
46. *Id.* at 7:43.
47. *Id.* at 8:49-50.

resumed classes in January 2016, she was a changed woman: relations with her family were strained, she was in treatment at a private psychiatric clinic, she was being prescribed multiple medications, and she had abandoned her dream of becoming a sports journalist.[48]

On December 11, 2018, Bailey Kowalski requested a jury trial and judgment against Michigan State University for sex-based harassment that was so severe, pervasive, and objectively offensive that it deprived her of access to educational benefits provided by the university.[49] This claim is widely known as a Title IX violation.[50] Bailey's complaint also alleges several other female Michigan State students were sexually assaulted by male athletes, and were treated by the university in a similar manner.[51] Bailey's complaint further refers to trends noticed by the director and counselors of the MSU Sexual Assault Program,[52] and also to Michigan State's responses to sexual assault and harassment prior to Bailey's complaint.[53]

In addition, Bailey alleges the manner in which the medical records of sexual assault survivors are reviewed by Michigan State University's general counsel before they are released to them essentially deters students from seeking counseling services.[54] The complaint states that: "[w]hen students request their medical and counseling records from the Sexual Assault Program they are 'interviewed' by counseling department personnel who ask the purpose for requesting their personal counseling records."[55] Then, students are informed "their records will have to be reviewed by [MSU]'s General Counsel before the records are released."[56] The complaint also alleges that at MSUCC "[t]here is an undeniable

48. *Id.* at 9: 53-56.
49. *Id.* at 27:172.
50. 20 USC § 1681(a).
51. First Amended Complaint and Jury Demand, Case 1:18-cv-00390-PLM-RSK, Docket No. 23, 11-20 (11 Dec. 2018).
52. *Id.* at 20–21 (stating that a MSU sexual assault counselor from 200–2015 expressed "concerns about a possible pattern" of sexual assault by MSU basketball players).
53. *Id.* at 21–24 (stating that professionals at MSU who were not trained in "sensitive, trauma-based response discouraged victims from reporting sexual assaults." Further, the complaint alleges that faculty and staff "experienced a culture of minimizing or ignoring sexual harassment," particularly among athletes).
54. *Id.* at 24:156–27:171.
55. *Id.* at 24:156.
56. *Id.* at 24:157.

culture of fear around reporting assaults committed by perpetrators of power, particularly athletes."[57] Why? Because sex offenders at MSU, "particularly athletes, are not held accountable for their actions."[58]

This was addressed in a letter sent by The U.S. Department of Education's Office of Civil Rights (OCR) to Michigan State University:

> A number of students stated that the University's athletes have a reputation for engaging in sexual harassment and sexual assault and not being punished for it, because athletes are held in such high regard at the University. Based on OCR's discussions with the student athletes and University staff, the student athletes receive more training on the topics of sexual harassment and sexual assault from the University than other students; however, at least one male athlete stated that athletes may not report an incident involving a fellow athlete to the I3 office. The male athletes also referenced the "Branded a Spartan" training the athletes receive, which covers upholding the Spartan name, and stated that making a report about sexual assault might tarnish the Spartan brand; however, they stated that their response would depend on the severity of the situation.[59]

Although the focus of this chapter is on institutions of higher education,[60] this book has made it clear sexual assault occurs everywhere and must not be construed as limited to college campuses.[61] To think otherwise is to not hear survivor voices and to miss what they have told us throughout this book. That is something we cannot allow ourselves.

In spite of the drum beat of media attention, water cooler discussions, and social media chatter, this seeming epidemic of sexual assaults has not

---

57. *Id.* at 22:145.
58. *Id.* at 22:148.
59. Meena Morey Chandra, Letter from United States Department of Education Office of Civil Rights, Region XV to Michigan State University, (Sep. 1, 2015), https://www.documentcloud.org/documents/2644770-OCR-Letter-to-Michigan-State-Closing-Investigation.html.
60. For simplicity and readability, generally, I collectively refer to colleges, universities, and other higher education institutions as "university" and "universities."
61. *See, e.g.,* Amy B. Cyphert, *Objectively Offensive: The Problem of Applying Title IX to Very Young Students,* 51 Fam. L.Q. 325 (2017) (discussing various problems with Title IX in elementary school settings).

received due attention.[62] Society has tolerated two wrongs: the predator's assault and the enabler's protection of the assailant. The repercussions are magnified when the enabler is an institution the survivor has every reason to believe will extend unlimited resources and protections. Until the moment the institution and individuals in positions of authority make the deliberate decision to walk away, there is no reason for the survivor to think protections would not be afforded him or her.

Indeed, all the institutions examined in this book consistently and loudly articulate their primary concern as the welfare of those for whom they are ostensibly responsible. As we have come to learn, painfully, there is a deep gulf—an overwhelming disconnect—between words and actions. That is the reality that we must acknowledge, for the institutions have chosen not to honor their commitment. It is incumbent upon us to punish that deliberate failure because this was not an off chance, flick of the wrist decision. The call to punish reflects that disturbing reality, the consequences of which are undeniable. Recommending imposition of punishment on institutions, and individuals in positions of authority is the only logical conclusion; the consistent, willful, and deliberate refusal to either proactively or reactively address this epidemic demands our immediate attention. While we have, throughout this book, focused on specific individuals, we must recall that they are representatives of a much larger pool of survivors whose number we do not know with accuracy and never will. Punishing those who facilitated, enabled, failed to prevent, ignored, or made a calculated decision to protect the institution is an important step in aggressively addressing what is a terrible reality for, literally, an untold number of survivors.

Bailey Kowalski's case is not unique, but her story illustrates with striking clarity the institutional deficiencies that foster enabling in sexual assault. Failure to enforce Title IX exacerbates those deficiencies. We will never know how many victims have, like Bailey, been coerced into "getting on with their lives." How many were told by people in positions of authority, specifically tasked with providing them assistance, protection, and support: *Forget about it. Pretend it did not happen.*

---

62. The word, "epidemic" is not used lightly given the severity of the COVID-19 pandemic.

Other Michigan State survivors echo Bailey Kowalski:

Everything that they were trying to do was to get me to go away, to get me to leave, to get me to be quiet.

She sat me down. "Look, you're a female coming in here accusing the Michigan State basketball team of this." And I'm like, "Woah. What? It happened, like, you saw what happened." And she goes, "I know, but look, you're gonna have to be a lot stronger than you are." I mean, she brought me to tears. And she says, "Look, if you can't even handle me, you're not gonna be able to handle a jury."[63]

Regardless of gender, geography, or status, sexual assault occurs in every aspect of our lives and at every level of the educational world. A 2000 survey by the American Association of University Women surveyed 2,064 students in grades 8 through 11 and found that 81 percent reported experiencing some form of verbal, visual/nonverbal, or physical sexual harassment at school.[64] More specifically, 58 percent of these students reported experiencing some form of *physical* sexual harassment at school.[65]

A 2017 National Woman's Law Center survey found that 21 percent of girls between the ages 14 and 18 are kissed or touched without their consent.[66] LGBTQ students and Native American, Latina, and black minority students reported even higher rates of sexual assault.[67]

In 2015, 647 university presidents were surveyed anonymously.[68] Only 32 percent of those surveyed strongly agreed or agreed that sexual assault was "prevalent" at universities.[69] Further, only 6 percent strongly

63. Carolyn Schaner, "Spartan Silence: Crisis at Michigan State," https://player.vimeo.com/video/310658133.
64. "Hostile Hallways: Bullying, Teasing, and Sexual Harassment in School." American Association of University Women," 2001, https://files.eric.ed.gov/fulltext/ED454132.pdf.
65. *Id. See also* Nicole Conroy, Journal of School Violence, "Rethinking Adolescent Peer Sexual Harassment: Contributions of Feminist Theory," 9 September 2013, https://www.tandfonline.com/doi/abs/10.1080/15388220.2013.813391?journalCode=wjsv20.
66. Kayla Patrick and Neena Chaudhry, National Women's Law Center, Let Her Learn: Stopping School Pushout for Girls Who Have Suffered Harassment and Sexual Violence 1 (2017), https://nwlc-ciw49tixgw5lbab.stackpathdns.com/wp-content/uploads/2017/04/final_nwlc_Gates_HarassmentViolence.pdf.
67. *Id.* at 3.
68. Scott Jaschik and Doug Lederman, The 2015 Inside Higher Ed Survey of College & University Presidents, INSIDE HIGHER ED 18 (2015), https://www.insidehighered.com/news/survey/2015-survey-chief-academic-officers.
69. *Id.*

agreed or agreed sexual assault was "prevalent at their institution."[70] These responses do not fit with available data. Whether they reflect willful ignorance or true ignorance is irrelevant, especially to the survivors. But there is no doubt that this institutionalized ignorance represents systemic failure by those most directly responsible for the welfare and safety of students. The consequences are dramatic and painful.

Myriad sources verify the widespread problems of sexual assault at universities. Many studies show that between 1 in 5 and 1 in 4 women are sexually assaulted while attending a university in the United States.[71] Other studies have found that 23.1 percent of female undergraduate students experience sexual assault.[72] Among male undergraduate students, 5.4 percent experience rape or sexual assault while enrolled at a university.[73] Major studies of campus crime also report that as many as 50 percent of university students experience some form of dating violence, a form of sexual assault, while attending school.[74]

Male university students between the ages of 18 and 24 are 78 percent more likely than males in the same age range who are not students to be victims of rape or sexual assault.[75] By contrast, female university students between the ages 18 and 24 are in fact 20 percent less likely than female nonstudents in this age range to be victims of rape or sexual assault.[76]

The fact that 23.1 percent of female university students experience sexual assault is distressing. Of that there must be no doubt. In that

---

70. *Id.*

71. *See, e.g.*, Corey Rayburn Yung, Is Relying on Title IX a Mistake, 64 U. Kan. L. Rev. 891 (2016); Christopher Krebs et al., Campus Climate Survey Validation Study: Final Technical Report, Bureau of Justice Statistics Research & Dev. Series (2016), https://www .bjs.gov/content/pub/pdf/ccsvsftr.pdf; Nick Anderson and Susan Svrluga, What a massive sexual assault survey found at 27 top universities, The Washington Post (Sept. 21, 2015), https://www.washingtonpost.com/news/grade-point/wp/2015/09/21/what-a-massive-sexual -assault-survey-showed-about-27-top-u-s-universities/.

72. David Cantor, Bonnie Fisher, Susan Chibnall, Reanna Townsend, et. al. Association of American Universities (AAU), Report on the AAU Campus Climate Survey on Sexual Assault and Sexual Misconduct (September 21, 2015).

73. *Id.*

74. Hoover, N.C. (1999). National survey: Initiation rites and athletics for NCAA sports teams. Alfred, NY: Alfred University.

75. Department of Justice, Office of Justice Programs, Bureau of Justice Statistics, Rape and Sexual Victimization Among College-Aged Females, 1995-2013 (2014).

76. *Id. See also* Facts about Sexual Violence, Centers for Disease Control and Prevention, https:// www.cdc.gov/features/sexualviolence/index.html (finding that about one in three women in the United States have experienced sexual violence).

vein, the fact that a majority of university presidents do not agree sexual assault is prevalent in American universities is remarkable and it raises serious concerns regarding those entrusted with protecting students on their campuses. That, after all, is their primary responsibility. The fact that those in the highest academic positions turn a blind eye—knowingly or unknowingly is irrelevant—to numbers that speak for themselves is devastating to survivors and serves as encouragement for predators and justification for enablers.

Why might so many university presidents fail to recognize a reality that should be otherwise obvious? The answers are predictable and discouraging. Some suggest that sexual assault among university students is difficult to identify because it often does not look like "real rape."[77] In general, our society has a narrow construction of what "rape" is and who "rapists" and "survivors" are, and the narrative that follows makes it much harder both to prevent rape and to respond when it occurs. Those who have been assaulted and the service providers who work with both survivors and perpetrators know, however, that most rapes are committed by someone the survivor knows and trusts.[78] The majority of perpetrators are seemingly "normal," "nice" individuals who hold positions of power and esteem within the community. The rapist is seldom a gnarly stranger hiding in a dark alley, poised and ready to attack—he is someone like Larry Nassar.

As a society, we need to be more informed about the dynamics of sexual violence; after all, the statistics suggest that most people likely know someone who has been affected in one way or another. Turning a blind eye—like the "three wise monkeys," who see no evil, hear no evil, speak no evil—may be convenient and easier than dealing with the uncomfortable truth. Seemingly that is the approach taken by those who deny what is clearly a reality; were that not the case, this book would

---

77. Tara N. Richards, No Evidence of "Weaponized Title IX" Here: An Empirical Assessment of Sexual Misconduct Reporting, Case Processing, and Outcomes, 43 Law & Human Behavior 180, (2019) (quoting Estrich, S. (1987). *Real rape.* Cambridge, MA: Harvard University Press).
78. Nat'l Institute of Justice, "Most Victims Know Their Attacker," (Sept. 20, 2008), https:// nij.ojp.gov/topics/articles/most-victims-know-their-attacker; Lucy Adams, *BBC*, "Sex attack victims usually know attacker, says new study," (1 March, 2018), https://www.bbc.com/news /uk-scotland-43128350.

be moot. Needless to say, the impact on the survivors is terrible and overwhelming.

Unlike the general populace, however, administrators and employees at universities such as Michigan State are *required* by federal law to be informed about the dynamics of sexual violence and to act on behalf of survivors. That is an essential aspect of their mandate. This is not an option; rather, university officials must recognize this as their primary responsibility.

It is, therefore, all the more heinous that Lou Anna Simon, then-president of Michigan State University, claimed to the university's Board of Trustees that "it is virtually impossible to stop a determined sexual predator and pedophile, that they will go to incomprehensible lengths to keep what they do in the shadows."[79] Simon's glib words are, at best, a cop out. They show her to be self-serving, self-pitying, and utterly dismissive of the pain of those assaulted.

It is impossible to understand then-president Simon's comments to the Board of Trustees without resorting to cynicism. Why she was not fired on the spot is an open question. Perhaps her words made the trustees feel better about the university's consistent failure to address a significant issue; they made it seem understandable that sexual predators were largely unhindered at Michigan State. One wants to shake Lou Anna Simon and confront her with her message as it is heard by the survivors: We [the institution] are helpless in the face of a determined and privileged assailant, and you [the survivor] just need to understand that. Don't expect us to help you; we have a more important consideration— the good name of MSU.

Had Michigan State University been as vigilant in protecting the survivor as in protecting itself, then perhaps Bailey Kowalski would not have been the profoundly "at risk" college student she was on the night three basketball players allegedly raped her. Moreover, Bailey, like many of the other survivors described in this book, had to deal with the additional challenge of not being believed. Many of those who came forward to report being sexually assaulted or raped were dismissed because the

79. Addy Baird, Think Progress, "Lou Anna Simon to remain MSU president amid uproar over Larry Nassar sex abuse," (Jan 19, 2018, 4:11PM), https://thinkprogress.org/simon-msu -larry-nassar-5d10971c22a4/.

alleged events were so hard to imagine: how could they have been hurt by people so hard to dislike?

Michigan State University is a case in point, but sexual assault and rape are widespread at universities. Similarly, the enabling of such violence is widespread and has catastrophic consequences. With that knowledge, and with the understanding that we cannot allow things to continue as they currently are, we turn our attention to Title IX. We do so with the explicit purpose of suggesting a path forward to address what is truly an epidemic harming vulnerable young people, whose protection must be understood as the primary obligation of those in authority. Not to do so would be to continue a pattern that can only be defined as, "same old, same old." The only problem, as we have come to learn, is that the pattern continues, largely unabated with minimal—at best—consequences incurred by those empowered to act.

Lou Anna Simon's words, seemingly left unchallenged by the Board of Trustees of a major American university, speak loudly in what they convey: there was nothing we could do. Truly. Were we to accept her self-justification, her thoroughly unacceptable rationalization for her failure to act on behalf of survivors then, indeed, we would raise our arms in defeat, enhancing the abandonment of those who truly suffered. That, however, is a road that we must not travel; doing so would only guarantee that the next Lindsey Lemke, the next Tiffany Thomas-Lopez, the next Peter Pollard, the next Sarah Shiley is just around the corner awaiting the combustible confluence of predator and enabler, who together ensure the continued pain of the survivor. With that, we turn to Title IX with two purposes: to explain its history and to recommend it as a means of punishing those who have so clearly failed.

Title IX

Title IX is a U.S. federal civil rights law enacted as part of the Education Amendments of in 1972.[80] Although the Civil Rights Act of 1964 was intended to end discrimination based on race, color, religion, sex, and

---

80. 20 U.S.C. § 1681(a).

national origin in many spheres, it did not directly address discrimination in federally funded private and public entities, such as schools.[81] Accordingly, Title IX was passed to eliminate "the continuation of corrosive and unjustified discrimination against women in the American educational system."[82] It states:

> No person in the United States shall, on the basis of sex, be excluded from participation in, be denied the benefits of, or be subjected to discrimination under any education program or activity receiving Federal financial assistance.[83]

These 37 words pertaining to gender- and sex-based discrimination in federally funded educational settings have been at issue in thousands of civil cases since they were passed. Understandably so. Title IX applies to any educational institution—college, university, high school, middle school, elementary school, or preschool—that receives funding from the federal government under the statute.[84] Currently, there are over 4,200 postsecondary educational institutions in the United States,[85] attended by roughly 19.9 million students.[86] In addition, there are 50.8 million public school students in pre-kindergarten through grade 12 in the United States,[87] and that number is expected to keep growing.[88]

---

81. § 703(a)(1), Civil Rights Act of 1964, Pub. L. No. 88-352, 78 Stat. 241, 255 (July 2, 1964).
82. 118 Cong. Rec. 5803 (1972).
83. 20 U.S.C. § 1681(a).
84. *Haffer v. Temple*, 688 F.2d 14, 17 (3d Cir. 1982) (finding "'education program or activity receiving Federal financial assistance' as used in Section 901 of [Title IX] includes programs or activities, such as Temple University's intercollegiate athletic program, which do not themselves receive earmarked Federal financial assistance, if such programs or activities benefit from the receipt of Federal financial assistance by other parts of the University and/or by students enrolled at the University"); *National Collegiate Athletic Association v. Smith*, 525 U.S. 459, 468 (1999) (finding "that Title IX coverage is not triggered when an entity merely benefits from federal funding. . . . Entities that receive federal assistance, whether directly or through an intermediary, are recipients within the meaning of Title IX; entities that only benefit economically from federal assistance are not").
85. John Moody, "A Guide to the Changing Number of U.S. Universities," U.S. News, February 15, 2019, https://www.usnews.com/education/best-colleges/articles/2019-02-15/how-many-universities-are-in-the-us-and-why-that-number-is-changing; Merle H. Weiner, A Principled and Legal Approach to Title IX Reporting, 85 TENN. L. REV. 71, 133 (2017) (stating that the United States has over 5,300 institutions of higher education).
86. National Center for Education Statistics, (last checked 2/15/2020), https://nces.ed.gov/fastFacts/display.asp?id=372#College_enrollment.
87. *Id.*
88. *Id.*

Title IX thus affects a considerable portion of the U.S. population.[89] Its importance cannot be overemphasized, especially as students are recognized as a vulnerable population.[90] The protections offered—at least, on paper—by Title IX to survivors of rapes and sexual assaults are particularly crucial at their greatest hour of need. It is for that reason that the failure of university presidents to recognize the harsh realities faced by women and men alike on U.S. campuses is so disconcerting.

Scope of Title IX

The range, and reach, of the statute is remarkably broad. In addition to the sexual assaults and rapes on university campuses that garner so much media attention, Title IX also covers university admissions processes,[91] university and high school athletic programs,[92] grooming codes,[93] fraternities and sororities,[94] educational programs in prisons,[95] and educational employment,[96] among other issues.[97] It also has bearing on a

---

89. Granted, not all of these schools are subject to Title IX, since not all schools choose to receive assistance through federal funding. However, tens of millions of students throughout the country are still directly affected by Title IX, especially since Title IX applies to schools benefiting from federal funding in indirect ways, such as though students who receive financial aid (which includes most universities). *See, e.g., Grove City Coll. V. Bell*, 687 F.2d 684, 693 (3d Cir. 1982).

90. The Supreme Court has pointed out that teachers and school authorities have had an *in loco patentis* role over their students since the time of Blackstone in 1769. *See Vernonia Sch. Dist. 47 J v. Acton*, 515 U.S. 646, 654–55 (1995).

91. *See* Tingley-Kelley v. Trustees of University of Pennsylvania, 677 F.Supp.2d 764 (E.D.Pa. 2010).

92. *See* National Collegiate Athletic Association v. Smith, 525 U.S. 459 (1999).

93. *See* Hayden ex rel. A.H. v. Greensburg Community School Corp., 743 F.3d 569 (Ind. CA 2014).

94. *See* Chi Iota Colony of Alpha Epsilon PI Fraternity v. City University of New York, 443 F.Supp.2d 374 (E.D.N.Y. 2006) vacated 502 F.3d 136.

95. *See* Roubideaux v. North Dakota Dept. of Corrections and Rehabilitation, 570 F.3d 966 (N.D. 2009).

96. *See* North Haven Bd. of Ed. v. Bell, 456 U.S. 512 (1982).

97. The average student in kindergarten through grade 12 in the United States will spend 180 days a year in school and roughly 1,000 hours per year at school. *See* "Average length of school year and average length of school day, by selected characteristics: United States, 2003-04," National Center for Education Statistics, (last checked 2/15/2020) https://nces.ed.gov/surveys/pss/tables /table_2004_06.asp; Jennifer Craw, "Statistics of the Month: How Much Time Do Students Spend in School?" National Center on Education and the Economy, February 22, 2019, http:// ncee.org/2018/02/statistic-of-the-month-how-much-time-do-students-spend-in-school/.

medical school's age policies,[98] and whether both male and female high school coaches were equally informed on how to receive funds from groups supporting athletic programs.[99]

The chief purpose of Congress in enacting Title IX was "to avoid use of federal resources to support gender discriminatory practices and provide citizens protection from those practices in educational settings."[100] Broadly speaking, discrimination under the statute includes conduct that denies or limits any student's ability to benefit from a school's programs or activities on the basis of that student's sex.[101] The critical question is whether university administrators honor its intent by establishing guidelines and protocols intended to facilitate its implementation. The question is not asked in the abstract; failure to do so has clear consequences and therefore the requirement to establish and implement protocols is paramount.

A survivor of sexual assault or rape has several courses of action under Title IX. He or she may file a Title IX complaint with their school or file a lawsuit in court based on Title IX violations. In the former instance, the intent is to get the university to administratively enforce the survivor's rights not to be denied the benefits of education under Title IX.[102] In the latter, the lawsuit is intended to remedy having been "excluded from participation in, . . . denied the benefits of, or [having] be[en] subjected to discrimination under any education program or activity receiving Federal financial assistance."[103]

---

98. *See* Cannon v. University of Chicago, 648 F.2d 1104 (Ill. 1981).

99. Ollier v. Sweetwater Union High School District, 858 F.Supp.2d 1093 (S.D. Cal. 2012).

100. *See* Cannon v. University of Chicago, 441 U.S. 677, 704 (1979); Gebser v. Lago Vista Independent School Dist., 524 U.S. 274, 286 (1998).

101. *See* 34 C.F.R. § 106.31(a) (2011); Office for Civil Rights, U.S. Dep't of Educ, Revised Sexual Harassment Guidance: Harassment of Students by School Employees, Other Students, or Third Parties (2001) at 4.

102. *See generally* "Title IX and Sexual Harassment: Private Rights of Action, Administrative Enforcement, and Proposed Regulations," EveryCRSReport.com, (Apr. 12, 2019), https://www.everycrsreport.com/reports/R45685.html.

103. 20 U.S.C. § 1681(a).

Universities under Title IX offer various recourses and accommodations to survivors of sexual assault. Some of these resources and accommodations include the following:[104]

Implementation of an Interim "No Contact Order"	Assistance with connecting to the University's Safe Rider program
Change in University-related work schedules or job assignments	Access to academic support services
Change in University-owned housing	Rescheduling of exams and assignments
Assistance from University staff in completing housing relocation	Availability of alternative course completion option, including, but not limited to the opportunity to change class schedules by transferring course sections or withdrawing without penalty
Assistance in addressing off-campus living arrangements	Voluntary leave of absence
Restricting a student's access to certain University facilities or activities pending resolution of the matter	Assistance with contacting the appropriate police department
Access to counseling services, including assistance in arranging an initial appointment, on/or off campus	Access to and assistance with connecting to pastoral care and support through the University's Chaplain Office
Access to and assistance with obtaining necessary medical services	Assistance in contacting community resources, such as Pittsburgh Action Against Rape, or other support services
Assistance in contacting legal resources such as County Bar Association Legal Referral, or other legal support	Guidance and support with filing a report through the University's disciplinary system, and Title IX Office and/or through the criminal justice process

The following are examples of the reporting processes for sexual assault
at a range of institutions:[105]

---

104. Katie Pope, Title IX Accommodations and Interim Measures, https://www.titleix.pitt
.edu/sites/default/files/Understanding%20Title%20IX%20Accommodations%20and%20
Interim%20Measures.pdf.
105. See also, e.g., "Sex- and Gender-based Misconduct Response and Prevention," Ohio State
University, (last checked Mar. 8, 2020), https://titleix.osu.edu/navigation/report-incident/report

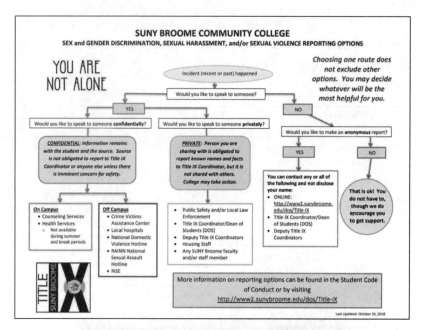

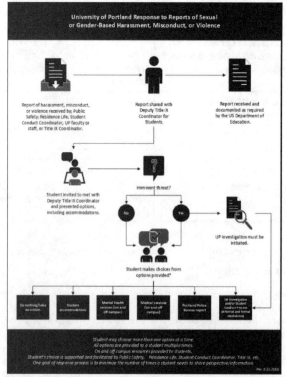

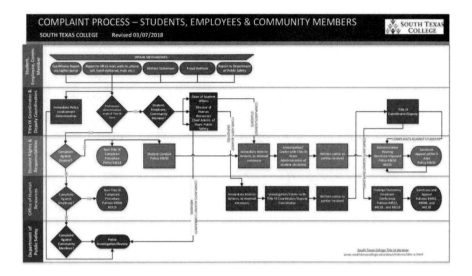

As discussed ahead, the implementation of Title IX at universities is rife with problems, particularly in regard to sexual harassment and how it is enabled. In part, this is due to the language of the text of Title IX. Title IX itself does not expressly mention within its language the term "sexual harassment."[106] In fact, it took the Supreme Court two decades to find that sexual harassment was included under Title IX. Additionally, Congress and the Supreme Court have been silent about Title IX for decades, even though Title IX cases have greatly increased in recent years.[107] Consequently, many universities have felt that there has been a lack of clear guidance on how to comply with Title IX. That lack of guidance has, as we have seen, enabled universities to minimize their responsibilities and obligations to sexual assault survivors. The lack of clarity has not worked to the advantage of the survivor, quite the opposite. Ambiguity and lack of clear guidance have provided "wiggle room" for too many universities. And the decision to see lack of guidance as wiggle room has made possible the conduct experienced by survivors

-incident.html; "File a report," Michigan State University (last checked Mar. 8, 2020), https://civilrights.msu.edu/file-a-report/index.html.

106. *See* 20 U.S.C. § 1681.

107. *See* Title IX: Tracking Sexual Assault Investigations, (2020), http://projects.chronicle.com/titleix/. *See also* Alia E. Dastagir, It's been two years since the MeToo Movement exploded. Now What?, USA TODAY (Sept. 30, 2019 6:00 AM), https://www.usatoday.com/story/news/nation/2019/09/30/me-too-movement-women-sexualassault-harvey-weinstein-brett-kavanaugh/1966463001.

like Bailey Kowalski. If guidelines, obligations, and responsibilities were firmly in place, then Bailey and other survivors would have likely received protections that they were never offered. The net result of a lack of clarity has been harm to survivors. Universities have a duty to defend their students zealously, regardless of the clarity of language of Title IX. Accordingly, universities should instinctively and automatically extend Title IX protections to survivors. As we know, this if often not the case.

As public consciousness of schools' duty to protect their students from sexual assaults has grown,[108] many advocates of survivors point specifically to Title IX as the source of that obligation. On May 6, 2020, Secretary of Education Betsy DeVos issued the much-awaited Final Title IX Rule.[109] According to the Department of Education:

> This new regulation requires schools to act in meaningful ways to support survivors of sexual misconduct, without sacrificing important safeguards to ensure a fair and transparent process. We can and must continue to fight sexual misconduct in our nation's schools, and this rule makes certain that fight continues.[110]

The Regulations, which are to go into effect on August 14, 2020,[111] were met with immediate criticism.

> "We will fight this rule in court, and we intend to win," said Emily Martin, a vice president at the National Women's Law Center, an advocacy group. She said the core of the challenge would be that the department was "arbitrary and capricious" and in violation of the Administrative Procedure Act, and that the agency has ignored evidence showing that the rules would harm survivors of sexual violence.[112]

---

108. *See* Edward J. Mentell, What to do to Stop Sexual Harassment at School, 51 Educational Leadership 96, 96–97 (1993), https://eric.ed.gov/?id=EJ472618.

109. https://www2.ed.gov/about/offices/list/ocr/docs/titleix-summary.pdf

110. https://www.ed.gov/news/press-releases/secretary-devos-takes-historic-action-strengthen-title-ix-protections-all-students

111. https://www.educationdive.com/news/title-ix-regulations-released/566248/

112. https://lawprofessors.typepad.com/gender_law/2020/05/dept-of-education-announces-new-rules-on-title-ix-for-campus-sexual-assault-requiring-a-more-judicia.html. For additional discussion regarding Title IX, please see "Pepper Hamilton Higher Education 'In Brief' Series, 'Title IX In Limbo: Practical Steps for Summer 2019', June 18, 2019, https://www.pepperlaw.com/events/pepper-hamilton-higher-education-in-brief-series-title-ix-in-limbo-practical-steps-for-summer-2019-2019-06-18/ and https://sports.yahoo.com/new-title-ix-regulations-no-longer

To better understand Title IX, we turn our attention to the legislation's history.

The History of Title IX in Relation to Sexual Harassment and the Proposed Regulations

The relationship between Title IX and sexual harassment has evolved over decades and has been marked by controversy.[113] Its purpose, in the words of its co-author, Senator Birch Bayh (D-Indiana),[114] was to fight "the continuation of corrosive and unjustified discrimination against women in the American educational system."[115] In introducing the bill, Senator Bayh declared:

> The field of education is just one of many areas where differential treatment [between men and women] has been documented but because education provides access to jobs and financial security, discrimination here is doubly destructive for women. Therefore, a strong and comprehensive measure is needed to provide women with solid legal protection from the persistent, pernicious discrimination which is serving to perpetuate second-class citizenship for American women.[116]

In 1975, three years after the adoption of Title IX, the Department of Health, Education and Welfare promulgated regulations under the

---

-require-coaches-to-report-sexual-misconduct-150637906.html?guccounter=2. To view a one page summary of the rule, see "U.S. Department of Education Proposed Title IX Regulation Fact Sheet," https://www2.ed.gov/about/offices/list/ocr/docs/proposed-title-ix-regulation-fact-sheet.pdf; for more general information, see "Secretary DeVos: Proposed Title IX Rule Provies Clairty for Schools, Support for Survivors, and Due Process Rights for All," U.S. Department of Education, November 18, 2018, https://www.ed.gov/news/press-releases/secretary-devos-proposed-title-ix-rule-provides-clarity-schools-support-survivors-and-due-process-rights-all; Sarah Brown and Katherine Mangan, "What You Need to Know About the Proposed Title IX Regulations," The Chronicle of Higher Education, November 16, 2018, https://www.chronicle.com/article/What-You-Need-to-Know-About/245118.

113. See, e.g., R. Shep Melnick, "The Strange Evolution of Title IX," National Affairs, 2018, https://www.nationalaffairs.com/publications/detail/the-strange-evolution-of-title-ix.

114. https://www.politico.com/story/2019/03/14/birch-bayh-indiana-senate-239688.

115. 118 Cong. Rec. 5803 (1972).

116. Id. at 5806-07.

statute.[117] These regulations required institutions that received Title IX funding to have a Title IX coordinator, to create and make available policies for nondiscrimination based on sex, and adopt and publish grievance procedures for individuals wishing to file a complaint alleging a Title IX violation.[118] However, these regulations did not directly address sexual harassment.[119]

In 1979, the U.S. Supreme Court found that, although Title IX did not provide a cause of action for monetary damages, it had an implied cause of action.[120]

It was not until the 1990s that the U.S. Supreme Court recognized sexual harassment as a form of gender discrimination that deprives an individual of their right to equal access to education under Title IX. In 1992, the Court held in *Franklin v. Gwinnett Cty. Pub. Sch.*[121] that money damages were available for private actions under Title IX based on sexual harassment and abuse by a high school coach/teacher against a student. As a consequence of *Franklin*, courts began to confirm other ways that sexual harassment could violate Title IX.[122]

Six years later, in *Gebser v. Lago Vista Ind. Sch. Dist.*,[123] the U.S. Supreme Court determined the standard for liability under Title IX, ruling that money damages are not recoverable "unless an official of the school district who at a minimum has authority to institute corrective measures on the district's behalf has actual notice of, and is deliberately indifferent to, the teacher's misconduct."[124] Finally, in *Davis v. Monroe*

117. 34 CFR § 106.1 *et seq.*
118. Nondiscrimination on the Basis of Sex in Education Programs or Activities Receiving Federal Financial Assistance, 83 FR 61462-01, 61463; 34 CFR § 106.1 *et seq.*
119. 34 CFR § 106.1 *et seq.*
120. *Cannon v. Univ. of Chicago*, 441 U.S. 677, 717 (1979) (finding that because Title IX was modeled after Title VI which provides a cause of action, Title IX did as well since it was "not inconsistent with an intent on its part to have such a remedy available to the persons benefited by its legislation").
121. 503 U.S. 60 (1992).
122. *See, e.g.,* Doe By & Through Doe v. Petaluma City Sch. Dist., 830 F. Supp. 1560, 1576 (N.D. Cal. 1993); Morse v. Regents of University of Colorado, 154 F.3d 1124, (10th Cir. 1998); Bosley v. Kearney R-1 Sch. Dist., 904 F. Supp. 1006, 1025 (W.D. Mo. 1995), aff'd, 140 F.3d 776 (8th Cir. 1998); *Franks v. Ky. Sch. for the Deaf,* 956 F.Supp. 741 (E.D. Ky. 1996), aff'd, 142 F.3d 360 (6th Cir. 1998).
123. 524 U.S. 274, 277 (1998).
124. *Id.*

County Bd. of Educ.,[125] the U.S. Supreme Court held that schools themselves are liable for student-on-student harassment.[126] Specifically, the Court held:

> Damages are not available for simple acts of teasing and name-calling among school children . . . even where these comments target differences in gender. Rather, in the context of student-on-student harassment, damages are only available where the behavior is so severe, pervasive, and objectively offensive that it denies victims the equal access to education that Title IX is designed to protect.[127]

The Court noted that the "deliberate indifference" standard in *Gebser* "makes sense as a theory of direct liability under Title IX only where the funding recipient has some control over the alleged harassment."[128] The Court reasoned that a recipient of Title IX funds "cannot be directly liable for its indifference where it lacks the authority to take remedial action."[129] Accordingly:

> recipient's damages liability [under Title IX is restricted] to circumstances wherein the recipient exercises substantial control over both the harasser and the context in which the known harassment occurs. Only then can the recipient be said to "expose" its students to harassment or "cause" them to undergo it "under" the recipient's programs.[130]

It is important to note that these cases address the issue of when a recipient of Title IX funds has violated the statute. In *Gebser*, the U.S. Supreme Court noted that Title IX was "designed primarily to prevent recipients of federal funding assistance from using the funds in a discriminatory manner."[131]

---

125. 526 U.S. 629 (1999)
126. *Davis,* 526 U.S. at 652.
127. *Id.*
128. *Id.* at 644.
129. *Id.*
130. *Id.* at 645.
131. *Gebser,* 524 U.S. at 292.

Franklin, Gebser, and *Davis* require a survivor to allege the following in order to bring a claim of Title IX violation against the university they attend:

1. That the university is a recipient of Title IX funds;
2. That the university had actual knowledge of the sexual harassment;
3. Which was so severe, pervasive, and objectively offensive;
4. To which the university exhibited deliberate indifference; and
5. That the victim was effectively barred from access to an educational opportunity or benefit as a result of the sexual harassment.[132]

These three cases represent the U.S. Supreme Court's guidance concerning Title IX and sexual harassment.[133] *Davis* reflects the last case in which the Court addressed the standard of liability for sexual harassment under Title IX. Consequently, during the past two decades, lower courts have been left to apply *Davis* to numerous fact patterns that none of *Davis, Franklin, Gebser,* and Title IX themselves address.

Since *Davis,* the U.S. Department of Education's Office for Civil Rights (OCR) has been the clearest guide for universities on how to comply with Title IX. The OCR was created by the Department of Education Organization Act of 1979[134] in order to investigate alleged violations of Title VI of the Civil Rights Act of 1964.[135] Its stated purpose was to "ensure equal access to education and to promote educational excellence throughout the nation through vigorous enforcement of civil rights."[136] Eventually, the OCR's duties grew to include ensuring that

---

132. Corey Rayburn Yung, *Is Relying on Title IX a Mistake,* 64 U. KAN. L. REV. 891, 896 (2016). *See also K.T. v. Culver-Stockton Coll.,* 865 F.3d 1054, 1057 (8th Cir. 2017) (stating "[w]here a plaintiff's Title IX claim is based on harassment, the school is liable in damages only where it is '(1) deliberately indifferent (2) to known acts of discrimination (3) which occur under its control'" (quoting *Ostrander v. Duggan,* 341 F.3d 745, 750 (8th Cir. 2003))).
133. To be clear, the Supreme Court also addressed Title IX again in *Jackson v. Birmingham Bd. of Educ.,* 544 U.S. 167 (2005), where it held that retaliation against a person for complaining about sexual discrimination is also a form of intentional sex discrimination within the meaning of Title IX. However, this case is not directly on point with this discussion.
134. Pub. L. 96-88.
135. Department of Education. Office of Civil Rights. (5/4/1980–) Organization Authority Record, https://catalog.archives.gov/id/10518452.
136. *Id.*

schools receiving Title IX funding were in compliance with Title IX; one means of doing so was by issuing guidance letters.[137]

Although the OCR issued "Dear Colleague" letters to schools addressing how to comply with Title IX prior to the U.S. Supreme Court cases of the 1990s, it began to do so more regularly after *Gebser* and *Davis*.[138] Both in 1997 and again in 2001, the OCR expressly informed all schools receiving Title IX funding that they must respond to sexual assault within their schools.[139]

In 2011, the Obama administration, through the OCR, released what subsequently came to be known as the first Obama-era Dear Colleague letter. The letter specified how schools were to comply with Title IX on matters of sexual harassment and violence and provided examples of a school's responsibilities. Notably, the 2011 Dear Colleague letter provided a broad definition of what constitutes sexual harassment:

> Sexual harassment is unwelcome conduct of a sexual nature. It includes unwelcome sexual advances, requests for sexual favors, and other verbal, nonverbal, or physical conduct of a sexual nature. Sexual violence is a form of sexual harassment prohibited by Title IX.[140]

The letter also commented on the scope and jurisdiction of Title IX, who may file a Title IX complaint, and the consequences for a school if it failed to comply with Title IX:

> Title IX protects students from sexual harassment in a school's education programs and activities. This means that Title IX protects students in connection with all the academic, educational, extracurricular, athletic, and other programs of the school, whether those programs take place in a school's facilities, on a school bus, at

---

137. To view various letters and publications issued out by the OCR, *see* U.S. Department of Education, "Reading Room," (March 3, 2020). https://www2.ed.gov/about/offices/list/ocr/front page/faq/readingroom.html.

138. Sex Discrimination: Policy Guidance; *see* https://www2.ed.gov/about/offices/list/ocr/front page/faq/rr/policyguidance/sex.html.

139. Office for Civil Rights, Revised Sexual Harassment Guidance, Dept. of Educ. 2, 6 (Jan. 19, 2001), https://www.ed.gov/about/offices/list/ocr/ docs/shguide.pdf.

140. *Dear Colleague Letter (Sexual Violence Letter)* April 4, 2011. Available at: https://www .ed.gov/about/offices/list/ocr/letters/colleague-201104.html.

a class or training program sponsored by the school at another location, or elsewhere. For example, Title IX protects a student who is sexually assaulted by a fellow student during a school-sponsored field trip.

. . .

Regardless of whether a harassed student, his or her parent, or a third party files a complaint under the school's grievance procedures or otherwise requests action on the student's behalf, a school that knows, or reasonably should know, about possible harassment must promptly investigate to determine what occurred and then take appropriate steps to resolve the situation.

. . .

When a recipient [of Title IX funding] does not come into compliance voluntarily, [the OCR] may initiate proceedings to withdraw Federal funding by the Department or refer the case to the U.S. Department of Justice for litigation.[141]

Although the Dear Colleague letter was not a legally binding document, universities worked quickly to follow its guidance.[142] In part, this was because the OCR increased its investigation of universities for Title IX compliance and publicly posted a list of schools under investigation for noncompliance.[143]

The Obama Dear Colleague letters coincided with a dramatic rise in Title IX litigation throughout the country;[144] the number of cases brought is higher than before the letter was issued.[145] The climate changed sharply in September 2017, however, when U.S. Secretary of Education Betsy Devos withdrew the Obama-era Dear Colleague

---

141. *Id.*

142. *See* Naomi M. Mann, *Taming Title IX Tensions*, 20 U. Pa. J. Const. L. 631 (2018).

143. *Id.* at 643 (stating "[b]etween 2011 and 2016, OCR dramatically increased the number of schools that it proactively investigated for Title IX compliance, and broke with prior practice by publicly listing the names of schools under investigation.").

144. *See* Title IX: Tracking Sexual Assault Investigations, (2020) http://projects.chronicle .com/titleix/; Deb Muller, Title IX and the Growing Wave of Litigation on American Campuses, HRACUITY, November 25, 2014, https://www.hracuity.com/blog/title-ix-growing-wave -litigation-american-campuses.

145. Title IX: Tracking Sexual Assault Investigations, (2020) http://projects.chronicle.com /titleix/.

letters.[146] One reason the Department of Education gave for the withdrawal of the Obama-era guidance was that

> current regulations and guidance do not provide appropriate standards for how recipients must respond to incidents of sexual harassment. To address this concern, we propose regulations addressing sexual harassment under Title IX to better align the Department's regulations with the text and purpose of Title IX and Supreme Court precedent and other case law.[147]

Secretary DeVos also stated that "instead of working with schools on behalf of students, the prior administration weaponized the Office for Civil Rights to work against schools and against students."[148] In November 2018, DeVos released the department's proposed Title IX regulations for public comment. In response, over 100,000 comments were received.[149] The Department of Education claims that the proposed regulations:

---

146. Dear Colleague Letter on Campus Sexual Misconduct, September 22, 2017, https://www2
.ed.gov/about/offices/list/ocr/letters/colleague-title-ix-201709.pdf. *See also* Valerie Strauss, "DeVos
withdraws Obama-era guidance on campus sexual assault. Read the Letter," the Washington
Post, September 22, 2017, https://www.washingtonpost.com/news/answer-sheet/wp/2017/09/22
/devos-withdraws-obama-era-guidance-on-campus-sexual-assault-read-the-letter/; Jeannie Suk
Gersen, *Assessing Betsy Devos's Proposed Rules On Title IX and Sexual Assault"* The New Yorker,
Feb. 1 2019; https://www.newyorker.com/news/our-columnists/assessing-betsy-devos-proposed
-rules-on-title-ix-and-sexual-assault (stating "[u]nder Betsy DeVos, the Department of Education
has rescinded more than twenty Obama-era policy guidelines on anti-discrimination laws").
147. Nondiscrimination on the Basis of Sex in Education Programs or Activities Receiving Federal Financial Assistance, 83 FR 61462; *see also* Jeannie Suk Gersen, *Assessing Betsy Devos's Proposed
Rules On Title IX and Sexual Assault"* The New Yorker, Feb. 1 2019; https://www.newyorker.com
/news/our-columnists/assessing-betsy-devos-proposed-rules-on-title-ix-and-sexual-assault (stating that "Universities reacted with panicked overcompliance" in response to the Dear Colleague
letter and that "in recent years, it has become commonplace to deny accused students access to
the complaint, the evidence, the identities of witnesses, or the investigative report, and to forbid
them from questions complainants or witnesses").
148. Kreighbaum, A. (2017, September, 8). DeVos to replace Obama-era sexual assault guidelines. Inside Higher Ed. Retrieved from https://www.insidehighered.com/news/2017/09/08
/devos-says-federal-title-ix-guidelines-have-'failed'-will-seekpublic-input-new; *but cf with* Tara
N. Richards, No Evidence of "Weaponized Title IX" Here: An Empirical Assessment of Sexual
Misconduct Reporting, Case Processing, and Outcomes, 43 Law & Human Behavior 180, (2019)
(discussing the lack of information regarding investigations and adjudication of Title IX cases,
thus calling into question DeVos' argument about weaponization of Title IX).
149. Tovia Smith, Trump Administration Gets An Earful On New Campus Sexual Assault
Rules, NPR, January 30, 2019, https://www.npr.org/2019/01/30/689879689/education-depart
ment-gathers-feedback-on-new-campus-sexual-assault-rules; Simone C. Chu and Iris M. Lewis,

would clarify and modify Title IX regulatory requirements pertaining to the availability of remedies for violations, the effect of Constitutional protections, the designation of a coordinator to address sex discrimination issues, the dissemination of a nondiscrimination policy, the adoption of grievance procedures, and the process to claim a religious exemption.[150]

According to the Department of Education, the proposed regulations reflect adoption of the U.S. Supreme Court Standards for Sexual Harassment.[151] Additionally, the proposed regulations provide numerous modifications to, and clarifications of how Title IX should be followed by schools.[152] One proposed regulation, 34 CFR § 106.44(a), would cover the response of a school that receives Title IX funding ("recipient") to sexual harassment.[153] It would state

that a recipient with actual knowledge of sexual harassment in an educational program or activity of the recipient against a person in the United States must respond in a manner that is not deliberately indifferent.[154]

Proposed 34 CFR § 106.44(a) would further state that "a recipient is deliberately indifferent only if its response to sexual harassment is clearly unreasonable in light of the known circumstances."[155] Under a companion proposed regulation, 34 CFR § 106.30, the Department of Education would provide definitions for both "sexual harassment" and "actual knowledge."[156] "Sexual harassment" would be defined as:

"What Happens Next With Title IX: DeVos's Proposed Rule, Explained," (Feb. 27, 2019), https://www.thecrimson.com/article/2019/2/27/title-ix-explainer/.
150. Nondiscrimination on the Basis of Sex in Education Programs or Activities Receiving Federal Financial Assistance, 83 FR 61462-01.
151. *Id.* at 61466.
152. For a simplified overview, see "U.S. Department of Education Proposed title IX Regulation Fact Sheet," https://www2.ed.gov/about/offices/list/ocr/docs/proposed-title-ix-regulation-fact-sheet.pdf.
153. Nondiscrimination on the Basis of Sex in Education Programs or Activities Receiving Federal Financial Assistance, 83 FR 61462-01.
154. *Id.*
155. *Id.*
156. *Id.*

either an employee of the recipient conditioning the provision of an aid, benefit, or service of the recipient on an individual's participation in unwelcome sexual conduct; or unwelcome conduct on the basis of sex that is so severe, pervasive, and objectively offensive that it effectively denies a person equal access to the recipient's education program or activity; or sexual assault as defined in 34 CFR 668.46(a), implementing the Jeanne Clery Disclosure of Campus Security Policy and Campus Crime Statistics Act (Clery Act).[157]

"Actual knowledge" would be defined to mean that a school is not in violation Title IX compliance unless there has been

notice of sexual harassment or allegations of sexual harassment to a recipient's Title IX Coordinator or *any official of the recipient who has authority to institute corrective measures on behalf of the recipient*, or to a teacher in the elementary and secondary context with regard to student-on-student harassment.[158]

The definition would further specify that

the imputation of knowledge based solely on respondeat superior or constructive notice is insufficient to constitute actual knowledge, that the standard is not met when the only official of the recipient with actual knowledge is also the respondent, and that the mere ability or obligation to report sexual harassment does not qualify an employee, even if that employee is an official, as one who has authority to institute corrective measures on behalf of the recipient.[159]

Another significant change between Obama-era Dear Colleague letters and the proposed regulations is that a university would be responsible for responding only to conduct that occurred within its "education program or activit[ies]."[160] On its face, this appears fair and broad: if alleged sexual harassment or misconduct occurs beyond a school's grounds or "any academic, extracurricular, research, occupational training, or other

---

157. *Id.* (emphasis added).
158. *Id.* (emphasis added)
159. *Id.* at 61496.
160. *Id.* at 61497.

education program or activity operated by a [school] which receives Federal financial assistance,"[161] it seems justifiable, at least at first blush, that a school need not respond. That, needless to say, is a proposal that is highly problematic given the realities of college life. Limiting Title IX's reach, which this proposal would achieve, leaves unprotected a broad swath of survivors and inherently favors institutions by narrowing the scope of their responsibility. That seems at odds with an institutions' primary obligation to protect members of its community; the proposal ostensibly creates a "loophole", whereby institutional liability is curtailed. The voices of the survivors should make clear just how problematic the proposal is.

After all, sexual harassment often takes place in off-campus student housing. Under the proposed 34 CFR § 104.44(a), a school would likely not be required to investigate allegations arising from events in such localities.[162] Bailey Kowalski's case, for example, would probably not fall within the scope of these regulations, since the alleged rapes took place at an off-campus apartment and not at an "education program or activity" as defined in 34 C.F.R. § 106.31(a) of the proposal. Such a limitation, were it to be promulgated, would reinforce—whether deliberately or not is irrelevant—the perception among survivors that protections that should otherwise be extended to them are limited in scope, enhancing the ability of institutions to avoid responsibility and liability. This harkens back to the words of Lou Anna Simon, which should be discounted at all costs, for they reinforce dismissiveness of the survivor and protection of the institution.

Admittedly, the proposed regulations constitute guidance for universities and do not purport to be the new legal criteria for bringing a Title IX violation to court. Historically, courts have not relied on OCR

---

161. 34 C.F.R. § 106.31(a) (West 2019).
162. *But see* Nondiscrimination on the Basis of Sex in Education Programs or Activities Receiving Federal Financial Assistance, 83 FR 61462, at 61468 (stating "[i]mportantly, nothing in the proposed regulations would prevent a recipient from initiating a student conduct proceeding or offering supportive measures to students who report sexual harassment that occurs outside the recipient's education program or activity"). *Compare with id.* (stating that "there may be circumstances where the harassment occurs in a recipient's program or activity, but the recipient's response obligation is not triggered because the complainant was not participating in, or even attempting to participate in, the education programs or activities provided by that recipient").

guidelines for determining violations of Title IX, since "the guidance provided by the [OCR] is obviously broader than the scope of liability for private causes of action for money damages under Title IX."[163] However, the importance of the proposed regulations must not be minimized.

In withdrawing the Obama-era Dear Colleague letters, Secretary DeVos stated that the 2001 OCR standards for Title IX should be considered the relevant guidance standard until new regulations take force. These 2001 standards distinguish themselves "from the standards applicable to private litigation for money damages."[164] Courts, including the U.S. Supreme Court, have concurred:

> We have never held . . . that the implied private right of action under Title IX allows recovery in damages for violation of those sorts of administrative requirements.[165]
>
> [T]he Supreme Court has cautioned that "alleged failure to comply with the [Title IX] regulations" does not establish actual notice and deliberate indifference and it has never held that "the implied private right of action under Title IX allows recovery in damages for violation of [such] administrative requirements."[166]
>
> The only relevant inquiry when a plaintiff seeks retroactive damages against a Title IX funding recipient is whether the recipient demonstrated deliberate indifference to known instances of sexual harassment.[167]

While courts have found that a private cause of action exists under Title IX,[168] it is fairly settled that OCR guidance is not determinative

---

163. Karasek v. Regents of the University of California, 2015 WL 8527338 at *13 (N.D. Cal. Dec. 11, 2015) (noting further that neither the plaintiff or court could find "any case in which a plaintiff has successfully relied on the DCL to establish deliberate indifference under Title IX")

164. Office of Civil Rights, Revised Sexual Harassment Guidance (2001), https://www2.ed.gov /about/offices/list/ocr/docs/shguide.pdf [PERMA].

165. *Gebser*, 524 U.S. at 291–92 (citations omitted).

166. Roe v. St. Louis University, 746 F.3d 874, 783 (8th Cir. 2014) (quoting *Gebser*, 524 U.S. at 291–92).

167. Ramser v. Laielli, 276 F.Supp.3d 978, 993 (S.D. Cal. 2017) (citing *Davis*, 526 U.S. at 643).

168. Cannon v. University of Chicago, 441 U.S. 677, 689–716 (1979) (finding that Title IX provides a private cause of action despite the although it does not expressly authorize it).

of liability under the statute.[169] In part, this reflects the understanding that "[t]he Supreme Court has been careful to limit the remedies available under Title IX because it views the legislation as enacted pursuant to Congress' authority under the Spending Clause."[170] When Title IX was adopted, it was passed through Congress' spending power under the Constitution's Spending Clause.[171] The U.S. Supreme Court has stated that when Congress exercises its spending power, it produces legislation "much in the nature of a contract: in return for federal funds, the States agree to comply with federally imposed conditions."[172] Accordingly, courts have been reluctant to expand remedies available to individuals under the statute beyond the "firm conceptual limitation on the contours of damages liability under Title IX."[173] However, the Office of Civil Rights has not provided any actual regulations since 2001. The Obama-era guidance letters did not have binding legal authority, whereas regulations can have legal effect. Thus, while the proposed regulations will not necessarily affect the legal rights of survivors, they may be more persuasive in compelling schools at a minimum to be in compliance with Title IX on matters of sexual harassment. Moreover, the proposed regulations have significant similarities with the holdings in *Davis, Gebser,* and *Franklin.*

Success on a Title IX claim in court is a high reach. As previously noted, a survivor who attends a Title IX funded school has to show: (1) that their school had actual knowledge of the sexual harassment (2) that it was so severe, pervasive, *and* objectively offensive (3) and to

---

169. *See, e.g.,* Karasek v. Regents of the University of California, 2015 WL 8527338, *13 (N.D. Cal. Dec. 11, 2015) (noting that OCR Dear Colleague letter guidance is broader than the scope of money damages action under Title IX and that neither the plaintiff or court could find "any case in which a plaintiff has successfully relied on the DCL to establish deliberate indifference under Title IX").

170. Mattingly v. University of Louisville, 2006 WL 2178032, *1 (W.D. Ky. 2006). *See also* Davis v. Monroe Cty. Bd. of Educ., 526 U.S. 629, 640 (1999) (stating that Title IX is "legislation enacted pursuant to Congress' authority under the Spending Clause").

171. United States v. Butler, 297 U.S. 1 (1936) (stating that Congress under Const. Art. 1, S 8, cl. 1 must use its power to tax and spend for the "general welfare" which in turn limits causes of action provided through the spending clause).

172. Pennhurst State Sch. & Hosp v. Halderman, 451 U.S. 1, 17 (1981).

173. Mattingly v. University of Louisville, 2006 WL 2178032, *1 (W.D. Ky. 2006).

which the school exhibited deliberate indifference, (4) that the survivor was effectively denied access to an educational opportunity because of the sexual harassment.[174] All these elements must be proven by a survivor.[175] And proving even just one of these points is a tall order.

Consider element two. Assume that a survivor is bringing a case similar to that of Bailey Kowalski, involving a single instance of sexual assault, such as rape, in which the alleged perpetrator is a peer.[176] Under U.S. Supreme Court case law, a court would need to consider whether that single instance of rape is so "severe, pervasive, and objectively offensive" that it can be said to have a "systemic effect."

A single instance of severe one-on-one peer harassment could, in theory, be said to have such a systemic effect, but it is unlikely that Congress would have thought so. The fact that it was a teacher who engaged in harassment in *Franklin* and *Gebser* is relevant. Peer harassment is less likely to satisfy the requirements that the misconduct breach Title IX's guarantee of equal access to educational benefits and have a systemic effect on a program or activity.[177]

Instances involving a single instance of sexual assault are also pose difficulties under element one. It is difficult to prove peer-on-peer sexual assault, because universities tend not to have knowledge of sexual violence between peers until after it has occurred.[178] Consequently, cases like Bailey Kowalski's remain challenging for survivors unless they can show "systemic" misconduct.[179]

---

174. Corey Rayburn Yung, *Is Relying on Title IX a Mistake*, 64 U. KAN. L. REV. 891, 896 (2016).
175. *Id.*
176. *See, e.g.*, Kollaritsch v. Michigan State Univ. Bd. of Trustees, 944 F.3d 613, 621-22 (denying a plaintiff's claim that her university violated her Title IX rights when she failed to plead more than one instance of sexual harassment to herself, even though other female students had been sexually harassed by the same individual, "[b]ecause the further harassment must be inflicted against the same victim, [and] the plaintiff cannot . . . premise the further harassment element of her Title IX claim on conduct by the perpetrator directed at third parties" (citations omitted)). *See also* David Jesse, "Federal appeals court continues to rewrite rules on campus sex assault investigations," Detroit Free Press, (Mar. 2, 2020), https://www.freep.com/story/news/education/2020/03/02/federal-court-continues-rewrite-rules-sex-assault-investigations/4805676002/.
177. Davis v. Monroe County Board of Education, 526 U.S. 629, 631 (1999).
178. Corey Rayburn Yung, *Is Relying on Title IX a Mistake*, 64 U. KAN. L. REV. 891, 911 (2016).
179. *Davis*, 526 U.S. at 631.

In this light, it is significant that the proposed regulations adopt the "severe, pervasive, and objectively offensive" element. This phrase is inadequate to address the true spectrum of sexual assault under Title IX because its coverage is so narrow that it essentially leaves out large swaths of conduct that could deny students their education rights. For example, repeated, unwelcomed, innuendo-laced comments about a student's appearance may be described as pervasive, but courts and schools would be less inclined to find that such conduct is troublesome under Title IX since it might be considered less severe or offensive than, for example, rape. Conversely, the rape of a student is objectively offensive and severe, but courts have often found that single instances of sexual assault, especially peer on peer, do not satisfy pervasiveness. By adopting the "severe, pervasive, and objectively offensive" language, the proposed regulations define sexual harassment in a way that will still permit some sexual harassment and assault. The proposed regulations should have instead adopted a phrase that more accurately encompasses behavior that may deny a student or survivor's ability to gain an education free of sexual harassment and assault.

The proposed regulations create further problems. For instance, it is not clear who exactly can receive notice that could satisfy the "actual knowledge" element above. The proposed regulations state that actual knowledge would exist only when notice is given to (1) a recipient's Title IX Coordinator or (2) any official of the recipient who has *authority to institute corrective measures on behalf of the recipient*.[180] While it may be clear who is an institution's Title IX coordinator for a school, "officials . . . with authority to institute corrective measures" are less easy to determine. The proposed regulation would place a new burden on survivors to determine whether someone to whom they feel able to report qualifies as such an official. This is a fact-based inquiry that is burdensome to place on a survivor of sexual assault.[181]

---

180. Nondiscrimination on the Basis of Sex in Education Programs or Activities Receiving Federal Financial Assistance, 83 FR 61462-01, 61467 (emphasis added).

181. *See* Doe v. Sch. Bd. of Broward Cty., 604 F.3d 1248, 1256 (11th Cir. 2010) (stating "the ultimate question of who is an appropriate person is 'necessarily a fact-based inquiry' because 'officials' roles vary among school districts.'" (quoting Murrell v. Sch. Dist. No. 1, 186 F.3d 1238, 1247 (10th Cir. 1999)).

The proposed regulations do not clarify the matter when they state:

> the mere ability or obligation to report sexual harassment does not qualify an employee, even if that is an official, as one who has authority to institute corrective measures on behalf of the recipient.[182]

It may not be prudent to designate all faculty and staff as mandatory reporters,[183] but everyone at a university should be responsible for helping to address sexual violence.[184] All employees should provide survivors with information on who is a mandatory reporter at their institution. Yet the proposed regulations do not clearly advocate for this.

Under the Obama-era Dear Colleague letters, schools were more likely to be held accountable by the Office of Civil Rights, given the administration's broad definitions and policies.[185] To the extent that the current administration seeks to withdraw the earlier guidance and replace it with standards that are more difficult for survivors to prove, universities may feel they need to provide even less support to survivors of sexual assault. If so, and universities slacken in complying with Title IX, survivors will find themselves in an even more hostile environment.

---

182. 83 FR 61462-01 at 61496. Furthermore, the Department of Education cites at 61467 to the following as justification for this standard: Plamp v. Mitchell Sch. Dist. No. 17-2, 565 F.3d 450, 459 (8th Cir. 2009) ("After all, each teacher, counselor, administrator, and support-staffer in a school building has the authority, if not the duty, to report to the school administration or school board potentially discriminatory conduct. But that authority does not amount to an authority to take a corrective measure or institute remedial action within the meaning of Title IX. Such a holding would run contrary to the purposes of the statute"). *See also* Santiago v. Puerto Rico, 655 F.3d 61, 75 (1st Cir. 2011) ("The empty allegation that a school employee 'failed to report' harassment to someone higher up in the chain of command who could have taken corrective action is not enough to establish institutional liability. Title IX does not sweep so broadly as to permit a suit for harm-inducing conduct that was not brought to the attention of someone with the authority to stop it") (internal citation omitted). *See also Gebser* (providing that an "appropriate person" is "an official who at a minimum has authority to address the alleged discrimination and to institute corrective measures").

183. Resisting State-Level Mandatory Police Referral Efforts, Know Your IX, http://knowy ourix.org/ask-survivors (finding that 88 percent of survivors reported that if universities were "required to turn rape reports over to the police," for instance, "(without the survivors consent), they believe fewer victims would report to anyone at all").

184. Merle H. Weiner, A Principled and Legal Approach to Title IX Reporting, 85 Tenn. L. Rev. 71, 188 (2017).

185. Naomi M. Mann, *Taming Title IX Tensions*, 20 U. Pa. J. Const. L. 631, 643 (2018).

Consequently, universities need to hold themselves to a *higher* standard under Title IX than the current Department of Education would hold them to.

Proposals for Moving Forward

The question is whether the Regulations announced by Secretary DeVos provide adequate protection to the survivors and sufficiently address the murkiness and amorphousness that characterizes implementation of Title IX. Prior to their release, the Department of Education received more than 100,000 comments in response to the Office of Civil Rights' proposed regulations. Whether the Bailey Kowalskis are left without clearly defined protections in the aftermath of a reported sexual assault or rape remains to be seen. Were that to be the case, then the profound concerns repeatedly raised by innumerable survivors would continue to go unaddressed. The immediate alarms raised by advocacy groups, legislators, and others gives serious pause regarding their efficacy from survivor's perspectives.[186]

Over the past year, we have encountered the consequences of the lack of clarity; we have been confronted with the voices of those who sought advice, help, and counsel only to be minimized, if not outright dismissed. That reaction—as deeply problematic as it is—must not be considered as a "one-off," a single incident reflecting the failure of a school official to understand their role and responsibility. We have twice referenced Lou Anna Simon's comments; we do so only because they are so profoundly, and disturbingly, telling. They highlight why the current status of Title IX—at least as implemented in the cases we have examined—in a manner that raises serious concerns regarding whose interests are to be protected.

Bailey's experience in trying to report her assault serves as a damning indictment of Michigan State University and its counseling center. A student who claimed to have been assaulted by three student athletes was, for all intents and purposes, left to fend for herself. As we have seen

---

186. https://www.educationdive.com/news/title-ix-regulations-released/566248/.

throughout this book, this is a familiar pattern. The collective voices of the survivors with whom I have engaged make it very clear that their minimal expectations were not met and thus they felt abandoned. For that reason, it is imperative that two interrelated points are addressed with crystal clarity: From whom should the survivor should seek protection? And, how are the relevant institutions to respond? Expectations must be clearly understood and consequences for failing to provide mandatory support must be punished. There is no alternative; otherwise the responses (such as they are) of today, will be the responses of tomorrow.

Title IX obligations must be both broad and clearly articulated. As has been amply illustrated, the instinctual institutional response is to minimize obligation and narrow the scope of care and duty extended to the survivor. The imposition of minimal standards on institutions will, for all practical purposes, ensure that the consistent failings of the past years will not be perpetuated.

These failures are not, however, limited to the universities where the assaults occurred. There is another institutional layer working against the survivor of sexual assault. Numerous survivors describe their hesitation in filing complaints with the police. As a case in point, a number of years ago, a female student shared with me that she had been raped. When she reported the episode to the local police department, she was left with two overwhelming impressions: it was her fault for putting herself in a bad situation, and the police had no intention of following up on her complaint.

The statistics underscore this troubling reality. Approximately, 3 out of 4 rapes are not reported to the police.[187] Clearly, therefore, the issue is not confined to reporting per se; we must also address the underlying causes of this failure to report. Out of 1,000 instances of sexual assault, 230 will be reported to police.[188] Of those 230 reported cases, 46 will

187. RAINN, "The Criminal Justice System: Statistics," https://www.rainn.org/statistics/criminal-justice-system (citing Department of Justice, Office of Justice Programs, Bureau of Justice Statistics, National Crime Victimization Survey, 2010-2016 (2017); Federal Bureau of Investigation, National Incident-Based Reporting System, 2012-2016 (2017)).
188. Department of Justice, Office of Justice Programs, Bureau of Justice Statistics, National Crime Victimization Survey, 2010–2016 (2017).

lead to an arrest, of which only nine will be referred to a prosecutor.[189] Also, many individuals, survivors included, do not want to feel "forced to participate in the criminal justice system" or go to trial.[190]

Furthermore, people of color and LGBTQ individuals, who are statistically more likely to be sexually assaulted, are also more likely to mistrust law enforcement.[191] These populations may experience further discrimination within the criminal justice system.[192]

Survivors may prefer to file a civil complaint, since the civil process affords survivors greater control over the case and requires a lower standard of proof than criminal charges brought by the state. Survivors may be consulted in the prosecutor's decision whether to issue charges or whether to offer a plea deal. But it is not the survivor's choice if or how a case is prosecuted once it is reported.

These facts and the seemingly endless anecdotal evidence of interactions between survivors and the police reinforce the survivors' sense of abandonment: door after door is slammed in their faces. The availability of robust Title IX protections is thus even more critical. That goal seems a long way off, however, given the present uncertainty about the status of Title IX and the consistently demonstrated determination of universities to under-deliver and under-protect those to whom they owe a duty of care. This is dangerous territory from the survivor's perspective, because guidelines are unclear and consequences and punishment are not being imposed on the institution. It is for that reason that we recommend the following measures, which would significantly enhance protection while ensuring compliance.

---

189. *Id. See also* Decision Making in Sexual Assault Cases: Replication Research on Sexual Violence Case Attrition in the U.S., https://www.ncjrs.gov/pdffiles1/nij/grants/252689.pdf.

190. Resisting State-Level Mandatory Police Referral Efforts, Know Your IX, http://knowyourix.org/ask-survivors (finding through a 2015 survey that 72% of survivors report not wanting to go to trial).

191. *Id.*

192. *See, e.g.,* Tom Caiazza, Center for American Progress, "Broken Criminal Justice System Disproportionately Targets and Harms LGBT People," (Feb. 23, 2016), https://www.americanprogress.org/press/release/2016/02/23/131547/release-broken-criminal-justice-system-disproportionately-targets-and-harms-lgbt-people/; Puzzanchera, C. Sladky, A. and Kang. W. (2017). Easy Access to Juvenile Populations: 1990–2016, OJJDP Statistical Briefing Book; The Sentencing Project, "Report to the United Nations on Racial Disparities in the U.S Criminal Justice System" (April 19, 2018), https://www.sentencingproject.org/publications/un-report-on-racial-disparities/.

In theory, Title IX offers important protections, but students and staff alike are all too frequently unfamiliar with federal protections and university resources, let alone reporting processes. Most troubling, as we have come to learn: it cannot be assumed that universities will prioritize safety over profit. To that end, the measures below must be understood as obligatory; failure to provide these critically needed resources and protections must be punished. Whether through financial reparations or sanctions, it is essential to impose penalties on universities that fail the survivor.

Universities must remain vigilant, ensuring that their policies and the implementation of these policies do not constitute a violation of Title IX by being deliberately indifferent to "providing adequate training or guidance that is obviously necessary for implementation of a specific program or policy."[193]

Universities should continue to provide, or implement, bystander training for faculty, staff, and students regarding how to respond to and prevent sexual harassment and assault.[194] Although not all faculty and staff should be designated as mandatory reporters,[195] universities should provide training to everyone to ensure that the proper responses to sexual harassment and violence are universally understood. This training should be provided regularly, and particularly at the very beginning of each academic year.[196] Training should also be specifically targeted to new students: statistics show that students are a heightened risk "during the first months of their first and second semesters at university."[197]

---

193. Simpson v. Univ. of Colorado Boulder, 500 F.3d 1170, 1178 (10th Cir. 2007).
194. *See, e.g.,* Harvard Title IX, "Types of Training," https://titleix.harvard.edu/trainings (providing lists of faculty and staff and student workshops).
195. Resisting State-Level Mandatory Police Referral Efforts, Know Your IX, http://knowyourix.org/ask-survivors.
196. RAINN, "Campus Sexual Violence: Statistics," https://www.rainn.org/statistics/campus-sexual-violence (finding that more than 50 percent of sexual assaults at universities occur between August and November (citing Campus Sexual Assault Study, 2007; Matthew Kimble, Andrada Neacsiu, et. Al, *Risk of Unwanted Sex for College Women: Evidence for a Red Zone,* Journal of American College Health (2008))).
197. *Id.*

Furthermore, *universities should make significant investments in campus law enforcement.* It is imperative that every campus law enforcement agency has staff members who are responsible and sufficiently trained to focus specifically on survivors of sexual assault and harassment.[198]

These proposals will not be inexpensive. However, the human cost of failing to implement robust measures far outweighs any financial outlay that may be incurred.

Albeit unwittingly, former Michigan State University president Lou Anna Simon made the strongest case for such stringent measures with her casual abrogation of all responsibility on behalf of the institution: "it is virtually impossible to stop a determined sexual predator and pedophile." The abysmal failure conveyed in that statement is an incontrovertible argument for why the U.S. Congress must step into the breach, and ensure that universities will pay heavily for the deliberate abandonment of those to whom they owe a duty.

Indeed, if the U.S. Department of Education is unable—or unwilling—to ensure that Title IX obligations provide the greatest possible protection to Bailey Kowalski and other survivors, then the need for legislative reform is clear. The stirring words of Senator Bayh highlighted the pressing need in American schools and universities in 1972 to eliminate corrosive, pernicious discrimination. And we know now that sexual assault is discrimination under Title IX and must be curbed. Today, it is beyond any doubt that additional protective measures are needed. Otherwise, our society will continue to support a reality that must not be tolerated. Survivors are dismissed, they are not protected, they are not explained their due rights and privileges, and thus a system is enabled whereby universities minimize their obligations and cower behind empty words and phrases.

Enough is enough.

---

198. RAINN, "Campus Sexual Violence: Statistics," https://www.rainn.org/statistics/campus -sexual-violence (stating that as of 2015 only "72% of campus law enforcement agencies ha[d] a staff member responsible for survivor response and assistance").

Conclusion

And I thought I was gonna have someone to help
me. And it wasn't that sense at all of getting help.
It was more a sense of, "Who have you told so far?"
and, "Let's not talk about this anymore."

—Anonymous student athlete[199]

Title IX is a vital resource for survivors at a time when they are most vulnerable and most in need.[200] But the statute has not proved optimal for curbing and holding accountable those who enable sexual assault. The elements required to bring a Title IX claim are demanding. Moreover, it seems unlikely that Title IX is the best vehicle for expanding liability, since Congress enacted it pursuant to its spending power.

If we shut our eyes to the reality of sexual assault at our universities, we are effectively saying, "I'm alright with more monstrosities." We cannot afford complacency in the face of sexual assault, rape, and sexual harassment. Yet the cases discussed in this book suggest an unwillingness to recognize both the profound trauma of sexual assault and the critical role played by enablers, individuals, and institutions alike. As we have come to learn, the survivor's trauma is twofold: the physical assault committed by the perpetrator and the subsequent emotional assault committed by the enabler.

Time after time after time, enablers have chosen the same path: walk away from the survivor in his or her greatest hour of need. Those who walked away were those best positioned to provide assistance, both practical and emotional. However, when standing at the decision fork, enabler after enabler chose the wrong path. There appears to be a culture of blaming the victim, of refusing to believe the survivor, which causes extraordinary harm and pain to the vulnerable persons who are owed a duty of care. In terms of sexual assaults on college campuses, it is clear the present system is not functioning as Congress intended.

199. *Spartan Silence: Crisis at Michigan State*, https://player.vimeo.com/video/310658133.
200. For more information regarding Title IX, *see* Title IX Legal Manual, United States Department of Justice, https://www.justia.com/education/docs/title-ix-legal-manual/department-of-justice-role-under-title-ix/.

An integral part of holding institutions responsible is the ability to penalize those that fail in their duty to protect. The punishments need to reflect the consequences of enabling and must serve as a powerful deterrent to other enablers and institutions. In reviewing the implementation of Title IX, one is left with the distressing sense that many survivors have been failed by the very institution that they trusted, if not loved.

From the survivor's perspective, in order to rectify the situation, the two most important issues to be addressed are how to ensure that an institution will protect the survivor rather than itself, and how those who fail the survivor will be punished. An institution-first approach is unacceptable:

> And lastly, I want the system surrounding Michigan State to change, and I want all people to be treated with dignity and respect, regardless of their status or the revenue they bring the university.
>
> At the time I needed help most, I went to the Michigan State Counseling Center where I was told during freshman orientation that I would find support. Instead, I was intimidated, and I was told that I was going to be swimming with some really big fish. I'll never forget that phrase and the immediate feeling of despair and isolation.
>
> I chose to come to Michigan State University. I did not choose to be gang raped. I did not choose to change my major. I did not choose the consequences that I and my family have been forced to bear. These decisions were made when I was 18 years old, and I know that the 18-year-old Bailey Kowalski is gone. I grieve who she once was, but I look forward to who I will become because I took this step.[201]

Sexual assault confiscates from a survivor the very person they once were. Too often, survivors of sexual assault are left with a new, unchosen identity: their survival. Sometimes they do not even survive.[202] And when a university fails to protect a survivor or offer resources and

---

201. Bailey Kowalski, transcription from my interview with her.
202. *See* Memorandum and Order, Case No. 8:17-cv-00031-JFB-CRZ Docket No. 188 (Aug. 22, 1029) (a case in which Fatima Larios died by suicide after being sexually assaulted while attending university).

accommodations, it can permanently rob a survivor of any chance of piecing back together the person that they once were.

We are all charged with taking a step forward. We are all charged with treating survivors with dignity and respect. And we are all charged with bringing to light and holding accountable those who enable sexual assault. We cannot give up and must be willing to grapple with universities, with administrations, with giants. The true spectrum of sexual assault requires us to be more vigilant than ever and to advocate for institutional changes. It is time to howl, flash our teeth, and beat back against the silence enablers would have survivors suffer. It is time to step forward.

"To believe in the future of gymnastics is to believe in change, but how are we to believe in change when these organizations aren't even willing to acknowledge the problem? It's easy to put out statements talking about how athlete care is the highest priority, but they've been saying that for years, and all the while this nightmare was happening. False assurances from organizations are dangerous, especially when people want so badly to believe them. . . .

A word of advice: continuing to issue empty statements of empty promises, thinking that will pacify us, will no longer work. Yesterday, USA Gymnastics announced that it was terminating its lease at the ranch where many of us were abused. I'm glad that it is no longer a national team training site, but USA Gymnastics neglected to mention that they had athletes training there the day they released the statement. USA Gymnastics, where is the honesty? Where is the transparency? Why must the manipulation continue?"

—*Aly Raisman, victim impact statement*

— 10 —

The Challenges Ahead

During the last stages of writing this book, I had the privilege of corresponding with writer and feminist organizer Gloria Steinem who offered valuable insights on the liability of the enabler from the survivor's perspective. In crafting a definition of the enabler, she had this to offer:

> If I can start with the goal, I think that will help. In *Trauma and Recovery*, Judith Herman's brilliant and healing book about all degrees of trauma—from child sexual abuse to torture of adult prisoners—she writes: "Remembering and telling the truth about terrible events are prerequisite both for restoration of the social order and for the healing of individual victims."
>
> Any one who obstructs this remembering and healing of the crime is guilty of enabling. Not all of them can be punished by the law, but all can be involved in healing and learning. For instance, a prisoner who sees prisoners raping other prisoners may have no safe recourse, and a battered wife who sees her children abused may not have a way of stopping the abuse. The degree of responsibility depends on the power of the witness to stop it. But if there is any way of stopping the abuse or getting out the truth about it, then a person who does not do this is an enabler who must be asked to take responsibility.[1]

---

1. Email communication, January 1, 2020. Steinem refers to Judith L. Herman, *Trauma and Recovery: The Aftermath of Violence—From Domestic Abuse to Political Terror* (Basic Books, 1992; rev. ed. 2015).

Throughout this book, we have heard the voices of the survivors. We have heard their pain; we have heard their overwhelming sense of anger and abandonment. Their words speak for themselves. If we, as a society, are truly determined to take decisive action against their enablers, it is imperative to acknowledge the depth of their emotions. This is no small task, and there will be many challenges along the way.

In the majority of cases, survivors who spoke out about their assaults were met with the assumption that they were making it up, exaggerating, or simply did not understand. Indeed, almost none of the survivors confided in their teammates, even when they were waiting in line outside Larry Nassar's room. On this, Steinem noted that, "when everyone is behaving as if something is normal, it comes to seem so, even if our individual instincts are saying, 'This is crazy!'"[2] Not one of the survivors with whom I engaged heard the simple words, "I believe you. Tell me what I can do." Instead, the individuals to whom they confided, despite being in positions of authority from which they could offer support, made a determined effort to minimize their stories or belittle them.

We have seen examples of the different categories of enabler—dismissive, discouraging, deceitful, punitive—in all the institutions discussed in this book. Ohio State athletic director Hugh Hindman was dismissive of Ron McDaniel. USA Gymnastics officials abandoned Mattie Larson. Walter Robinson described the Catholic hierarchy as discouraging and deceitful. Michigan State University gymnastics coach Kathy Klages was discouraging to Lindsey Lemke. Tiffany Thomas-Lopez's reporting to Michigan State trainer Destiny Trainor-Hauk had punitive results.

It is striking that in cases where female survivors described their assault by a male to female coaches and trainers, they were nevertheless discouraged from complaining. Gloria Steinem provides some insight into this apparent lack of gender solidarity:

It's definitely not excusable but it may be understandable. For instance, they may see their own safety or survival in being one with the more powerful class, "the only Jew in the club"; or they may have been convinced that complaining will only bring down more punishment; or they may have tried to make change themselves in

---

2. Email communication, January 1, 2020.

some intimate situation and suffered; or they may have such negative experience of male behavior that they think it's natural and
inevitable, "boys will be boys."[3]

The numbing regularity and similarity of these responses must both
give us pause and motivate us. While Jerry Sandusky and Larry Nassar
will die in jail, an innumerable number of priests will escape justice and
evade incarceration. The report of the Pennsylvania grand jury made
clear the institutionalized criminality of the Catholic Church.[4] It is less
clear whether church leaders will read the report carefully and internal-
ize its powerful words of condemnation or brush it aside on the comforting grounds that a few bad apples do not define the institution. If they
chose the second path, then we write with confidence that nothing will
change, and inevitably the same pattern of predator abuse and systematic
enabling will continue without end.

The same holds true for the reports written on Michigan State University, Pennsylvania State University, USA Gymnastics, and The Ohio
State University. In their painstaking detail, those reports are as damning indictments as the vivid victim impact statements heard in court.
But will they be heeded in order to protect future generations?

To date, as we have seen, all these institutions, to their ever-lasting
shame, have mounted expensive and determined spin efforts that cast
themselves as putting the survivors' interests first. These were so patently
false, so unctuous and self-serving, that they elicited perhaps even greater
contempt and rage from the survivors than did the perpetrators of the
assaults:

> We may be more angry at the person who had the power to protect
> us than at the one who hurt us. . . . Our anger at individuals may
> be dictated by our hopes for them, and so we have way less hope for
> the crazy or criminal than we do for those we depend on to protect
> us. The criminal is still the criminal, and the bystander is still the
> bystander. We need that principle in the law.[5]

---

3. Email communication, January 1, 2020.
4. As these lines were written, CNN published this story: https://edition.cnn.com/interactive/2019
/12/us/salesians-of-don-bosco-intl/.
5. Gloria Steinem, email communication, January 1, 2020.

The *direct* role of the enabler in sexual assaults and the enormous costs to the survivors require that we move the conversation from the court of public opinion to the court of law. Otherwise, there will be no concrete plan of action to address Tiffany Thomas-Lopez's rightful demand, "I wanted someone to get Larry the fuck off of me." Legitimate survivor expectation is one of the primary reasons to propose legislation that would criminalize the enabler.

Under current law in most jurisdictions, punishment is meted only to the perpetrator. The enabler may walk away unencumbered, free to roam the institution, protected by its walls. It is not a competition for who is worse or is more culpable. Perpetrator and enabler are attached. The enabler is of the utmost importance to the perpetrator. Both have injured the survivor. Both must be understood to be culpable and be held accountable for their actions. We can only answer Mattie Larson's "How the fuck did they let an adult be alone with me in a hotel room?" by criminalizing just that.

It is of the utmost importance to craft a viable plan to move forward. To this end, I have drawn on lessons learned from my significant involvement in bystander legislative efforts in Utah and other states. My experience with mandatory Holocaust education legislation is also relevant. Still, legislation alone cannot change behavior. Education must be viewed as walking hand in hand with any legislative undertaking.

The educational effort to sensitize the broader population to the role of the enabler will require dedicated resources and a willingness to confront the consequences of enabler conduct directly. In some circumstances this will be particularly challenging, perhaps nowhere more than in religious organizations. Nevertheless, survivor protection must outweigh any discomfort or hesitation.

Education will also involve engaging with institutional leaders at all levels who must be trained that their primary duty is owed to the individual survivor, not to the institution. For some, this will seem counterintuitive and potentially harmful to the institution. Yet even if such concerns might be valid, it must never be forgotten that the underlying premise of the proposed legislation is that the individual in a position of authority owes a duty to protect the survivor. Failure to legislate the crime of enabling ensures the protection of predators at the expense of those in peril.

The proposed legislation seeks to establish an incontrovertible resolution to the dilemma, whom and what do we protect? The enablers we have encountered, all of whom were in positions of authority, uniformly made the decision to protect the predator and institution. In doing so, they abandoned the person in peril. For that reason, the enabler must be subject to the criminal process and brought before a court of law.

The rationale for criminalizing the enabler builds naturally from 9-1-1 Duty to Act legislation. Both reflect the principles that duty is owed to the person in peril, and failure to act on that person's behalf is a crime. While arguments rejecting bystander legislation have carried the day in some jurisdictions, the consequence is continued failure to protect the person in peril. The recommendation for Title IX expansion has a similar justification.

The one question I asked all the survivors was: what did you expect from the enabler? The more survivors I spoke with, the clearer it became to me that without the enablers, the perpetrators would not have caused the terrible harm they did. I therefore trained my focus on the survivor–enabler–perpetrator relationship in order to build a case for legislation that would criminalize the enabler.

Enacting such legislation will signal to survivors that those who walk away, smirk, degrade them, deceive them, or humiliate them in the presence of others will pay a serious price for behavior that will no longer be merely unconscionable, but will be illegal. It will also serve as a powerful deterrent to institutional leaders, who will be mandated to ensure that those who have been placed in positions of authority recognize that their primary duty is owed to the vulnerable. Too many survivors over the course of too many years have paid a terrible price precisely because the legal expectation, responsibility, and accountability demanded of the enabler has not been clearly defined.

Steve Penny had not a care in the world about what was happening to the vulnerable young gymnasts for whom he bore ultimate responsibility. The same is true for Lou Anna Simon, Hugh Hindman, Andy Geiger, Cardinal Law, Bishop McCormack, and all their fellow travelers. This most undistinguished group, with their distinguished titles and positions of authority, were individually and collectively responsible for a colossal failure. Though they did not physically touch the survivors, they preyed on them psychologically and emotionally through their determined effort to protect the predator.

Legislation is of prime importance, but it is critical to ensure that it is properly enforced, and that leadership signals the appropriate messages. Unless the duty to protect is upheld in a firm and consistent manner, survivors will continue to suffer.

I finish with four requests of the reader:

1. Listen carefully to the survivors.
2. Then ask yourself, how can we *not* punish the enabler?
3. Then ask yourself, who represents me in my state legislature and in the U.S. Congress?
4. Then, please, write your representatives and senators, imploring they work for legislative action against the enabler.

If we do not follow these steps, we disrespect the voices of the survivors who courageously agreed to share their pain with me and with you, my readers, in the hope that future survivors would not be turned away. But if we do take action, there is hope that we will be able to:

Assure Tiffany Thomas-Lopez that, yes, we will punish those who failed to "get Larry the fuck of me."

Ensure that the next generation of Mattie Larsons will not have to ask, "How the fuck did they let me be alone with an adult?"

Assure Peter Pollard that a church leader who tells an abusing priest, "Turn off the lights when you are done," will be punished by a court of law.

Assure Sarah Shiley that your report of a priest who violated you will be believed and acted on forcefully, and failure to do so will be punished by a court of law.

Unless we act—each of us—the endless parade of survivors assaulted by a predator protected by enablers will continue.

Epilogue

On January 19, 2020, Peter Pollard and I met at the Hilton Washington D.C. National Mall Hotel. Peter had graciously agreed to read a working manuscript of the book, and I was eager for his feedback.

I was deeply grateful that he was willing to meet with me face to face. He graciously shrugged it off, but I am not convinced it was as easy as he suggested. Despite having communicated by Skype and email on several occasions, we had never actually met. Indeed, this was my only in-person meeting with any of my male survivor interviewees. By contrast, I met with five of the female survivor interviewees.

For two hours we discussed the book, its primary themes, a reader's possible takeaways, and the twin realities he confronted: as a young boy, when he was assaulted by his priest, with whom he otherwise had a very positive relationship; and as an adult, when he confronted Bishop McCormack and Cardinal Law, who were dismissive of his claims.

In preparation for our meeting, I asked Scott Allen, one of my assistants on the book, what questions he would like me to ask Peter. Scott suggested inquiring what the reader should take away from the book.

Perhaps reflecting his professional training as a social worker, Peter suggested a theme of *hope.* I countered that I did not see this as a book about hope, but rather as an effort to make sure the survivors' voices would be heard. To this he wisely replied that, if there is accountability—such as a misdemeanor charge—then the survivor could have a sense that the enabler will be held liable.

Peter was deeply concerned that the recommended crime of enabler would be a felony. I reassured him that it would be a misdemeanor. While I think we disagree about the need to criminalize the enabler, we may perhaps have found a *via media* in this classification.

227

Peter largely rejects the notion that there are good people and evil people. Rather, he believes that good people do bad things. In that context, he suggests—and his childhood trauma can be heard here—that "we are all capable of turning away, but that doesn't make us evil." Peter knows far better than I the reality of that statement and its terrible consequences.

We discussed Judith Herman's terrific book *Trauma and Recovery: The Aftermath of Violence—From Domestic Abuse to Political Terror,*[1] noting that in many cases the awfulness of the trauma of an attack is far outpaced by the trauma of dealing with the emotional implications of the attack: the sense of betrayal, the loss of any sense of safety, the self-questioning, the ongoing hyper-vigilance, and the difficulty in trusting other people's intentions. This was something new that I learned while working on this project, and it crystallized in my mind the power of the enabler and the terrible consequences of their actions.

I asked Peter what he would ask Bishop McCormack and Cardinal Law if they were sitting in on our conversation. He replied, "I'd ask them, what factors were at play that made it possible for you to let this happen?" Fair enough. Peter also noted that as the archbishop of Boston, Law's primary mission was to ensure the smooth functioning of the church and to protect the institution and its members, as a whole. Law chose what he mistakenly saw as "the greater good" over the well-being of certain individuals. From Law's perspective, I am sure Peter is correct. However, that is precisely how Law and all the other enablers discussed in this book failed the survivors, and it is exactly why they *must* be held accountable. We, as society, owe it to the survivors.

Before taking leave from Peter, I thanked him warmly for taking the time to meet and for being so open with me. We parted, but not before embracing. As he walked away, I could only note his courage, honesty, and strength. For that, Peter and all the other survivors who spoke with me truly have my everlasting admiration.

The end of a book is a moment of poignancy, finitude, and reflection. the course of twelve months, men and women who had no idea

---

man, *Trauma and Recovery: The Aftermath of Violence—From Domestic Abuse to* Basic Books, 1992; rev. ed. 2015).

who I was, shared with me the worst moments of their lives. They did so graciously, honestly, and bluntly. In this spirit, the book comes to an end with a piece written by Brooke Martin (University of Utah, 2020) that powerfully and painfully conveys many of the emotions running raw throughout this book.

Violated by Water

A Statement on Consent

By Brooke Martin

In my video installation piece, *Violated by Water*, I am pictured in a domestic setting that tends to be a safe space for people. In a home, the shower is a place where one can be alone in their own skin and reflect. The sensations felt in the shower are typically soothing, relaxing, comfortable, and pleasurable. Living with PTSD [Post-Traumatic Stress Disorder], the shower is a place where I process my trauma. The invigorating warmth of the water cleansing my skin elicits desires to cleanse my mind as well. In the process of this mind cleansing, I sift through the contents of my psyche, confronted by unresolved thoughts and flashes of vivid memories that tend to be malicious. In order to digest the reality of the trauma, I must confront it head on.

   In 2014, I began a series titled *People in Water*, as a way to nonverbally communicate emotions that I felt as I began to experience trauma. In correspondence to the series, I decided to portray myself in the comfort and safety of a bathtub/shower to comment on the importance of consent. The emotions I express through my face and body language don't follow the typical script for those of a being in the shower. Contextually the clothes on my body do not correspond with my process of self-cleansing. I shower nude. The sensation of the unwanted wetness contorts my face and body in an unpleasant way. I jump to the touch. My starch white bralette and freshly done make up ruin under the unsolicited downpour. I did not turn on the faucet, I did not ask for the water. The make-up that I so lovingly adorned my face with is not accompanied by sexual implications. It melts now, the artificial beauty. Blackness welling underneath my lower eye lids, I struggle to adapt to the water that violates my skin. As the downpour trickles to a stop, I am left to accept the defeat. Left with nothing but a cold chill, smeared face, and an unfathomable feeling of regret, I act instinctually. Fight or flight. The thoughts of regret and loathing flush my perception of reality. These illogical emotions create their own overwhelming downpour. I placed myself in the tub . . . was it naïve of me to not expect to get wet? Was I asking for the water even though my hand was not on the faucet?

Water is a powerful element. It has the power to give life and also drown it out. It has the power to cleanse and also inflict discomfort. The difference between bathing one's self and being subjected to the water paints a picture of the importance of consent.[1]

---

1. Brooke Martin, Final Artist Statement, ART 3420 Figure Sculpture, University of Utah, Fall 2019.

Index

About the Author

Amos N. Guiora is Professor of Law at the S.J. Quinney College of Law, the University of Utah. He is actively involved in bystander legislation efforts in Utah and other states around the country.

Professor Guiora has an AB in history from Kenyon College, a JD from Case Western Reserve University School of Law, and a PhD from Leiden University.

He has published extensively in both the United States and Europe on issues related to national security, limits of interrogation, religion and terrorism, the limits of power, multiculturalism, and human rights.

His books include *Populism and Islamism: The Challenges to International Law* (2019); *Earl Warren, Ernesto Miranda and Terrorism* (2018); *The Crime of Complicity: The Bystander in the Holocaust* (2017); and *Tolerating Intolerance: The Price of Protecting Extremism* (2014).

Professor Guiora is a Distinguished Fellow at The Consortium for the Research and Study of Holocaust and the Law (CRSHL), Chicago-Kent College of Law.

www.armiesofenablers.com